Contents

Part 1

American Ideals and Obstacles to their Practice

Introduction

Since America declared its independence from Great Britain in 1776 the U.S. population has gone from under 3 million to 327 million. What began as thirteen states along the continent's East coast has become the seat of world power. The frontier used to be what is now Tennessee and Michigan, not the moon or even Mars. The range of political issues one is now expected to have thoughts on is global. Expectations of the average democratic "informed voter" have expanded with specialized fields, from genetically modified crops to stem cell research. Modern governments enact policies in enumerable fields that are headed by scores of experts who themselves cannot arrive at certainty. As Walter Lippmann said in the 1920s, the world is now "too big, too complex, and too fleeting for direct acquaintance. We are not equipped to deal with so much subtlety, so much variety, so many permutations and combinations. And although we have to act in that environment, we have to reconstruct it on a simpler model before we can manage it."

In reaction to all of the topics and data, we simplify and generalize. If we didn't we could hardly talk about anything we see or read about the outside world. Unfortunately, too often our reconstructions of reality do not match up with the actual thing. Our ideas about politics, and of one another for that matter, often depend on second party sources conveyed by a medium likely dependent on advertising revenue, like television news or Facebook feeds. Presently, social media is besting television and radio, which bested print media. The delivery of the news and the pace at which we consume it is becoming faster and narrower, as the reality it supposedly conveys gets more and more complex and nuanced. Those who want votes or money play on the common desire to have the world neatly packaged into a narrative of good vs. evil where the consumer is always on the side of the good and normal. They have to keep us around for the commercial breaks.

In the absence of digital technology Americans encountered this information problem very early in U.S. history. The United States became too big and too connected to the world for citizens to judge national affairs by their personal experience. Beginning with the adoption of the Constitution in 1789, a faraway government made policy for millions. Local (state) legislatures enacting the policies voted on by majorities were subsumed under one national government. The Constitution re-channeled the flows of power from the states towards a central government. This distant national government linked itself to a world of trade, finance, and military adventure as foreign to most Americans then as other planets are today. They did not have National Geographic channels. Dora the Explorer had not been born. In place of accurate knowledge based on experience, citizens came to rely on gatekeeping journalists and other secondary sources that conveyed a simplified version of "the news."

Newspapers determined the entry of information in the early republic, acting as knowledge **gatekeepers**. Even then, each newspaper had its own bias and they all shared the need to sell copies. By the 1950s, audio-visual imagery from outlets dependent on advertising revenue overcame print as the gatekeeper of the public's knowledge. "News" increasingly came between commercials and entertainment shows. Americans began purchasing fewer newspapers and magazines and instead relied on advertisers to pay news outlets to provide the information everyday Americans consumed as reality. When people did pay for information, they were not willing to pay much. In 2019, the figure is about 30 cents a day. Walther Lippman quipped: "For a dollar, you may not even get an armful of candy, but for a dollar or less people expect reality/representations of truth to fall into their laps."

Even if the average citizen spends one-hundred times that on good information like books or journals, consider that most people work 40 hours a week. They have families and lives to maintain. When they are not working, they have to spend their money to "blow off steam" or relax so they do not burn out of the whole process. Between football games, Xbox sessions, workouts, and six-packs where is there time for the citizens to educate themselves even if they wished to do so? Does anyone expect a single parent struggling to pay the bills to read SCOTUS Blog or to have read the latest issue of Foreign Affairs?

Even so, with so much information, one would think that the voter is more informed than ever. The Internet made us all into journalists and freed us from the media monopoly in which a handful of companies produced all of the music, books, T.V., movies, and news, right? Wrong. While we have access to countless journal articles and primary sources, it turns out that when people seek information they are not seeking truth. They're seeking to reinforce the simple versions of the world they have constructed. We swipe the screen when something does not confirm what we already think or feel. By selecting the information we are exposed to, we end up getting news that echoes our own thoughts and feelings. Like much else we do in leisure time, this gives us a warm feeling of confidence that we see things correctly. Others and their views can be waived off with a label and reference to a news story.

Instead of compilations of expert analysis, which would be confusing and daunting, we instead use a grab bag of stereotypes, clichés and lazy generalizations to arrive at a sense of confidence that we understand the vast array of people, places, times, theories and events. Of course, one cannot possibly hold all of the nuance and complexity in one's head and make rational choices. However, instead of feeling constantly confused, we accept the authority of an information provider or turn off the noise completely.

The first generation of Americans had such problems. The framers of the Constitution saw voters in state governments being fooled into electing people who gave them simple versions of their problems and proposed they alone could solve the problems with ever simpler solutions. These "**demagogues**" and their voting majorities almost cast the country into chaos before it began. Then, uninformed publics formed voting majorities to make policy through democratic governments. These majorities were manipulated into making short-term decisions harmful to their own interests and the stability of their governments. From 1776 to 1789 what would become the United States almost descended into a chaotic conflict of warring states and classes. Forging one nation out of thirteen states led by passionate majorities of debtor farmers would be no easy task. Despite the difficulties, the framers built a structure of government that would best prevent uninformed, riled up majorities from running them into the ground through the election of men who talked like freedom lovers but behaved like dictators.

Turning from the natural wisdom of the common man, the architects of the Constitution sought to relocate the basis of government from voting majorities into the hands of a deserving elite. Elites, the best and the brightest, could better grasp the facts in all of their subtlety, variety, and combinations. The good operation of the Constitution's government would not rest on the assumption that Americans were by their nature--as farmers and artisans--perfectly fit to make good decisions because they ran farms and presumably knew how the world worked. Instead of assuming the best of property owner's human natures, the framers set up a kind of government-machine with different types of operators, most of them far removed from the mood swings of voting majorities. Some officials in under the new Constitution would be directly elected by the people (the House of Representatives) while state governments would select members of the federal Senate. The President would be elected in a small "electoral college" and have the power to appoint members of the third, least powerful branch, the judicial. The Senate would approve the President's choices, keeping the election of the President and federal benches out of the majority's reach. The government would be powerful but in no one group's hands, especially not in the hands of the uniformed majority.

However, the principles expressed by the Declaration in 1776 were honest reflections of the national spirit. How could a government not depend on majorities if the words of the Declaration were to be taken seriously? If "All men are created equal," should they not have an equal say in their government? The framers determined that the people could still direct the government through majorities in places (the House and local governments). However, voting majorities would be checked, would be tempered, by other branches made up of a select group of wiser men who could implement policies against the "popular will" when necessary. Ten years of mayhem was enough for the authors of the Constitution to see that power had to be held more refined hands. Matters like national **monetary and fiscal policy** were not to be left in the calloused hands of voting majorities as the states had done. Such matters would be entrusted to a select few whose experience and expertise would override their emotions and biases. As Broadway star Alexander Hamilton described the turn away from the citizen-farmer ideal:

"All communities divide themselves into the few and the many. The first are the rich and well-born, the other the mass of the people. The voice of the people has been said to be the voice of God, and however generally this maxim has been quoted and believed, it is not true in fact. The people are turbulent and changing; they seldom judge or determine right."

The driving motive of the Constitution builders was to devise a government that **factions**—or groups of special interests--could not control. At the founding, the faction causing the problem was voting majorities operating within states dominated by one-branch, legislative governments (**republics**). The **Constitution's structure** would keep them and other interest groups fighting for power and incapable of gaining complete control of the government. No group would have complete control since those with power would use it for their own benefit, hurting everyone else. In Madison's day, voting majorities of farmers were passing laws in their narrow self-interests to cancel their debts. If this went on, creditors would go out of business. With no banks, the farmers themselves would be able to survive the next bad season. Worse, without credit a nation cannot make investments in things like infrastructure and education that provide the basis for economic growth. Even farmers would need a national network of canals, roads, and bridges to get their crops to market.

Madison created a republic that could control the excesses of democracies while it adhered to democratic principles. In the state and local governments, democratic systems could even be preserved. However, the central government as defined by the Constitution would be a **republic** with few democratic features. Today we consider our nation a democracy because it adheres to principles like free and fair elections, a free press, and the rule of law (to name just three). However, the Constitution's aim was by no means to create a government that would be associated with the word "democracy" nor was it to be directed by a voting majority.

The founders saw that all other governments before them had become **dictatorhips** or too weak to defend themselves. This government would be new: no single person or interest would be in charge. The government that resulted would be slow moving and depend on compromise. The founders did not prevent leaders from wanting to become dictators, it created a government unsuited to them. Autocrats need fast-acting, centrally located governments they can control without compromising (which requires the acknowledgement that one could be wrong and certain at the same time).

Madison's system takes into account that the winners of elections will want to rewrite the laws to benefit their group and want more and more power to do so. He and the other framers broke power into opposing parts. No one part of the new government would likely be controlled by a single interest. If one interest pushed for laws that would benefit only itself at the expense of other interests in the society, those interests could push back through other **government institutions**. Also, they could use linkage institutions like a free press or fair elections to hold selfish officials accountable to representing the common good and not just the good of their narrow group.

Again, this is not to say that the U.S. is undemocratic. Principles like the Declaration's "all men are created equal" in their "pursuit of happiness" still had meaning. The U.S. would be the first modern nation in which neither God nor one's family determined one's destiny. Instead, power would belong to those who deserved it most. American elites would earn their places, not inherit them. Just ten years after the founding, a baby was born in a log cabin along a wild frontier. In no other country could Abraham Lincoln have risen from such humble origins. Because he entered a fair race, as designed by the founders, he was able to pursue his potential all the way to the White House. He then led the nation through a war that reinforced the commitment to fairness and equality. We take these values for granted today, but we should not. That the race be fair, rewarding the fastest, is a duty of each generation of Americans.

There was a viral video in 2017 of a coach who staged a 100-yard dash for a price of $100. At first, all of the participants were lined up evenly. Then he started asking questions. If a racer answered "yes" to a question, she took a step forward, leaving others at the original starting line. The questions were as follows:

- If your ancestors were forced to come to the USA not by choice, take one step back.
- If your primary ethnic identity is "American," take one step forward.
- If you were ever called names because of your race, class, ethnicity, gender, or sexual orientation, take one step back.
- If there were people who worked for your family as servants, gardeners, nannies, etc. take one step forward.
- If you were ever ashamed or embarrassed of your clothes, house, car, etc. take one step back.
- If one or both of your parents were "white collar" professionals: doctors, lawyers, etc. take one step forward.
- If you were raised in an area where there was prostitution, drug activity, etc., take one step back.
- If you studied the culture of your ancestors in elementary school, take one step forward.
- If you went to school speaking a language other than English, take one step back.
- If there were more than 50 books in your house when you grew up, take one step forward.
- If you ever had to skip a meal or were hungry because there was not enough money to buy food when you were growing up, take one step back.
- If you were taken to art galleries or plays by your parents, take one step forward.
- If one of your parents was unemployed or laid off, not by choice, take one step back.
- If you have health insurance take one step forward.
- If you attended private school or summer camp, take one step forward.
- If your family ever had to move because they could not afford the rent, take one step back.
- If you were told that you were beautiful, smart and capable by your parents, take one step forward.
- If you were ever discouraged from academics or jobs because of race, class, ethnicity, gender or sexual orientation, take one step back.
- If you were encouraged to attend college by your parents, take one step forward.
- If you have a disability take one step backward.
- If you were raised in a single parent household, take one step back.
- If your family owned the house where you grew up, take one step forward.
- If you saw members of your race, ethnic group, gender or sexual orientation portrayed on television in degrading roles, take one step back.
- If you own a car take one step forward.
- If you were ever offered a good job because of your association with a friend or family member, take one step forward.

- If you were ever denied employment because of your race, ethnicity, gender or sexual orientation, take one step back.
- If you were paid less, treated less fairly because of race, ethnicity, gender or sexual orientation, take one step back.
- If you were ever accused of cheating or lying because of your race, ethnicity, gender, or sexual orientation, take one step back.
- If you ever inherited money or property, take one step forward.
- If you had to rely primarily on public transportation, take one step back.
- If you attended private school at any point in your life take one step forward.
- If you were ever stopped or questioned by the police because of your race, ethnicity, gender or sexual orientation, take one step back.
- If you were ever afraid of violence because of your race, ethnicity, gender or sexual orientation, take one step back.
- If your parents own their own business take one step forward.
- If you were generally able to avoid places that were dangerous, take one step forward.
- If you were ever uncomfortable about a joke related to your race, ethnicity, gender or sexual orientation but felt unsafe to confront the situation, take one step back.
- If you were ever the victim of violence related to your race, ethnicity, gender or sexual orientation, take one step back.
- Imagine you are in a relationship, if you can get married in the State of __ take one step forward
- If your parents did not grow up in the United States, take one step back.
- If your parents attended college take one step forward.

By the end of the questions, many students were steps away from finishing the race while others stood despondently in the back. The coach blew his whistle and those with unearned advantages easily won. Yes, "all men are created equal," but we do not all get an equal start in life, and equal opportunity. The promise of the Declaration is that we do. The architects of our nation were not concerned that everyone end up equal, just that they started that way. This is why Thomas Jefferson was against inherited wealth, writing, "A power to dispose of estates for ever is manifestly absurd. The earth and the fulness of it belongs to every generation, and the preceding one can have no right to bind it up from posterity. Such extension of property is quite unnatural. Equality of citizenship was impossible in a nation where inequality of wealth remained the rule. North Carolina's 1784 statute explained that by keeping large estates together for succeeding generations, the old system had served "only to raise the wealth and importance of particular families and individuals, giving them an unequal and undue influence in a republic" and promoting "contention and injustice." Abolishing aristocratic forms of inheritance would by contrast "tend to promote that equality of property which is of the spirit and principle of a genuine republic."

The Declaration announces all can run the race or play the game, and the government should not stand in anyone's way. Seeing the curses hurled at refs at nearly every sporting event, it may seem that rules, that governance, is a bad thing. However, limitations like the time clock and three-point line in basketball award skill and keep leading teams from just passing the ball around to kill time once they have a lead. Good rules foster competition and reward skill. Political parties who win elections should not be able to write laws or limit rights just to give themselves an advantage in future elections. If the winners are allowed to rewrite the rules, the race quickly becomes unfair.

In the spirit of Jefferson's, "All Men are Created Equal," each team and each player—no matter what shoe deals they have—has the rules applied to them as do unknown rookies. No team is allowed to rewrite rules in their favor, no matter how good they are. The Golden State Warriors won the 2017 and 2018 NBA title through their 3-point sharpshooters. Many "treys" are taken well outside the 3-point line. If able to influence regulations, they might create a 4-point and 5-point line, virtually ensuring the next year's title. While this may seem like a simple point, winners of elections and the special interests that get them there construct policies with only their short-term gain in mind. Their goal is to get a head start in the race for power and wealth. While the founders were men of privilege and so many were hypocritical slave plantation owners, they were sincere in their desire that those with ability, not the descendants of the able, succeed and govern. They were rejecting the European system of land, power, and wealth passing down through generations regardless of effort or ability. They sought to create a nation of competitors who valued freedom and fair play. We, along with each generation, either embrace or reject these values.

To conclude, the whole purpose of democratic government is to foster fair competition for power and not let one person or group (faction) get too much of it. Free, fair, and regular elections act as legalized revolutions (when the people can "kick the bums out") and keep our leaders competing for our votes. The framers did not want to give "turbulent and changing" **majority factions** too much power. Nevertheless, the framers, elites as they were, did not want a permanent class of a wealthy few ruling (aristocracy) either. Moreover, they certainly did not want a king. They wanted to create a stable government that was not wholly in the hands of one, a few, or the many. These different factions from various classes of society would have to share power and balance one another's interests through various government institutions. If they could pull this off, they would have designed a government better than any that had existed before them.

This book will examine the nature of America's large republican form of government. It will also examine the citizen's place within it. As Walter Lippman warned, citizens in a large, modern nation cannot possibly be informed well enough to set policies on highly complex topics. What, then, does a government run "by the people, for the people" look like if not a democracy? How are we to have faith in democracy without having the ability or means of directing it ourselves? We will begin by examining the main source of what we think we know about the government, the media.

Chapter 1

The Declaration of Independence: A Revolutionary Beginning

IN CONGRESS, JULY 4, 1776

The unanimous Declaration of the thirteen united States of America

When in the Course of human events it becomes necessary for one people to dissolve the political bands which have connected them with another and to assume among the powers of the earth, the separate and equal station to which the Laws of Nature and of Nature's God entitle them, a decent respect to the opinions of mankind requires that they should declare the causes which impel them to the separation.

We hold these truths to be self-evident, that all men are created equal, that they are endowed by their Creator with certain unalienable Rights, that among these are Life, Liberty and the pursuit of Happiness. — That to secure these rights, Governments are instituted among Men, deriving their just powers from the consent of the governed, — That whenever any Form of Government becomes destructive of these ends, it is the Right of the People to alter or to abolish it, and to institute new Government, laying its foundation on such principles and organizing its powers in such form, as to them shall seem most likely to effect their Safety and Happiness. Prudence, indeed, will dictate that Governments long established should not be changed for light and transient causes; and accordingly all experience hath shewn that mankind are more disposed to suffer, while evils are sufferable than to right themselves by abolishing the forms to which they are accustomed. But when a long train of abuses and usurpations, pursuing invariably the same Object evinces a design to reduce them under absolute Despotism, it is their right, it is their duty, to throw off such Government, and to provide new Guards for their future security. — Such has been the patient sufferance of these Colonies; and such is now the necessity which constrains them to alter their former Systems of Government.

The Declaration of Independence (1776) was Thomas Jefferson's breakup letter with Britain addressed to "a candid world." Before he roasts King George III for a few pages, he lays down the philosophical principles of our nation, beginning with "All men are created equal." He and the first Americans flipped the script between ruler and ruled. In America, there would be citizens rather than subjects who would create and operate governments under whose rule they **consented to be governed**. In the modern world's first democracy, the American government's power would come from the people's willingness to obey it. This belief in people makes the American national project the most hopeful the world had seen.

By stating that all were equal, the Declaration is not saying that all will get the same paycheck or haze equal vacation time. In fact, the liberty the Declaration creates soon resulted in inequality as ability was rewarded in one generation and then those rewards were passed down as privilege to the next. Races have winners. Winners in politics are unlike racers in that they get to write the rules that govern future races. They even pass on their leads to sons and daughters, giving future generations head starts they did not earn. Jefferson was short on details (and personal example, he owned slaves) on how to have a government of equals after the first, fair races were run. Once the states ran for ten years, it became apparent that something more than the elegant language of the Declaration would be needed to keep the winners from gaming the system. As we have mentioned, voting majorities in states passed laws that benefited debtors at the expense of everyone else. Later in American history **minority factions** of creditors and land speculators would command government to serve their special interests.

The Constitution creates the basic framework for a government that keeps things fair for each generation. By placing protections against the winners of one election altering government institutions to ensure victory and riches to their heirs, power becomes accessible to all. The Declaration, then, is best seen as a philosophical statement of principles, not a plan of government. Like all philosophical principles, they tend to be discarded by lawmakers when faced with a crisis. Nevertheless, the Declaration is the repository for American ideals. It, rather than the Constitution, is most often quoted, and can be seen in famous rhetoric such as Lincoln's Gettysburg Address and King's "I Have a Dream" speech.

The Laws of Nature

According to the Declaration, the ideal government rests on a social compact between the government and governed. Those governed consent to a power that has specific, limited duties—protecting citizens' right to life, liberty, and property (Jefferson changed John Locke's "property" to "happiness")—based on the belief that all of us are equally given **inalienable rights** by "Nature's God" according to "**Nature's Law.**" Human equality is rooted in shared inalienable rights, or natural rights, that no government can violate. Jefferson explains that if the government violates our natural right to our lives, liberty, or fulfillment, it breaks the **social compact** between it and its people. In such a case, the peoples' consent would be voided, and they would enter into a state of rebellion against a tyrannical government. In justifying our break with Britain, Jefferson expressed great faith in our ability to govern ourselves rather than needing the authority of a king who acted as a god on earth.

Jefferson was a man of the Enlightenment which valued proved fact over received truth. With a king, the "truth" had no basis in fact. Instead, it rested on the authority of the one who revealed it. If like Galileo, one maintained that the earth revolved around the sun, but the King or church-king Pope did not find that to be True, one would have Galileo's choice: deny the facts or burn at the stake. He chose to deny what he proved to be true to avoid the horrifying consequences of using deductive reasoning. Jefferson's generation would be free from such authoritarianism. The rulers and the ruled played by the same rules, the **natural law** that made truth available to all who would gather facts and make non-contradictory conclusions.

For the first time, the common man could test ideas and beliefs instead of receiving them from a revealed source that usually came in a forgotten language from a social superior. Blame the printing press, but the rabble gained confidence in their ability to judge the truth for themselves in the century and a half leading up to the American founding. A statement that could not be tested and verified would not be deemed valid in Jefferson's America, no matter what a King or church leader said.

It is ironic that Jefferson's Declaration is the only of the founding documents that mentions God, "Nature's God." Lest one confuses this with a proclamation of his Christian faith, here is Jefferson on religion:

"I have examined all the known superstitions of the world, and I do not find in our particular superstition of Christianity one redeeming feature. They are all alike founded on fables and mythology. Millions of innocent men, women, and children since the introduction of Christianity, have been burnt, tortured, fined, and imprisoned. What has been the effect of this coercion? To make one half the world fools and the other half hypocrites; to support roguery and error all over the earth."

Unsurprisingly, it is from one of his letters that the phrase, "separation of church and state" originates.

Self-evident Truths

Truth, until the 1700s, had been given from on high. The Declaration rejects that laws descend from mountaintops and emanate from cathedrals. Instead, the law is found in Nature using reason to discover it. How does this reasoning to self-evident truth work? Let us say, you are in nature, under Nature's Law and Nature's God and you see a fruit tree. There is no private property and no man-made law, so picking the fruit is just fine. You are hungry, so you pick some apples and head back to the hut. On your way, a fellow villager sees your fresh apples and asks for one. You explain that that apple is yours and he should go pick his own. He argues that the apple cannot be yours because the tree does not belong to you. Again, he demands the apple. Do you give it up? Most of my students say "no" and see a fist fight happening. So, what makes the apple yours? You picked it, that's what. Your labor makes it yours. Duh. You have arrived at the natural law of private property.

That process we just went through, posing a hypothetical and then reasoning through the scenario, brought us to self-evident truth/inalienable right/natural law Number One: what you work for is yours. Apple pickin' and eatin' is the pursuit of happiness if nothing else is. What we work for is our property: not the King's, not the government's. In most other places in 1776 that apple would have belonged to a king or royal family or village strongman. In America, freedom was something everyone already had, and it was the government's job to guard it. Such ratiocination seems possible for the ordinary farmer, no?

Jefferson thought such reasoning processes could guide legislators in state governments. The problem came in when the same natural law, common sense approach was used to determine complex issues like trade policy and currency values. Voters work best with simple, "I'm for" and "I'm against" issues. Some issues can seemingly be grasped intuitively like abortion and gay marriage. What few facts find their way into discussions of such topics are usually the ammunition of one side against the other. A discussion about abortion rarely resembles two researchers puzzling over a difficult problem. Instead, the two sides (that there are two sides is a strong indication of an over-simplified problem) follow their gut feelings and emotions. It is not long before those engaged in such questions fall into one of two camps: those for and those against. The problem with such voting blocs is that the most complex issues must be simplified to a point where the information they are given is so simple it is false. "Informing" an ignorant public about a complicated issue is a petri dish for propagandists. The first thirteen independent state governments were cases in point. In our own time, voters in democratic republics have been given wide authority to determine massive policy decisions.

Brexit, although not an American issue, is a perfect example of a complicated issue that was dumbed down for a voting public. The politicians who "informed" the UK's voters of the merits of leaving the European Union used the most modern propaganda techniques to target voters' gut feelings to get the results they wanted. Research showed the attention merchants whom to target and tailored well-fitting, narrowcasted phrases using well-worn stereotypes of immigrants stealing jobs and open borders that created dangerous societies. The latter included heavy doses of fear mongering to a population that felt left behind by the modern world. After a majority of Brits voted "Yes" to leave the European Union, their government had to navigate hundreds of complex facts and webs of relationships to execute the majority's will. In the span of a few years the UK will have seen three Prime Ministers and a befuddled Parliament try to transpose a simple vote onto a complex problem that the UK's voters hardly ever grasped. Instead, those voters acted on slogans and outright lies.

Jefferson's ideal of the self-governing, democratic citizens depends on the proper use of words and facts and a humble willingness to act in light of the truth once it becomes self-evident. A Jeffersonian citizens changes his mind constantly as new data is collected rather than stand uncompromising by received "knowledge." Another way to question our commitment to the Declaration's vision is, have we, the commoners, ever been capable of thought that overrides our base emotions of fear and anger? I am remembering what Alexander Hamilton said about majorities: "turbulent and changing; they seldom judge or determine right."

H.L. Menken snarked that "for every complex problem, there is a solution that is simple, neat, and wrong." Reflection, reading, and fact gathering are the best defenses against the manipulation of our emotions. The "Information Revolution" is in full swing, and we are still trying to figure out its implications for how we find the truth. All of the data has seemingly stupefied us. We must filter so much "fake news" and noise to get to any shared truth, doing so seems to require a master's degree in political science. If you do not need an advanced degree, you certainly need an excellent civics class.

Today claims are rampant that powerful elites are manipulating working class voters to vote in ways that hurt their long-term interests and make the rich even richer. In his "What's the Matter with Kansas," Thomas Frank sees a situation similar to the ailment of state governments under the Articles. Just like in the thirteen state republics, demagogues use the language of the people only to gain power in pursuit of policies that would lead to more wealth and power for themselves and worsening conditions for the voters. Frank poses a hopeless picture of the modern voters: "Push them off their land, and next thing you know they're protesting in front of abortion clinics. Squander their life savings on manicures for the CEO, and there's a good chance they'll join the John Birch Society" (they will vote to cut the CEO's taxes).

In the next chapter we will pause in our study of the formation of the American republic will consider the relationship between citizens and the press. As we begin our study of the U.S. government we must understand how easy it is to be misinformed while growing certain in the feeling of one's knowledge about politics or "the way the world works."

Chapter 2

Media

"Nothing can now be believed which is seen in a newspaper" --Thomas Jefferson in a letter

"FAKE NEWS media ... makes up stories and 'sources.'" --Donald Trump in a Tweet.

"...the ordinary citizen must rely on signals transmitted by the mass media. He immerses himself in the metaworld of shows, commercials, news, and televised sports events and allows them to represent a larger world that he cannot experience firsthand. He knows better than to expect truth from the endless stream of programs. Instead he seeks satisfaction, titillation, and a minimal level of real information. He rests content in the belief that if anything does happen, there will be a televised special on it.
The gap between the realities of the world and the pictures individuals have of that world grows ever greater...most persons are caught between the narrowness of their everyday concerns and a bedazzlement at the works of civilization. Beyond a certain point they simply do no know or care about things happening in their surroundings. With the overload of information so monumental, possibilities once crucial to citizenship are neutralized. Active participation is replaced by a haphazard monitoring. The idea that civilized life consists of a fully conscious, intelligent, self-determining populace making informed choices about ends and means and taking action on that basis is revealed as a pathetic fantasy."
--Langdon Winner

Langdon Winner describes the ideals embodied in the Declaration of Independence as "pathetic fantasy." Jefferson and other Enlightenment thinkers were hopeful that humans had evolved from hunter gatherers to fact finders. In Jefferson's universe the wisest would science, discovering that knowledge which leads to power over nature. Nature has laws that good government would use. As an engineer would use calculus to direct the placement of artillery, so would governments arrange societies according to natural laws. Beneath the guidance of an elite knowledge class would be

Jefferson's landowning farmers tending to their manors and conducting their local affairs, leaving complex matters to complex minds. Before the time of the industrial revolution and electricity, before radio, television, or social media, before globalization, before cat viral cat videos, this picture seemed reasonable. However, it is difficult to imagine Jefferson, with his library of books in mostly Greek and Latin, finding kindred spirits in today's news consumer who receives information between his Netflix binging, Youtube journeying, and online gaming.

A snapshot from a 2018 Pew survey of the Millennial "informed citizen": Millennials spend far less time-consuming news overall than older adults, and the time they do spend is concentrated on digital consumption. Millennials ages 21-37 consume only about 30% of the amount of news as adults age 38 and older, per Nielsen. This amounts to 8,766 minutes of news a year on average compared to 30,103 minutes for older adults. But millennials have largely abandoned traditional TV formats for digital platforms. While adults aged 38+ average 54 minutes a day watching TV news, millennials register just 12 minutes a day. And digital news reaches 88% of millennials while national TV news reaches just 61% of them, compared to digital news reach of 80% and TV news reach of 90% for older adults.

Broadly, a study of "the media" is to consider how one finds the truth about the world. For those who think with their gut, finding truth means following the biases and emotions their experience has bequeathed. Those led by feelings never gain the sense that experience gives a minimal picture of reality. They are not able to acknowledge that their own vision goes no further than a cell phone flashlight.

To go from using one's intuition, "my gut tells me," to our brains requires us to practice humility and lower our expectations of what we can know. Most of all, we have to give up the warm blanket of **selective perception and exposure**: choosing information sources that confirm our biases and even hearing what we want to hear when our ideas are flatly disproved. Feeling right, and knowing without doubt that others are wrong (idiots!) is a sure sign one is wrong. Ironically, the feeling of certainty is a strong indication that one is wrong. In 1999 two psychologists, Kruger and Dunning conducted now-famous experiments from which they concluded that there are two groups of people who feel certain in their opinions. The first is those who know nothing. This group is remarkable in its ability to "know everything" without doubt or question. The second group is more justified to feel like their knowledge is superior to others since they are experts in their fields. Not every field, though. So this second group is made up of, say, the oral surgeon whose training makes him an expert on everything from healthcare policy to the science of global warming to the nature of God and His angles. Since they are authorities in one field where their confidence is justified they carry their authoritative clarity into of which they have no more knowledge than a high school graduate.

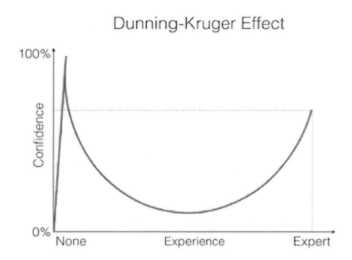

The media, TV, Youtubers, vloggers, and print know that most will spend their lives seeing no farther than their flashlight beams but will quickly believe they are correct in their view of the world. Modern propagandist **spin** information and **narrowcast** messaging to reinforce their audiences' feelings of certainty and even superiority. Desirous of making money by attracting advertisers, news producers must show soap to car companies that they have a critical mass of attention ("Like my channel!" "Stay tuned!"). The subtext to their "news" is, "HEY, LOOK OVER HERE!" The most effective programming to this end is to prey on consumers' fear, anger, and feelings of being right. The news media's job becomes to confirm viewers biases and give them a sense that they were right all along.

Jefferson's idea that every day, 9-5 folk would gather self-evident truths and apply reason when acting or speaking is to society what Santa Clause is to Christmas, cute mythology parading before the great churning of a market economy. Guiding emotions like fear and anger must be replaced by courage and the hard work of critical thinking to move from a Santa Clause version of reality. Resistance to dramatized "news" forwarded by a friend is built by reading books and thoughtful reflection in the company of others. One must be determined not to be manipulated. For those who produce the news have given up on treating voters as intelligent, capable citizens. Instead of complexity, they dole out simple narratives of good vs. evil and use scare tactics in place of persuasion. "The only true wisdom is in knowing you know nothing," said Socrates. One thing to know for certain is that very, very few of us should claim to know anything with a confidence that keeps us from considering the likelihood that we are mistaken.

The press is a vital **linkage institution** connecting citizens to the government through information and access to the publication. What it reports determines what people talk about and think is important (**agenda setting**). It is the primary way citizens can hold the officeholders accountable (it has a **watchdog** role). The media's watchdog, gatekeeping, and agenda-setting functions are of supreme consequence. Without responsible media that refrains from sensationalism, citizens cannot be expected to self-govern or act beyond the dim light of their casual experiences. However, media driven by advertising is unlikely not to dramatize events. A Pulitzer Prize winning journalist Theodore H. White observed the following of his profession after the 1968 presidential election: "American journalists are the most efficient, honest and accurate presss corps in the world. Yet since time on air is always limited and space in print is always tight, all reporting must be a snatching of fragments, chosen by each reporter's own judgement." But this judgement must lead to news people will want to consume, so news reports better not be "kind, soft or tolerant in judgement..." Reporting "must have bite: TV shows must 'march.'" Twenty-four hour news channels seek drama, excitement. News dependent on advertising revenues "dare not be dull." In providing "infotainment," information providers avoid challenging viewers to think differently. The viewer changes the channel or swipes the screen (after clicking a thumbs down) instead of gathering new facts and feeling doubt over certainty.

The Business of Information

The news has become a business. All but one television channel (the Public Broadcasting Service) and one radio programmer (National Public Radio) are dependent on advertising revenues. The public owns PBS and NPR, and these get their funding through donations and government funding, not advertising. The rest of the news programming must cultivate a consumer base—viewers. When there were three television channels, newsgroups competed with one another for tens of millions of viewers. Today's most popular network news show gets 8 million viewers tuning in on a good day.

Numbers for the week of June 6, 2016:

	ABC	NBC	CBS
• Total Viewers:	8,227,000	7,341,000	6,367,000
• Age 25-54:	1,792,000	1,720,000	1,397,000

by Taboola

Cable news shows can hope for around 2 million viewers.

Advertisers are especially interested in the 25-54 age group—they are the ones with jobs out buying stuff. If a news program has impressive statistics there, it can charge top dollar to advertise during its show. On what kind of stories are they going to focus?

Unlike the viewers who watched the news before cable TV, today's viewer has hundreds of channels through which to get the "news." To attract eyeballs, news shows target smaller audiences by appealing to their ideological biases. The result: the two most popular cable news shows are the most partisan with MSNBC on the left and Fox on the right. When covering the same event, their commentary will vary wildly. Headlines will vary as well:

Sarah Sanders Apologizes for False Claim About Black Jobs Growth Under President Trump

White House Press Secretary Sarah Sanders apologized for falsely claiming that President Trump has created three times as many jobs for black people as former President Barack Obama did during his entire eight years in office. The economy added 2.95 million jobs for African-Americans during Obama's term, whereas 708,000 have been created since Trump took office.

From the Right
Sarah Sanders Issues Correction on Black Employment Numbers, but Refuses to Apologize for One Critical Thing
The Daily Caller
L L C R **R**

From the Center
Sarah Sanders sorry for false claim that Donald Trump created more jobs for blacks than Barack Obama
USA TODAY
L L **C** R R

From the Left
Sarah Huckabee Sanders made a false claim about black employment. She's issued a rare apology
Los Angeles Times
L L C R R

Those who still watch TV keep watching personally tailored programs, and politicians know it. Just like product advertisers, politicians have to "pay to play." Pay they do. In 2012, the Republican and Democratic nominees spent nearly a billion dollars on TV advertising (88% of which covered negative ads towards the opponent). In 2004, for every minute of news coverage in **swing states** of candidates, there were 17 minutes of candidate TV ads. However, most voters are not likely to see these ads unless they live in a competitive market—a swing state.

Once a candidate is elected president, his use of the media does not stop there.

The President's Bully Pulpit

With the advent of the radio in the early 20th century, Americans could listen to the same things as a nation in real time. Baseball players like Babe Ruth and boxers like Jack Dempsey became national heroes. While newspapers informed the nation, radio spoke more directly to Americans' emotions.

Presidents have used this power to step up to the mic and develop a personality, the most notable being Franklin D. Roosevelt. Using the radio, he gave a talk to his constituents every night at primetime, branding them "Fireside Chats." His portrait was hung on millions of dining room walls as countless families invited him into their homes each night.

Obama followed suit. From an article by Kenneth T. Walsh in the July 2015 US News and World Report magazine:

More than ever, President Barack Obama is deftly using the White House **bully pulpit** to illuminate the nation's problems and highlight his proposed solutions. In addition to educating the country, his goal is to frame the political debate and **set an agenda** that the next Democratic presidential nominee can run on next year – an agenda that Obama hopes will put opposition Republicans at a significant disadvantage.

Obama has been getting lots of attention for bypassing the Republican-controlled Congress and using his **unilateral powers**, such as executive orders, to get his way. However, his power to persuade is another vital weapon in the president's arsenal, since he can command media and public attention almost whenever he wants. Increasingly, that's what Obama is doing as he promotes his major initiatives. He appears to be using President Theodore Roosevelt, a progressive Republican who served from 1901-1909, as his model. TR was a firm believer in a president's ability to influence the public and famously said when discussing his vigorous campaigning, "I suppose my critics will call that preaching, but I have got such a bully pulpit!" He was using "bully" as a synonym for "excellent" or "powerful," and this remains true for Obama.

Bully, dude!

In a media environment that treats politicians as though they are fighters in a ring, the president has a crucial advantage in getting his nose out in front of congressional adversaries. With devoted followers, modern Presidents like Trump even have a fan base.

News Consumption

A friend of mine spent his twenties in a punk band. No longer a punk, Bobby is a responsible adult who likes to keep up with the news as well as new artists. He has, ah, strong tastes in music. A few years ago, one of his favorites was a Swedish heavy metal group his wife would not let him play when she was around. I called it devil music. One day, Bobby opened his Internet browser, and there was his favorite, obscure band on the front page. He relayed this story to me, excited his possibly evil favorite band had gotten so famous. I had to burst his bubble and tell him about the echo chamber and algorithms.

Yahoo, Google, and Facebook are not news sites. They are platforms that run on algorithms designed to show what is "trending" and deliver content based on an Internet user's clicks and searches. If you shop for shoes, you will soon see shoe advertisements on your social media platforms. If you visit conservative websites, Facebook will feed you conservative news. Bobby's news included his devil band, but he, being old, still has a news mindset that the same news broadcasts to the country at once.

We live in the "Information Revolution" indeed. One hundred eighty-nine news channels are covering breaking events 24 hours a day. When Bobby and I were kids, three stations covered the news for one hour a day. We should be so much better informed today, right?

With so many messengers, viewers do not know whom to listen to and end up resting on their biases and **political socialization**--by the beam of our cell phones. As the world gets bigger, people become more tribal—they stick with the ideas and values handed down to them because those seem much more trustworthy than the bustling storm of information coming through screens and memes.

Even when Americans watched the same news programs, the **selective perception** bias applied. Even then people saw and heard what they wanted to while ignoring ideas and facts that challenged their beliefs. The tendency to seek information that only confirms biases—**selective exposure**—is what puts one in an **echo chamber**.

Once there, the news consumer only hear "news" that which conforms to the ideas already in their heads. Many never hear facts and points of view that conflict with their own.

Selective perception and exposure amount to the same thing: **confirmation bias**. If one thinks something is true and new information confirms his "truthiness" feeling, he will most likely believe the information to be factual. Taking advantage of this, modern-day propagandists create their own "facts" so that their message will hit the desired "truthiness" feelings of their target audiences.

Manufacturing Facts

When citizens with differing **ideologies** interact, they increasingly bring their own sets of facts to the table that the other side is entirely wrong. It is getting rare for partisan citizens and politicians to agree on what the problem is and how to fix it. Multiple experts claiming diametrically opposing facts is a new problem those wishing to be genuinely informed face. Increasingly, the dogged citizen has to fact-check to a study's source. The useful first question is to ask who would be incentivized to lie?

The tobacco industry once found itself on the losing end of facts—it sold a highly addictive product that caused cancer. The evidence supporting this was considered conclusive by scientists in 1964. However, it was not until 1997 that an executive of a tobacco company admitted the truth. In those thirty years, millions died of cancer caused by cigarettes, yet no **regulations** were put in place to protect the public from the noxious product.

Why did Congress not pass any laws to help save citizens from tobacco? It is important to realize that members of Congress do not do their independent cancer research, and thus need experts to give them data. **Lobbyists** and the media provide those experts. In this case, the tobacco industry funded studies that contradicted those that concluded tobacco smoking kills. Back to the question, which side was more incentivized to lie? Tobacco, of course. Being right did not profit those who claimed the truth. A similar dynamic has gone on between energy companies and climate scientists over the issue of global warming. The following pattern emerges in studies that cast doubt on whether global warming is occurring and its human cause.

HOW TO MAKE UP A FACT:

1.   Have a motive. If you are the owner of a tobacco company, you need a different set of facts that will distract from the conclusion your product is killing people. As recently as 1990, tobacco companies were spending $20 million a year to fund studies saying smoking was not harmful.

2.   Form an organization or company to commission "studies." You want to hide your involvement, as you do not want Marlboro's brand on a study that says smoking is not bad for you. The tobacco's lobby firm, Hill & Knowlton, came up with the Council for Tobacco Research.

3.   Find an expert willing to speak on your behalf. The scientist willing to lend his name to biased studies will be well paid and will get lots of media attention. Dr. Clarence Cook Little did the job for the tobacco industry, insisting cancer is caused by genetics, not smoking.

4.   Send your expert(s) out to the media, getting them on talk shows and before congressional hearings. The most respected journalists included the tobacco industry-sponsored studies and experts to avoid bias and to be fair to both sides. Hindsight, of course, shows that it was never a two-sided issue.

5.   Buy ads. One of Hill & Knowlton's first acts was to spend $250,000 on pro-smoking ads that denied smoking's dangers. The ad reached 43 million people (out of a US population of 163 million). That was just the beginning of the ad onslaught that would continue through the 1990s.

6.   Hire your personal freelance writers to compose articles in support of your cause. Articles like "Phony Cigarette Scare" started being published in magazines such as People and Popular Medicine. TV coverage would routinely include Dr. Little and the Council for Tobacco Research (Hill & Knowlton), as reporters attempted to present "the other side of the issue."

The goal of manufacturing information is to confuse the issue. In the absence of solid information, the citizenry remains passive and the special interest gets its way. No action is taken in the form of laws or agency regulations.

When the government makes policy, there are economic winners and losers. If Congress sees that there is a debate among scientists over a technical issue, then Congress will not pass a law hurting the finances of such major political donors. The confusion was the goal and continues to be for a legion of industry shell companies, non-profits, and think tanks representing industries that will lose money if anything changes.

Media Bias

A common refrain when discussing the media is its **bias**. In most cases, ideological bias acts as the monster that is the horror movie of the media landscape. However, ideological bias can only exist if those with it can profit. If it did not sell it would be of minor concern, making media company's proclivity to make money the first bias to consider.

PROFIT BIAS

The news is not free, and advertising pays the bills. To get advertisers, a news outlet must show that it has viewers.

If a liberal bias costs news organizations money, they will not be news organizations long. News programs, like any, target and cultivate audiences. Like the makers of Gossip Girl or Pretty Little Liars will tell you, they do not make their shows for everyone: they target pre-teen girls. Fox News broadcasts for people with conservative bias; MSNBC does the same with liberal biases. Their goal is more to find the market for the bias and sell it rather than creating it. This bias is already there, in its viewers: the outlets want to capitalize on it. To media companies, a conservative is like someone who likes Coke and liberals their Pepsi, and they deliver the product 24 hours a day, 7 days a week.

Sound bites, "breaking news," and **horse-race journalism** characterize coverage generally. Network television stations must compete with social media, online sources, and cable TV for viewer's attention. TV time is costly, so the political messengers who buy ad time want to get as much emotional effect as they can with the precious seconds they have with an audience. As a result, the press abandons its **watchdog roll** and becomes lapdog to those who can pay to play.

Jefferson's citizen self-governors are the losers. If a product is poisoning a people or voters are being duped by elected officials, the only defense is a free press. Good reporting can have a huge impact, but make no money. In 2013, ProPublica spent two years and $750,000 to produce a report on the dangers of Tylenol's principal active ingredient, acetaminophen. The report saved thousands of lives. Each year sees a decrease in the number of local newspapers and investigative journalists who unearth stories like this. Since 1990, newsroom employment in the US has gone from 55,000 to 33,000 (2014). As mobile devices replace print media for news sources, long-term investigative reporting becomes a rare commodity. If news is to be "free," what sort of reporting can we expect? You get what you pay for...

SCREEN BIAS

Newspapers are on the decline, and the trend will only increase as the population ages. Local papers have historically done the heavy lifting, covering in-depth reporting on local matters. In a given year, a local paper is the one that will discover a school-board bribery scandal, botched homicide investigations, or deception among environmental regulators. Good **investigative reporting** pushes businesses and governments to make better choices because they know they are watched.

Overall, news organizations are losing money as they go digital, losing their capacity to cover local stories in-depth. Thus, stories become more general and sensationalized.

NATIONAL STORY BIAS

Once local newspapers fold, downsize their local reporting budgets, or are bought by one of the "Big Six," their audience is no longer local. They have to sell to a national audience, so reporting on local draining/flooding issues or dirty water is out of the question. Even when small town newspapers manage to survive, they receive most of their stories from national news organizations like the Associated Press or Reuters. The news in Tulsa, OK is the same as it is in Bangor, Maine. "All politics is local" becomes a quaint quote taken from another age.

SOFT NEWS BIAS

"Infotainment" takes the place of "hard news" when profit drives coverage. Most news has little chance to be ideologically biased because most news is not "news" at all. More and more news is soft: not relevant but entertaining. Celebrities, sports, crime, movies, music, and stories about a boy saving puppies from drowning crowd out complex stories about policy issues like trade, education, or healthcare. Local TV news stations produce stories each day with the same people reporting doing the "investigating." A well-known secret is that TV news reads the local paper every morning to decide what stories to "cover" (make a two-minute segment about). While puppies and murders grab attention, such information does not result in more clarity regarding issues like healthcare or education policy.

CONFLICT BIAS

"IF IT BLEEDS, IT LEADS"

Since the news has to cater to an audience socialized by popular entertainment, the news we receive reflects the movies we watch and the music we listen to. If there is video footage of shootings, burnings, verbal rants, or someone mauled by an escalator, it will get top-slot coverage.

When covering political elections, the news media often treats politics as a horse race instead of a set of common problems with various possible policy solutions. When covering issues like climate change, gun control, immigration, trade, or the debt, the media features quotes, barbs, gaffes, and personal insults to heighten the conflict between the candidates rather than define their policy differences. When it does cover issues, like the Democrat's "Green New Deal," the proposal itself is ignored. **Horse race journalism** "news" commentators act more like ESPN personalities as they consider what effect making such a proposal will have in determining who wins the next election. On their shows political parties are more like sports rivals. The fact that sports teams are not expected to run the government seems unimportant when such models of journalism pay network bills.

GOOD STORY BIAS

Donald Trump is a good story. Every week during the 2016 primary season, he seemed to do or say something inflammatory. The controversial real estate billionaire turned reality TV star turned presidential candidate followed a narrative line too tempting for television, print, or online media to pass up on. The New York Times estimates that Trump got $2 billion of free advertising in the form of "news coverage"—whatever he did was news according to network **pollsters** and **ratings**. The same is not true regarding his opponent. While Obama benefitted from the narrative of "First African-American President," Hillary Clinton has not yet received the same narrative boost for possibly being "First Woman President." Back to the profit bias, we get stories that we "buy," and we purchase them simply by viewing and clicking.

As for the issues themselves, **wedge issues** make better stories than policy. These are the topics such as abortion, gun control, or gay rights that divide people into "for" and "against" sides. Trade policy affects the average American much more than wedge issues do but is no fun to talk about. Even considering the annual 8% rise in tuition costs, high school juniors and seniors, along with their parents who will struggle to pay for university, are more likely to engage in a debate over gay marriage than education funding policies.

IDEOLOGICAL BIAS

The latest study reports that 28% of journalists identify with the Democratic Party while only 7% say they are Republicans. The others identify as "Independents." Reporters tend to be against corporations and those in power. On the other hand, the executives above them tend to be "establishtarian" with few liberal tendencies. Much ideological bias is intended to attract viewers into a network's echo chamber. News shows become places where tribes met to converse in their stereotypes and myths, their fables and allegories.

The media can wield as much power as the voters or officials themselves. With an electorate that spends an average of twelve minutes a day getting "news" through mostly social media is it a wonder that those seeking power chose to manipulate voters instead of educating them? The result? Modern Daniel Shays vote for the banker who took his land rather than stoking a rebellion. This was Thomas Frank's conclusion is elites convince common voters that it is another group of elites, the "liberal elite," who cause their suffering and go on to focus on issues that have emotional appeal like gay rights or abortion. By giving their voters scapegoats and simple causes, a rich elite can pursue their self-interested policies of **privatization**, tax cuts and **deregulation**.

In conclusion, in a republic as large as America's the idea of "making a difference" is daunting. Far away systems, be they Snapchat or governments, boards of education or Play Stations, determine much of our daily existence. Rather than call on our courage and creativity, they evoke the smallest, the least creative, least trusting, least loving, and least lovable traits in us all. Our society is technological, requiring that we fulfill narrow, often mindless tasks. We are unimaginably far from Jefferson's self-reliant farmer living under a small republic, self-sufficient on his own property. Instead of independent thought and self-dependence, our socialization is too often an exercise in conformity and adaptation to a gadgets and techniques. If nothing else is at stake, one's sanity and dignity are surely reasons enough to seek to see things accurately in their full complexity. Without fear or panic stoked in our hearts we might experience the unpredictable and exciting journey human enlightenment can be. While a student, turn off the streaming TV and take a break from social media. The pursuit of happiness as "full grown men and women" requires seeing the world accurately and taking action to find a noble place there.

Chapter 3

Shaping Public Opinion

Polling

At their core, polls are sets of questions whose answers will reveal what people want. From there, politicians try to tailor their message and platform to get votes. Popularity builds on itself, and as soon as a politician gets good results, he will use the results of the poll as evidence of his appeal, hoping to create a **bandwagon effect**. If "everyone" likes someone, why shouldn't we like them, too?

Polling is the air politicians and their strategists breathe. For instance, Donald Trump received the Republican Party's nomination in 2016 despite being generally disliked by the elites of his party. They could have decided to kick him out of their club and tell him to run as an Independent. What held them back? Polling showed them that Trump was popular with voters. 80% of Republican voters like him, making him the most popular primary candidate on their side. Polls also showed Trump consistently within three percentage points of Hillary Clinton. So it does not matter that the Republican Party leadership did not want him because enough people did.

Some polls are better than others, though do not expect politicians to criticize the methods of a poll that is favorable to them. In case you are inclined to test the veracity poll numbers presented as fact, here is a brief guide to evaluating the quality of a given poll. Whenever a statistic is used to say what the American people think or feel, a poll is the source of information.

Types of Polls

Opinion Polls-- many people are asked the same questions in order to find out what most people think about something.

Benchmark Polls--Conducted early in a campaign to gauge the name recognition, public image, and electoral prospects of a candidate.

Tracking Polls--Frequent polling using overlapping samples to provide daily updates of the status of the race

Entrance Polls--Taken before voters have cast their ballots to get an early sense of who won and why

Exit Polls--Taken after voters have cast their ballots to get an early sense of who won and why

Push Polls--A biased set of questions geared for a specific outcome disguised as scientific polls.

Poll quality depends on sample size, the quality of the questions, and whether it was a mass poll or focus group. A poll's rate of **sampling error** is a shortcut in finding out whether a poll has truthful information or not. A sampling error is an error that arises as a result of taking a sample from a population rather than using the whole population — the bigger the sample size, the better. Number crunchers like Nate Silver can help us tell if a poll is validly scientific or not.

- The first standard is whether the firm participates in the American Association for Public Opinion Research Transparency Initiative. This poll monitoring group is a member of the National Council on Public Polls or contributes its data to the Roper Center for Public Opinion Research archive. Polling firms that do one or more of these things abide by industry-standard practices for disclosure, transparency, and methodology and have historically had more accurate results.
- The second standard is whether the firm usually conducts its polls by placing telephone calls with live interviewers and calls cellphones as well as landlines. Automated polls ("**robopolls**"), which are legally prohibited from calling cellphones, do not meet this standard. It is increasingly essential to call cellphones given that about half of American households no longer have a home landline. Master statistician Nate Silver comments on one firm's, Zogby, methodology used in its Internet polling: "These polls are conducted among users who volunteer to participate in them, first by signing up at the Zogby site and then by responding to an e-mail solicitation. These Internet polls, to the extent they rely on voluntary participation, violate the most basic precept of survey research, which is that of the **random sample**. And as you might infer, they obtain absolutely terrible results."

Making Polls Say what the Pollster Wants: Push Polls

Because of the central place polling has in our democracy, politicians find ways to get polls to say what they want. **Push polls** are a biased set of questions geared for a specific outcome, and they sneakily disguise themselves as run-of-the-mill polls. Pollsters use **robocalls**, in which a computer calls, asks a question with a series of possible answers, and utilizes pushing a numbers on the phone to indicate an answer. If the questions are generally fair, it is merely a poll. However, if the questions are being asked to sneakily "inform" voters of an opposition candidate's unworthiness for office or profound inner evil, it is a push poll. Examples of push poll questions from a mayoral race in which one Rodney Wiltshire was push-polled by his opponent:

"Are you aware or unaware that Council President Rodney Wiltshire missed two crucial budget votes while vacationing in Florida? Press 1 for aware press 2 for unaware."
"As City Council president, how would you categorize Rodney Wiltshire's leadership: Press 1 for advocate for the people. Press 2 for egocentric and blinded by ambition. Press 3 for self-serving. Press 4 for responsible for city gridlock."
"Which one word best describes the City of Troy City Council under President Rodney Wiltshire: Press 1 for dysfunctional. Press 2 for obstructive. Press 3 for leaderless. Press 4 for self-serving."
"After losing the Democratic primary, do you believe Rodney Wiltshire should have bowed out gracefully and supported the winner of the primary? Press 1 for yes. Press 2 for no."

Testing Public Opinion: Trial Balloons and Leaks

Before taking action, elected officials like to dip their toes into the waters of public opinion to test the temperature. By sending out **trial balloons**, policymakers can test the popularity of a given policy or decision. Most of us have sent out our fair share. You dye your hair pink. However, before posting a selfie on your Snapchat story, you ask your closest friends what they think of the new hairdo. They try to be supportive and muster what compliments they can. "It's different." "I've never seen hair that color before." You conclude from the Snapchat selfie your pink hair will not go over well and you dye it back as close to the original color as soon as possible. Side note: go with pink hair and cut off the Snapchat.

In the political world, actors will often allow **leaks**—information that is not officially released—to the media to see how the public reacts. For instance, after Obama leaked his position in favor of gay marriage and polls showed the public's opinion to be on his side, he took a public stand. The trial balloon sailed. Challengers in elections will often intimate that they are thinking about running, commission a poll, and go from there. If polls show donors and voters seem interested, they will run. As campaign costs continue to rise, throwing one's hat into the ring often means throwing away a perfectly good hat. Fewer and fewer potential candidates are willing to become challengers without polls showing they have a chance at winning.

In our age, good polling is political gold. Mining for it has gotten much harder, in any case. A poll depends on someone answering a phone or going to a screen and answering questions. In 2016 major polls were still conducted by calling landlines. Do you have a phone with a wire that only goes to your house? If not, you were not accessible to pollsters in 2016. Pollsters will eventually find ways to measure the publics' opinion. The information is too valuable to stay buried for long.

Manufacturing Public Opinion

Consider the importance of public opinion to our elected officials in light of the gap between the realities of the world and the pictures individuals have of it. All that is seen and heard goes through emotional layers of primal emotions, preconceptions, and lazy assumptions. Truth itself becomes fluid. Propagandists and political consultants get to work molding public opinion from the raw emotional and intellectual material pre-socialized, pre-sorted groups offer. Shaping perceptions is a lot easier than devising and enacting government policy. Real policy solutions require educating and persuading **voting coalitions** and gaining legislative majorities.

Much easier is to appeal to what groups think they know. Each political group has its own facts within its own echo chambers, each thinking the other unreasonable, vile, and probably part of a conspiracy. To win the public opinion game, politicians learn to tap into and ride on the currents of emotion and myth groups hold in their collective psyches. Campaigns pay top dollar to the firm that can get their sails into the winds of a majority coalition's moods.

Whole industries thrive in the gray area between the way things are seen and what is there. Politicians hire public relations firms to shape a constituency's perception of a problem so they can propose solutions to phantom problems. What is more, the process of manipulating people takes no more energy on their part than staying awake. Again, the "Brexit" referendum in the UK serves as an apt cautionary tale. Paul Flynn of The Guardian newspaper there reported in 2017, April 17:

"Artificial intelligence, algorithms and invisible money sources can overwhelm democratic rules. An elite group is shaping world politics to suit their private beliefs, and their behaviour has untold and unquantifiable effects. While the plot reads like a comic book, this cyber-manipulation is no fiction and played a role in the EU referendum and Donald Trump's election.
When interviewed by Cadwalladr, Leave.EU's communications director admitted Facebook was the key to the entire campaign. A Facebook 'like' was their most potent weapon. 'Using artificial intelligence, as we did, tells you all sorts of things about that individual and how to convince them with what sort of advert. And you knew there would also be other people in their network who liked what they liked, so you could spread. And then you follow them. The computer never stops learning and it never stops monitoring.'

There is contempt for the electoral process.
Lobbyists and billionaires are willfully manipulating the media and public opinion in defiance of **transparency regulations.**
A large group of bots can misrepresent public opinion. 'They could tweet like real users, but be coordinated centrally around a specific topic. They could all post positive or negative tweets skewing metrics used by companies and researchers to track opinions on that topic.' Bots can even 'orchestrate a campaign to create a fake sense of agreement among Twitter users where they mask the sponsor of the message, making it seem like it originates from the community itself.'
Evidence from Oxford Internet Institute suggests that a third of all Twitter traffic prior to the EU referendum was actually bots.
Together, this evidence makes it clear that democracy is struggling to stand tall in a disturbing era where lobbyists can weaponize fake news for the highest bidder. Malign forces can track voters' personal data and manipulate public opinion as if it were in fact using cyber-deception. All of this they can do under cover of anonymity and free of regulation or **oversight**.
The EU **referendum** was a battle of dishonesty. It was won by the side with the means to distribute the most plausible lies."

Prophetically, Walter Lippman expressed no hope in the use of reason and self-evident truths as guides to happiness. In 1922, the dawn of mass propaganda, he paints a bleak picture of the targets of the bots and opinion-shapers. The public, Lipmann writes, forms its views "by scanty attention, by the poverty of language, by distraction, by unconscious constellations of feeling, by wear and tear, violence, monotony. These 'limitations' lead us "to substitute misleading fictions for workable ideas, and to deprive us of adequate checks upon those who consciously strive to mislead." It is the purpose of this book to give the reader the tools necessary to grasp such realities and possess the vocabulary necessary to address them.

Part 2

The Founding

Chapter 4

Making One Nation Out of Independent States

America's First Constitution: The Articles of Confederation

The American colonies decidedly broke the chains of colonialism by winning the Revolutionary War (1781); as a group of states fighting a common enemy they fought as **"a league of friendship"** without a central government. As this friendly league, they defeated the most formidable military power of the age. Remember this when Federalists throw shade on the Articles.

The **Articles of Confederation**, in place from 1781-1789, was more like a treaty. The states were more like countries and less like satellites orbiting a dominant central government as they are today. The central government created by the Articles is now known mainly for its weaknesses, primarily its lack of taxing power and military. The newly independent states did not coordinate their policies, which were made through single-branch governments with no judiciary or executive to check the will of majorities. Dominated by legislatures, state laws and were determined by Jeffersonian electorates who knew more about farming than statecraft.

The conducting of commerce between the states looked more like foreign exchanges rather than interstate commerce. States had different banks and currencies. South Carolina had a little green bill while Rhode Island had a pink square bill the size of a small pizza box. When a South Carolinian went to Rhode Island, the value of his money would go down based on the person taking it. If the bill looked unofficial or from far away, it would go from being worth ten dollars to say, six. This was no way to do business.

Adding to its inability to act and get the states in line was the structure of the Articles' central government. A **confederation**, it lacked a unifying center that provided an underlying national identity to the collection of states. Like most state governments, the Articles national government only had one branch, made up of delegates the states could **recall** within one year. Each state got one vote and amendments required a **unanimous vote**. Small states like Rhode Island liked having equal standing relative to big states like Virginia, but this arrangement left the majority of Americans underrepresented. There was no executive branch to make decisions for the national defense. Nor was there a court system (judicial branch). On the eve of the Constitutional Convention, the central government was subservient to the states and showed little signs of vigor. The states were hardly models of good government. The solution would lie in finding a balance between the central government and state government power.

After the war, it did not take long for order to break down in the states. In contrast to the tyranny of King George and monarchical regimes, the states had swung from legislatures having no power to having all power. State legislatures and the majorities that swayed them had no brake system. State representatives in their 13 respective legislatures were passing laws that would lead to bankruptcy, internal chaos, and even conflicts between the newly independent states. New York and Vermont nearly went to war over a border dispute as the original 13 states were extending their domains as far west as the Mississippi River. A conflict arose in 1787 that encapsulated the weaknesses of the Articles of Confederation and the crisis of state governments.

Shay's Rebellion (1786-1787)

Daniel Shays, a Revolutionary War veteran, returned from the war to his Massachusetts farm to find that the bank was going to take it. He had not paid his debts because the underfunded national government lacked the money to pay its heroes. Big city banks in places like Boston were taking farmers' land at an astonishing rate and selling their farms off to speculators ever eager to grab cheap land to sell for high profits. What is more, states raised land taxes on common folk fivefold during the 1780s to pay off war debt. High taxes and transport costs produced an economic downturn some historians consider worse than the Great Depression of the 1930s. True to Jefferson's vision, Shays and thousands of farmer-vets found this to be a violation of the social compact/contract. As they saw it, the government broke a promise to protect their property—pay them for their service—and was allowing banks to take their land.

Channeling the Declaration's justification of rebellion, the farmers took up arms. When state militias were ordered to fight the farmers, they refused to do so. Shays and the gang were arrested, but local juries freed the rebels, and many of those who took up arms were even elected to their state legislatures. Once in office, they proudly acted as Madison's majority faction and passed laws allowing farmers to pay debts in fruit and vegetables. Some state legislatures even passed outright debt-forgiveness laws. Debtors passing laws that canceled their debts was what Madison feared. To him, debtors were the most dangerous threat to property and liberty--the tyranny of the majority seemed to be using democracy to take property for themselves. Bankers, too, have a social compact with the government regarding their money, and allowing the dissolution of debts was no way to honor that compact.

Fearing civil war or rule by the debtor class (as well as broke governments paid in carrots), city elites pushed back against the rabble. The Massachusetts governor suspended habeas corpus (the rights of the accused/arrested to be lawfully tried) and arrested key leaders of the rebellion who were close to Boston. Those in the Massachusetts countryside prepared themselves for a full-out war. The weak central government, including future first president George Washington, looked on with empty pockets as the Articles gave all taxing and military power to the states. All the central government could do was ask the states for cash, requests the states honored at a 37% rate during the Articles' duration.

Thus, it was up to the Massachusetts governor to put down a rebellion that could quickly spread to other states and lead to a more extensive insurrection. The governor took up a collection from 125 wealthy Bostonians and hired over 3,000 troops to put down the 1,500 farmer-vets. In the fighting that followed, the casualties were low, and the farmers ultimately surrendered. State courts granted most rebels, including Shays, amnesty. Two unlucky insurgents were hung.

Addressing the Weaknesses of the Articles of Confederation

The lesson to the framers was clear. The threat to good government no longer came from a tyrannical government led by a king and aristocrats. As a founder put it, "In our opposition to monarchy, we forgot that the temple of tyranny has two doors. We bolted one of them...but we left the other open." The other door, according to Benjamin Franklin, was "a defect of obedience in the subjects." The rabble, John Adams warned, were emboldened by the freedom given to local governments under the Articles of Confederation and were being led by demagogues – "self-appointed leaders of the people who for dark, ambitious purposes" bully state governments into serving their interests. Adams saw state-level governments in the hands of men with "popular talents" able to manipulate the rabble to get power for themselves. To the traditional governing elite, such people-power in legislatures was as dangerous as a single tyrannical dictator: "40 tyrants at our doors exceeds that of one 3,000 miles away," exclaimed a South Carolina newspaper describing its unruly state legislature. "Liberty," Madison warned, "may be endangered by the abuses of liberty as well as the abuses of power." Freedom was not enough. Order became the priority of those thinking about the type of central government necessary to tame the states and majorities within them. Whew! How to have a government by and for the people when they were the problem?

The problem was one of the access points to the government's power. By giving local and state governments power over armed forces, taxes, and currencies, people everywhere--even debtors--could shape military and economic policy. Majorities in states should not be able to steer taxing and military policy. A more refined hand was needed to control those levers of power.

From the perspective of the ruling class, the "elites," the men behind the Declaration and the nation's independence, were seeing their revolution get hijacked by "lesser" men and majoritarian rule. Beer making rabble-rouser Samuel Adams had even changed his Jeffersonian tune from that of a revolutionary to that of a white-gloved aristocrat. When responding to Shays' Rebellion, he declared, "In monarchy, the crime of treason may admit of being pardoned or lightly punished, but the man who dares rebel against the laws of a republic ought to suffer death."

The Constitution is the response of men like James Madison to demagogues and the majorities they represented. State legislatures seemed to have been captured by "an interested and overbearing majority" led by local loudmouths who stoked people's fears and resentments to get votes. Such men controlling armies and budgets was the immediate problem the Constitution had to solve. However, they had to keep their eyes on the long run. The framers also had to address the perennial plagues that killed good government. In every country before them, too much power fell into the hands of one, the few, or the many, and in choosing which of these was best, the framers created an "All of the Above" answer. An executive would govern alongside a **bicameral legislature**, one part from the people and the other sent by state governments. An independent judiciary would monitor them both. Their plan would be bold and highly inventive. The Constitution they would devise would combine elements of **participatory**, **pluralist**, and **elite** democratic models. In the process, practical solutions to pressing problems had to come with the plan they devised. Pirates, border disputes, currency conflicts, and the general failure of governance plagued the new nation.

Chapter 5

The Great Debate: Anti-Federalists vs. Federalists

The Opponents of the Constitution: Antifederalists

Perhaps the most significant debate in American history concerned the ratification of the Constitution. **Anti-federalists** - opponents of the Constitution who wanted the Articles of Confederation to be strengthened but not abandoned - reacted to the suggestion of the Constitution in fear and some confusion. Anti-federalists like Patrick Henry refused to participate in the Constitutional Convention after it was clear that the 55 delegates intended to write a new constitution. In fairness to Anti-Feds like Henry, the Convention was called to edit the Articles, not to write a new Constitution. Claiming he "smelled a rat," Henry warned that an elite group of Americans was going to become worse than the British had been. While the problems of state governments concerned him, he was much more afraid of the Federalists' centralized government with its kingly executive branch.   He pleaded against the abandonment of a confederate structure: "The Confederation; this same despised Government, merits, in my opinion, the highest encomium: It carried us through a long and dangerous war: It rendered us victorious in that bloody conflict with a powerful nation: It has secured us a territory greater than any European monarch possesses: And shall a Government which has been thus strong and vigorous, be accused of imbecility and abandoned for want of energy? Consider what you are about to do before you part with this Government."

The divisions in **ideology** formed during this time still echo in policy debates today. The divisions between Republicans and Democrats, liberals and conservatives, go back to the founding. The Federalists and Antifederalists would morph and change into America's first two political parties which in turn would evolve into the Democratic and Republican parties in gridlocked battle today.

The two **coalitions** differed in outlook, temperament, and their place in society. The Federalists, intellectual, conversant in the intricate language of political science had a clear edge. The great minds of the American founding were Federalists. Anti-federalists, the "out-of-doors" crowd worried that intellectual and financial elites from a central government would concentrate on trade and manufacturing over the interests of agriculture. The Anti-federalists envisioned an America of Jeffersonian farmers living under municipal and state governments. There, knowledge of the world, currency values, or interest rates would be European concerns. America to them would be a nation of doers, of makers. Commercial and manufacturing interests saw the farmer's produce as raw goods to be bought for the lowest prices possible and sold elsewhere for a trading firm's profit. Antifederalists asked, would the government be for the few at the expense of the many or would the people govern themselves? Two versions of the American future conflicted: Jefferson's agrarian utopia with its small republics versus Madison's complex division of power run by an elite insulated from the whims of majorities.

Antifederalist Fear vs. Federalist Vision

In order to govern themselves, local majorities needed governments near their homes. For farmers and artisans, time was money. They could not afford to travel to a capital city for weeks at a time to debate and vote on laws. They needed the government to be down the street. At the farthest, the state capital - but certainly not in the swampy terrain of what is now Washington, D.C.

Additionally, they did not think it possible, nor did they trust, that educated, wealthy men from established families could represent the interests of the bulk of the population. What did a Boston banker know of the needs of a Western Massachusetts blacksmith? Rural farmers with little schooling saw no point in giving a national government power to solve problems that were unique to merchants and bankers.

Alexander Hamilton's vision of a wealthy, powerful America dominant on the world stage did not inspire them at all.

Different Visions of The Future

Federalists like Hamilton and Madison looked eastward to the Atlantic and saw shipping lanes to the world's riches. They wanted to become a nation mightier and more productive than any in Europe. Coastal banker types who lived in places like Boston and New York had more in common with their counterparts in London and Paris than inland farmers in their states. They wanted big banks that could finance a big central government as it grew its army, navy, canals, bridges, courts, and post offices. Federalists saw a commanding central government with subservient states as the best solution. A unified nation could best face the pressing debt left over from the Revolutionary War, the Native American threat to the west, and the British and Spanish still hanging around the new country like vultures. The U.S. seemed to be on the brink of breaking into city-states and regional powers that European rivals could play off one another.

Anti-federalists feared the East coast, big-city elites dominating western and southern agrarian interests and were content with the confederation supplied by the Articles of Confederation. In its confederated structure, the central government was barely worthy of being called a "government" at all, and the states were free to govern themselves. They saw the future of America heading westward to the Pacific Ocean, where a generation of people was already heading to stake its claim. To the east, the Atlantic Ocean provided the protection of a hundred navies. Instead of wishing to be centered in cities like the Europeans with their class system of lords and subjects, these Americans valued the equality and hard work that farming and craftsmanship engendered. They saw America as the land of the "yeoman farmer," as Jefferson dubbed them, rather than a nation of importers and exporters making vast sums through banks, speculation, and currency exchanges. The American economy rested on the skill and independence of men and women who had bravely made lives for themselves. With all of that Western land, generations to come could continue reinvigorating the American spirit and governing themselves under small legislative bodies.

Let us pause to remember that Jefferson would have only white male property owners practicing the art of self-government. In his more democratic moods, Jefferson would tolerate those owning 25 acres having the vote. To the founders, citizens without property work for others and have no independence of mind or body. Better to give them land than access to power without it. It would be majorities of limited groups of property owners who made policy for the rest. One group's freedom may be another group's tyranny.

Even still, Antifederalists put their faith in the self-sufficient farmer whose independent spirit would expand with the frontier. Hard work and land would produce a sturdy breed of Americans capable of voting responsibly. No book smarts required. An America based on agricultural production and wise leaders, Jefferson surmised, would be self-reliant and immune from the need to trade with outsiders. Unlike industrializing Europe, America would not concentrate its people in polluted cities and make unskilled hourly workers of them. Indeed, **Federalists** like Hamilton seemed to look forward to the day when youth "at a tender age" and their sisters and mothers could be put to work for manufacturers in Eastern cities. Jefferson sought to prevent this fate and thought them better off in the fields, in guilds, or prying land away from the Native Americans to turn into their homesteads.

Counter to this vision, Federalists wanted a government powerful enough to create its own money and regulate the commerce of all states. In this way, it could finance national projects like constructing roads and canals (and later, railroads) to connect its urban centers. Such a government acting in the national interest would surpass all others in wealth and power.

PROBLEMS UNDER THE ARTICLES OF CONFEDERATION

External Threats	Internal Threats
War Debts	Popular Majorities
Spain on the Mississippi	Taxes
Britain still around	Broke national government
Western lands	Currency Chaos

Chapter 6

The Constitution: A Network of Compromises

When shaping the new Constitution, the framers got to the root of the Articles' problem: it was the wrong structure of government for their situation. It provided a cure for the wrong disease. The government framed by the Articles provided a one-branch, unicameral legislature with no judicial or executive branches. Going back to the Magna Carta and the English Bill of Rights, legislatures and bills of rights had been set up to protect property owners from the King. After the War of Independence (1783), America did not have that problem. It had thirteen of the most representative, responsive legislatures in the world with no King to hold them in check. None of the states had judicial branches, and many of them had no executive governors. Unbalanced, the state legislatures put all government controls in the hands of populations that were vulnerable to mood swings and manipulation by selfish leaders. These elites disguised in overalls spoke the farmers' language but acted against the working man's interests just a Thomas Frank claims happened in his native Kansas. Even when elected officials tried to do right, they did not have much room to make unpopular decisions under the Articles. They were elected annually and could be **recalled** at any time, tying lawmakers to the whims of their constituents and making long-term policy making unlikely.

The Constitution Sent to the States for Their Approval: Nine Must Ratify

In 1787, 55 delegates from 12 states met in Philadelphia to edit the Articles of Confederation. When Rhode Island did not send delegates, the prospect of legally changing the Articles became impossible, as amending them required a unanimous vote of 13 states. From the start, the delegates decided to scrap the Articles and perform a constitutional do-over.

The framers would trust the people as little as possible while forming a government that rested its power in the hands of the people. How to stay true to the principle of government "for and by the people" while taking control away from them? The key to this riddle was the idea of **popular sovereignty** - that the people were ultimately in power (but not immediately exercising it). The people's power would rest in a law above the laws of their representative legislatures in ratifying state conventions. Once a supermajority of state legislatures ratified the written Constitution, it would become "the supreme law of the land." This supreme law would keep all levels of governments faithful to the will of the people as they had expressed it in their state ratifying conventions. Such state bodies assembled to debate and vote on the ratification of the proposed constitution. For "the Supreme Law of the Land" to be changed, the people could gather again in state conventions to give direction to all lawmaking in federal and state legislatures.

If a statute contradicted the people's Constitution, the Supreme Court would strike it down as "unconstitutional." If SCOTUS failed in this duty, the people could reconvene to pass an amendment per Article 5 of their Constitution. If the Federalists had indeed created a Frankenstein as the Anti-Federalists feared, at least the amendment process allowed the people to put the beast back on the table for modification.

If **popular sovereignty** seems complicated, that is probably because the idea is stretched to mean more than it does. The high status of the Constitution, the judicial branch's power of **judicial review**, and the incredibly formidable amendment process are hardly banners that scream PEOPLE POWER! Remember, the framers were divorcing the state governments from the people. These democratic marriages suffered economic ruin and internal discord. Concepts like popular sovereignty gave the people the right to visit the children on special holidays, giving them minimal access to the Federalists' government. Let's not abandon the word "democracy" altogether, though. We still have a "**representative democracy**" in which the people elect those who govern and pass laws. In short, a republic.

The debate over the Constitution happened in two places. The first was at the Constitutional Convention in 1787. The second took place over two years in the national press. Once the convention of delegates sent the proposed constitution for publication in every newspaper in the country, the debate took place there, in newspapers. The 85 articles written in favor of the Constitution by John Jay, James Madison, and Alexander Hamilton are now a book available at your local bookstore titled "**The Federalist Papers**."

Debates at the Constitutional Convention

The most profound cleavage between the framers was the Northern/Southern--non-slave/slave--divide. Before even taking part in writing a new constitution, the slave state delegates made clear to their abolitionist peers that debating the existence of slavery was off the table. All agreed. Apart from slavery, small and large states bitterly disagreed on whether representation should be equal in the legislature or based on population. Small states were accustomed to equality with the most significant states under the Articles. Moving to a **popular**, population-based representation system would take up the most time of any issue at the convention. It was within the context of representation and voting power that slavery would come up, though not by its name.

THE COMPROMISES OF 1787

The Great Compromise

The Slavery Compromises

- **3/5 Clause**
- **Fugitive Slave Clause**
- **Slave Trade Clause**

THE GREAT COMPROMISE

Not surprisingly, populous slave states favored a republic based on proportional representation rather than the equal representation the Articles' congress afforded small states. The **Virginia Plan** gave large states a share of seats that reflected its large population in a single legislative body. Small states put their hopes for a weaker central government and equal representation in the **New Jersey Plan**. Under the small states' scheme, Congress would still be the most powerful branch, with each state represented equally in a unicameral body. Apart from a Senate with equal representation, the framers approved the main features of the Virginia Plan.

The final compromise, the Connecticut or "The Great Compromise," had the people directly elect the **lower house** of Congress. State legislatures would send two of their best to serve in the Senate, Congress' **upper house**. While we may call this arrangement undemocratic today, for their time this was a radical way to run a government.

GRAPHIC: NEW JERSEY v. VIRGINIA PLAN (Venn Diagram)

Slavery and the Constitution: Compromising Against Principle

Looking back, a conflict between slave and free states seems inevitable. The only question is when this conflict should have occurred. The founders chose to form one nation at the cost of leaving nearly 700,000 enslaved people within it (total U.S. population: 3.8 million). The slave states made clear that they would not hear any talk of abolition, though many of the founders were die-hard abolitionists. While acknowledging its evil, the framers left it to later generations to end this "peculiar institution." Three states had already done so, and many others were considering it. As founder Oliver Ellsworth saw the issue, "poor laborers will be so plenty as to render slaves useless. Slavery in time will not be a speck in our Country."

Of course, slavery did not end. Many of the next generations of Americans considered the Constitution to be "a covenant with death and agreement with hell," as William Lloyd Garrison phrased it in a Fourth of July speech in 1854. Even at the time of the founding, many founders spoke of slavery's evil. Activists since the end of slavery have fought for the long-due inclusion of African-Americans in the **franchise**, public offices, congressional districts, and public schools. Legal segregation is U.S. history though social, housing, and education segregation remains.

Although there were several clauses addressing slavery in the document, the word "slave" never explicitly appears. The framers avoided such a stark contradiction to the expressed values of the Declaration like "all men are created equal." Slave state delegates threatened to walk out of the convention if their abolitionist brethren proposed abolishing slavery. So while the perpetuation of "America's original sin" was off the table, there were three areas of contention regarding the issue of slavery: representation, the slave trade, and escaped slaves.

The Three-Fifths Compromise. Southern states wanted to increase their population count to maximize their representation in the House (based on population) and in the Electoral College by extension. So, ironically, they wanted

slaves to count along with freemen in their populations. Non-slave states gave them a majority of what they wanted, counting each slave as 3/5 of a person. The **3/5 Compromise** gave slave states an edge in national politics, in both congressional and presidential elections, until after the Civil War.

The formation of the Electoral College

At the Philadelphia convention, the visionary Pennsylvanian James Wilson proposed the direct national election of the president. However, the savvy Virginian James Madison responded that such a system would prove unacceptable to the South: "The right of suffrage was much more diffusive [i.e., extensive] in the Northern than the Southern States; and the latter could have no influence in the election on the score of Negroes." In other words, in a direct election system, the North would outnumber the South, whose many slaves (more than half a million in all) of course could not vote. Standard civics-class accounts of the Electoral College rarely mention the real demon dooming direct national election in 1787 and 1803, which was slavery. The Electoral College let each Southern state count its slaves, albeit with a two-fifths discount, in computing its share of the overall count.

Virginia emerged as the big winner—the California of the Founding era—with 12 out of a total of 91 electoral votes allocated by the Philadelphia Constitution, more than a quarter of the 46 needed to win an election in the first round. After the 1800 census, Wilson's free state of Pennsylvania had 10% more free persons than Virginia but got 20% fewer electoral votes. Perversely, the more slaves Virginia (or any other slave state) bought or bred, the more electoral votes it would receive. Were a slave state to free any blacks who then moved North, the state could lose electoral votes. If the system's pro-slavery tilt was not overwhelmingly obvious when the Constitution was ratified, it quickly became so. For 32 of the Constitution's first 36 years, a white, slaveholding Virginian occupied the presidency.

Slave Trade. The slave trade would remain legal until 1808. That gave the slave states enough time to import the slaves necessary to sustain an "in-house" slave trade (slave owners became slave merchants). This provision seems only to have applied to South Carolina, the only state not to have outlawed the slave trade by 1787.

Fugitive Slave Clause. Those in free states must return escaped slaves to their owners in slave states. Tragically upheld in Dred Scott v. Sandford (1857).

Federalists' last Compromise with the Antifederalists: Protections for Individual Rights

If nothing else, the adoption of the Bill of Rights (adopted by the first congress in 1790) shows that the Constitution was anything but stone tablets the framers brought down from a mountaintop like Moses and the Ten Commandments. Just about everything in it is the result of a compromise of values and ideas, even the first ten amendments, The **Bill of Rights**. How could a list of freedoms have been controversial?

One might not think of the Bill of Rights as being a key compromise in getting the Constitution ratified. Nevertheless, Federalists like James Madison mocked the Antifederalists for demanding a Bill of Rights. From the Federalists view, calling such a list a "parchment barrier" that an overly powerful government or a **tyranny of the majority** could easily crumple up. Regular elections, three branches that checked one another's power, the preservation of local governments, trial by jury, and habeas corpus protect liberty more effectively than a limited list of rights. To Madison's credit, authoritarian governments around the world have splendid lists of rights that citizens never get to enjoy. Federalists like him warned such a list of rights could be used against someone who "discovered" a new right. Prohibiting someone from doing something implies that they can do it. To the Federalist mind, violating speech or personal property was not possible since such powers were not enumerated. The Federalist Constitution lists the new federal government's power in order to limit it. For example, the "right to privacy" and "freedom of expression" are not listed. Does that mean Americans do not have such rights? Making a list of all rights that does not include these suggests the U.S. Constitution does not. In the end, the Federalists did not see much harm in passing the Antifederalists' Bill if it led to more states ratifying the Constitution.

Indeed, at the beginning of the nation's history, citizens needed little protection from the federal government; it was small and distant and underfunded. State and local governments were the principal seats of power. Additionally, states had their own bills of rights that protected individual liberties like freedom of speech and religion.

Over time, the Bill of Rights would become central to the role of the Constitution in American's lives. However, the federal government did not start making states protect rights such as individual freedom of speech or freedom from unreasonable searches for a century and a half after the framing.

In addition to their arguments that a federal bill of rights would be a meaningless "parchment barrier" or worse, used against individuals claiming rights not listed in it, the founders pointed to the text and structure of the Constitution to claim that individual rights would be protected:

- Article One, Section 9, clause 2 reads, "The privilege of the writ of **habeas corpus** shall not be suspended, unless when in cases of rebellion or invasion the public safety may require it."

- Aritcle One, Section 9, clause 3 reads, "No **Bill of Attainder** or **ex post facto** Law shall be passed.

- The Constitution's federal structure. The federal government had only the powers listed in Article I, Section 8. If not in that list of **enumerated powers**, the **10th Amendment** makes clear that those "powers not delegated to the United States by the Constitution, nor prohibited by it to the States, are reserved to the States respectively, or to the people."

Habeas Corpus

In its barest form, a writ, or order, of **habeas corpus** is someone in jail sending a note to a judge asking the court to provide due process. If the federal government were to violate individual rights, habeas corpus gives the wronged party a way to seek the court's help. Meaning, "show the body," the writ requires the government to follow steps like providing a jury and attorney in a public trial. When a judge considers a habeas petition she determines whether a detention is authorized. The most recent habeas corpus cases have involved the executive branch's detainment of terrorism suspects in overseas locations.

Bill of Attainders and Ex Post Facto Laws

Bills of attainders are death sentences passed by legislatures. Not only would the practice be a breach of the separation of powers principle, such actions were clear examples of rule by law instead of rule of law. These were usually used against political enemies of the crown. Not only bills of attainer condemn the accused to death, they aimed to corrupt his blood—preventing any heirs from inheriting land or riches, ending a family's high status and economic security.

Ex Post Facto laws deem a past action illegal, though there had been no law against it when the act had been carried out. While bills of attainder prevented the law from singling out one person, the ban on ex post facto laws kept it from making one deed illegal in order to use the law as a weapon instead of a rule for order. If the government could use laws to make innocent conduct when committed punishable, then the law would be no more than the personal mood of those in power at a given time. Together, these two provisions show the strong commitment the framers had to a rule of law system under which all would be equal. Tellingly, the next part of Article I, Section 9 prohibits state and federal governments from granting titles of nobility. Americans would be judged on their behavior under a system of laws, not men.

Structural Protections of Individual Rights

In addition to habeas corpus protections, the Federalists thought the structure of the Constitution, not a list of rights, would protect individual rights from being stamped out by the federal government. A case in point, consider the case of one high school senior, Alfonso Lopez and how the federal system protected him from a powerful central government:

U.S. v. Lopez (1992)

Eighteen-year-old Alfonso Lopez Jr. was just six weeks short of his high school graduation when, in March 1992, he was caught carrying a .38-cal. handgun on school grounds. The San Antonio, Texas senior suddenly found himself in deep trouble. Thanks to a law Congress had passed two years earlier that banned guns within 1,000 ft. of a school, Lopez had little chance of escaping a six-month prison sentence.

Little chance, that is, until Lopez's court-appointed defense attorney decided that his client's case was hopeless enough to warrant a bold gamble. Lopez had a daring lawyer who threw the equivalent of a Hail Mary pass in the final two seconds of the Super Bowl. Lopez's lawyer argued that the federal government acted in violation of the principle of federalism. Pushing back against the federal Gun-Free School Zones Act, Lopez's side wanted to draw the line between state power and federal government overreach. Going back to the arguments in **McCulloch v. Maryland**, the state of Florida (representing Lopez) saw the federal government's dominion as limited to only those powers explicitly spelled out in the U.S. Constitution in Article 1, Section 8. Remaining areas of authority, such as law enforcement and education, are jealously cloistered behind the 10th Amendment's powers reserved to the states. Up until Lopez's case, however, the Supreme Court had permitted the federal government to breach certain portions of this wall, using the **Commerce Clause**.

In a shocking majority ruling, SCOTUS agreed with Lopez's lawyer that the Gun-Free School Zones Act of 1990 is unconstitutional.   The court rejected arguments based on the Commerce Clause, like guns in schools contribute to violence, which in turn hampers students' learning and hurts the economy by making students less productive. In doing so, the court went against decades of precedent in clipping the wings of the Commerce Clause. The court was deeply divided, however. Justice Stephen Breyer, who called the majority ruling "extraordinary," took the unusual position of reading from the bench a portion of his dissent, which argued that "gun-related violence in and around schools is a commercial, as well as a human problem."

Lopez won his case and faced state, non-felony charges. Avoiding a federal charge allowed him to handle firearms for a living in the U.S. Marine Corps, something he could not have done with a felony conviction. An irony of federalism: extra layers of governments over him gave Lopez more, not fewer, rights. Lopez's case worked out just as Hamilton predicted in Federalist Paper 51:

In the compound republic of America, the power surrendered by the people, is first divided between two distinct governments, and then the portion allotted to each subdivided among distinct and separate departments. Hence a double security arises to the rights of the people. The different governments will control each other; at the same time that each will be controled by itself.

.

Chapter 7

Federalism: The Power Flow Between Federal and State Governments

In 1789 the Federalists got their way. The Federalists assured the states that the Constitution left state and local governments with most of the powers they enjoyed under the Articles. States could still put their residents in prison for not going to church, for instance. The Bill of Rights only applied to actions of the federal government, so individuals and their states worked out the boundaries of speech and religion. While the federal or central government is way more powerful than the states today, the states still have considerable **powers reserved** for them, especially over criminal law and education. In a federal system in which multiple layers of government govern the same land and people, laws can differ wildly from state to state. Consider the following:

In Alabama, it is illegal to wear a fake mustache that causes laughter in church.
In Maine, shotguns must be taken to church in the event of a Native American attack.
It is illegal to have Christmas decorations up after January 14.
In Massachusetts it is illegal to own an explosive golf ball.
In Mississippi one can be fined up to $100 for using profanity in public.
In Nebraska it is illegal for a mother to give her daughter a perm without a state license.
In New York City, it is illegal to fart in church with the intention of causing a disturbance.
In North Carolina, elephants may not be used to plow cotton fields.
In Nicholas County, West Virginia no clergy members may tell jokes or humorous stories from the pulpit during church services.

The Constitution's federal system divides power and responsibilities between different governments that rule the same land and people (**federalism**). Conflicts are inevitable in such a setup. The framers devised a structure with many **access points**.

A stronger central government along with weaker, yet still powerful, state governments would give everyone a chance to vote, run for office, and see their policymakers at the market. For the day to day operations, local institutions - state legislatures, city councils, and school boards, along with their local court systems, agencies, and enforcement bodies - would be the government with which most of the population interacted. The problem was that the states had powers national in their scope, especially **fiscal**, **monetary**, and military powers.

The framers were careful to list—to enumerate--the powers they were taking away from the states through the Constitution. Namely, the central government claimed the powers to tax, raise armies, make treaties, and regulate interstate and international commerce. Such a concentration of vital powers made those in favor of states' power--the Anti-Federalists--very nervous. To reassure them, the Constitution gives the states a sort of guarantee: the **Tenth Amendment**. This darling of the Anti-Federalists reads, "The powers not delegated to the United States by the Constitution, not prohibited by it to the States, are reserved to the States respectively, or to the people." Putting undelegated, unlisted, powers in the hands of the people instead of a central monarch was revolutionary at the time. Powers came from the center in those countries. All power was the king's while the people possessed what he willed. The 10th Amendment showcases the revolutionary character of the Constitution: unclaimed powers belonged to the people in their state governments.

State governments continue to cling to the promise of **state sovereignty**, that states keep those powers not explicitly granted to the federal government in the Constitution. Based on the wording of the 10th Amendment, powers of state governments are known as **reserved or delegated powers**. Such areas like criminal law, housing codes, infrastructure, education curriculum, healthcare, welfare, and institution funding come from state and local revenues, regulated by locally elected officials. Who else better to serve the communities' needs than those who live in them? However, the boundary between powers, even over areas like education and crime, did not remain clear for long.

Madison and the framers would put the burden on the courts to keep the states (and other branches of the federal government) in line with the Constitution.

While states could pass and enact unconstitutional laws, the judiciary could later declare such laws void. How much power the Court had was not clear. Unlike the executive branch with its **expressed powers** or the legislature's **enumerated powers**, SCOTUS had to establish and build its strength. First, it would have to prove itself equal to the other federal branches. Secondly, it would show it could assert federal power over the states.

SCOTUS Becomes an Equal Branch

Marbury v. Madison (1803)

The story began in the third presidential election (1800) between America's two new political parties, The Federalists and Democratic-Republicans (Anti-Federalists). The Federalists had put the first two presidents in office (Washington and John Adams) and had dominated Congress. This changed in 1800 when Thomas Jefferson won the presidency, and his party took control of Congress.

John Adams determined to make the central government as Federalist as he could before state-friendly Jefferson took over. He and Congress would spend the next few months, the lame-duck period, trying to keep the government as federalist as possible. Until 9:00 pm of his last night in office, Adams was sending out "You're Hired!" notes with the seal of the President on them. Marbury's was not delivered by a neglectful clerk and was still sitting on the desk when Jefferson's new Secretary of State, James Madison, came to work. Jefferson told Madison not to deliver it. Wanting the job Adams gave him, Marbury sued, submitting his case before the Supreme Court with John Marshall at its head. John Adam's son Henry remembered Marshall's one fault: "he detests Thomas Jefferson." In his turn, Jefferson hated Marshall as well. Surely Marshall would rule in favor of Adams and enjoy ordering Jefferson around.

There was a catch. Marshall knew that Jefferson would not comply with a court order to deliver the job notice. As Hamilton pointed out in Federalist 78, while the executive had an army at its command, SCOTUS had no **enforcement power** at all. As Alexander Hamilton saw it in **Federalist 78**, the judicial branch would be the "least dangerous" because it had "neither FORCE nor WILL, but merely judgment." This was certainly true in 1803 when the court met in the Senate basement, a moldy and murky origin far from the temple from which "The Nine" issue rulings today. It would take John Marshall to elevate the Supreme Court's status from the basement. If he ruled against the executive only to have the ruling ignored, the court would sink further. So he did something characteristically clever. He found a way for Marbury and Jefferson to lose while claiming that the court had the power to declare actions of the president and Congress unconstitutional. That is, Marshall avoided a showdown he could not win while still claiming the Court's power of judicial review over the other two branches of government.

Marshall ruled that Marbury should have gone to a lower court first as the Supreme Court has **original jurisdiction** only over those matters listed in **Article III**. It reads that the court can first hear cases that affect "ambassadors, other public ministers and consuls;--to all cases of admiralty and maritime **jurisdiction**;--to controversies to which the United States shall be a party;--to controversies between two or more states;--between a state and citizens of another state;--between citizens of different states;--between citizens of the same state claiming lands under grants of different states, and between a state, or the citizens thereof, and foreign states, citizens or subjects." In Marbury's case, his case should have been heard first in a lower court then appealed to SCOTUS. SCOTUS is primarily a **court of appeals** and has minimal **original jurisdiction**.

Getting to the court's power over the executive, Marshall ruled Congress's Judiciary Act unconstitutional which would have required the president to give Marbury a job. It was a genius maneuver. Marshall overruled an act of Congress and claimed, on the record, that SCOTUS could also review acts of the executive.

Federal Power Over the States

Having established the court's clout among the other two federal branches, Marshall waded into those waters the framers intended the Court to navigate--the area between federal and state power. After establishing the court's power as co-equal to the legislative and executive branches, Marshall's court would fulfill Madison and the Federalists' vision for its role: to impose the will of the federal government on the states.

Generally, the national government would use a combination of powers to become supreme over the states. Through two vague clauses in Article I, Section 8, and the **Supremacy Clause** in Article 6, the federal government's power relative to state governments has grown much over time. The Commerce Clause and the **Necessary and Proper clause** are the conduits for powers implied by those expressed in the Constitution.

If the national and state governments are in a tug-of-war, the Commerce and Necessary and Proper clauses are the rope. Officiating the contest, the Supreme Court has become a central player in the national government's growth. This was no accident; the Court was designed to navigate the murky, choppy waters between the state and national governments. Moreover, lest the student forgets Brutus' argument, SCOTUS is on the federal government's, not the states', team.

The Necessary and Proper Clause

Article 1, Section 8 of the Constitution provides the basis of **implied powers** through the **Necessary and Proper Clause**. This provision is also known as **the Elastic Clause** because its application and meaning can be stretched to achieve the necessary ends of an effective national government. The exact text of the provision reads, "The Congress shall have Power ... To make all Laws which shall be necessary and proper for carrying into Execution the foregoing Powers, and all other Powers vested by this Constitution in the Government of the United States, or in any Department or Officer thereof." The elastic clause is state rights people's worst nightmare, as it can be loosely interpreted to serve federal wishes. One monumental case ushered in a period of the federal government's increasing supremacy over state governments and its ability to enact laws not explicitly written in Article I, Section 8's enumerated powers.

McCullough v. Maryland (1819):

Story:

Remember **Shay's Rebellion**? Come on, that was just a chapter ago! Well, Shays and his farmer kind were having their land taken by banks. In response, they shut down foreclosure courts and even took up arms. This scenario was beginning to play itself out again in the 1810s. This time around, state banks had made loans to farmers. When the economy fell, farmers were not able to pay on their loans, and the state banks began foreclosing. State legislatures responded by taxing the federal bank to give relief to debtors. James McCullough, the manager of the federal bank in Maryland, refused to pay the tax. Maryland sued, claiming that establishing a national bank was not an enumerated power. The federal government drew their trump card: the Necessary and Proper Clause (banks being necessary to foster commerce in a national economy).

In the case that followed, old Federalists and Antifederalist wounds reopened. Those in favor of a strong central government like Alexander Hamilton saw a central bank as "necessary and proper" to carry out the central government's role. Antifederalist Jeffersonians pointed to the list of enumerated powers of Congress to tax, spend, and raise a military in Article I, Section 8 and found no mention of a bank. Maryland's lawyers pointed to Federalists' assurances that Congress could not - would not - go beyond the enumerated powers found in the Constitution. That was 1788; it was 1819 now and the last of the Federalists, like Supreme Court Chief Justice John Marshall were intent as ever in building a strong central government. Using the Necessary and Proper Clause, Marshall spoke for the court: "We are unanimously of opinion, that the law passed by the legislature of Maryland, imposing a tax on the Bank of the United States, is unconstitutional and void." Citing the commerce, the supremacy, and the necessary and proper clauses, John Marshall vaulted federal power over state governments and won a decisive victory over the Anti-Federalists.

The Commerce Clause and the Growth of the National Government

Article I, Section 8, Clause 3, establishes that Congress has the power to regulate foreign and interstate trade. This gives the federal government ultimate authority when states do business with one another (**interstate commerce**). However, the federal government has no constitutional right to interfere when states do business within their respective borders (**intrastate commerce**). Although this seems clear enough, which level of government is in charge of trade is murkier.

Confusingly, the meaning of the term "commerce" has been interpreted in different ways, depending on the **judicial philosophy** of Supreme Court justices. Around 1900, SCOTUS refused to interfere with intrastate trade no matter the injustice (i.e., child labor and unsafe working conditions) if money exchange over state lines was not the issue. However, by 1964, the Commerce Clause was being used to combat a whole range of activities, including racial segregation.

While the Commerce Clause may seem lackluster and technical, an analogy from Jab Abumrad, host of a podcast about the Supreme Court, helps in understanding the potency of the clause.

For me, the experience I had learning about the commerce clause was a little like watching the X Men movies. Like, initially, I was like, 'Why is Magneto the head of the bad guys.' Why would they follow him? He has the most boring power. I mean he can control metal. Ok. Mystique can shift into any shape she wants! Storm can control lightning!... I didn't understand the true, deep nature of his power. But then you see these scenes where he's being attacked by a thousand policemen and he just kinda, 'whew'--makes their bullets freeze in mid-air. Or he picks up a bridge just by pointing at it. And then it hits you...he has the best power!

Like metal, money is in everything. So, the commerce clause touches every aspect of our lives. Or can, depending on who sits on the SCOTUS bench. Once the student gets past its "shell of boring," the commerce clause has a lot of great stories to tell.

Commerce Clause Cases

Commerce Clause Victories

Gibbons v. Ogden (1824):

Story: Aaron Ogden had been given exclusive rights by the state of New York to operate his steamboat business on the river between New York and New Jersey. Thomas Gibbons, however, said, "You can't do that, Ogden, because federal law gives me the right to operate my steamboats there, too."

Legal question: Did the state of New York infringe on the federal government's Commerce Clause power?

Decision: Yes! The federal government has the power to settle disputes between states regarding interstate commerce.

This case established the federal government's ability to settle disputes among the states through the commerce clause.

Heart of Atlanta Motel v. United States (1964):

Story: A racist hotel owner sued the federal government after it outlawed his prejudice against African American would-be customers. He was trying to challenge **the 1964 Civil Rights Act**. The owner, Moreton Rolleston, who also happened to be a lawyer, represented himself in court and argued that the federal government's Commerce Clause power did not reach so far as to dictate whom he did business with on his personal property. He also argued that the imposition of the law made him a slave who should be protected by the **13th Amendment**!

Legal question: Was the 1964 Civil Rights Act's prohibition against discrimination in public places (including businesses) based on race, color, religion, sex, or national origin stretching the Commerce Clause too far?

Decision: No. The Commerce Clause extends to private businesses. The 1964 Civil Rights Act was upheld as constitutional because of the Commerce Clause. To no surprise, Rolleston was not regarded as a slave by the court.

Raich v. Gonzalez (2005)

Story: California voters passed a **referendum** legalizing marijuana in 1996, in clear violation of federal law. The Controlled Substance Act of 1971 (CSA) classifies marijuana as a Schedule 1 drug, equal in severity to heroin and cocaine. Angel Raich, a patient whose doctors testified that she needed medical marijuana to stay alive, received prescribed weed from two anonymous caregivers. The caregivers wanted to be sure that they would not be arrested under federal law and filed an **injunction** against the enforcement of the CSA.

Legal question: Does the Commerce Clause supersede state laws like CA's referendum, giving the federal government implied the power to outlaw marijuana? Alternatively, do states retain their reserved power to legislate on issues not expressly mentioned by the Constitution? The Constitution contains no references to drugs, food, or medicine. Further, does the Commerce Clause apply to a case in which there is no interstate commerce? After all, the exchanges between Raich and her doctor as well as the growing of the marijuana were intrastate transactions—no aspect of the trade or growth of the weed left California's borders. Lastly, Raich did not even pay for the marijuana—it was given to her to avoid "commerce" specifically.

Decision: The Commerce Clause does indeed prevail. Raich's actions, as well as her doctor's and caregivers', were illegal and punishable under federal law. Confused how the case has anything to do with commerce? The Supreme Court said the case fell under the authority of the Commerce Clause as "the regulation is squarely within Congress's commerce power because the production of the commodity meant for home consumption, be it wheat or marijuana, has a substantial effect on supply and demand in the national market for that commodity."

Commerce Clause Losses

(Victories for states' reserved powers)

Two recent cases put limits on the power associated with the Commerce Clause.

United States v. Lopez (1995):

Story: A 12th-grade student, Alfonzo Lopez, brought a concealed gun to school. The state of Texas arrested him, as it was illegal to possess a gun on a school campus. The next day, the national government charged him with violating federal law as well, the Gun-Free School Zones Act of 1990. The law aimed to prevent gun violence at schools, but it had little constitutional ground to stand on. The federal government argued that gun violence negatively affects the health of communities and their economies (e.g., property values).

Legal question: Can the national Congress enact laws that apply to individuals within states under the authority of the Commerce Clause?

Decision: The Commerce Clause does not stretch so far. The law belongs in a state's criminal statute book and is a reserved power of states, having no direct effect on economic activity.

United States v. Morrison (2000):

Story:

The U.S. Supreme Court struck down as unconstitutional a key section of the 1994 Violence Against Women Act (VAWA). That section allowed a victim of rape or other violence "motivated by gender" to sue the perpetrator for **civil damages** in federal court for violating her civil rights.

The act established both a federal right to be "free from crimes of violence motivated by gender" and a federal remedy for violating that right. Namely, sexually assaulted women could more readily seek compensatory and punitive damages in federal courts. The federal claim was not meant to replace punishment by state criminal statutes but to supplement them. In 1995, Christy Brzonkala became the first person to sue under the act, over a rape that allegedly occurred in her dormitory room while she was a student at Virginia Polytechnic Institute. The men accused, two football players named James Crawford and Antonio Morrison, had been cleared by both a university judicial committee and a criminal grand jury.

Legal Question:

Had Congress exceeded its constitutional authority in passing VAWA?

Outcome:

In 1999, the U.S. Court of Appeals for the Fourth Circuit (Richmond, Virginia) ruled against her, saying that Congress had exceeded its constitutional authority in passing VAWA.

U.S. v. Morrison eventually came before the Supreme Court. The Court stated that the issue under consideration was "Did Congress exceed its powers when it gave victims of sex crimes the right to file **civil lawsuits** against their attackers?" The Court answered, "yes." Referencing Lopez, Chief Justice Rehnquist deflated the commerce clause again:

"....the Commerce Clause...is subject to outer limits.....the scope of the interstate commerce power 'must be considered in the light of our **dual system of government** and may not be extended so as to embrace effects upon interstate commerce so indirect and remote that to embrace them, in view of our complex society, would effectually obliterate the distinction between what is national and what is local and create a completely centralized government.'"

In its ruling, the Court seemed to address Brutus' fear:

Of..."all ideas of confederation are given up and lost. It is true this government is limited to certain objects, or to speak more properly, some small degree of power is still left to the states, but a little attention to the powers vested in the general government, will convince every candid man, that if it is capable of being executed, all that is reserved for the individual states must very soon be annihilated, except so far as they are barely necessary to the organization of the general government. The powers of the general legislature extend to every case that is of the least importance — there is nothing valuable to human nature, nothing dear to freemen, but what is within its power. It has authority to make laws which will affect the lives, the liberty, and property of every man in the United States; nor can the constitution or laws of any state, in any way prevent or impede the full and complete execution of every power given."

Special Sections: Marijuana and Transgender Bathrooms

MARIJUANA LEGALIZATION

Perhaps no other issue illustrates the conflict between the federal and state governments as does this question.

The federal government made marijuana an illegal substance on par with heroin and cocaine through the Controlled Substances Act in 1970. Since then, citizens have gotten extreme prison sentences for selling small amounts of the drug. Consider Patricia Spottedcrow of Oklahoma who received a 12-year prison sentence for selling $31 worth of weed. Her arrest was one of the millions since 1970. In 2014 alone, there were 620,000 arrests—1,700 a day—despite the drug being recreationally legal in

Washington state and Colorado, and medicinally legal in 32 states. These states are acting as laboratories for the legalization of marijuana, but this experiment is in direct defiance of the Controlled Substances Act. Such enforcement of the act was ruled constitutional in Raich v. Gonzales (2005). To recall, the decision in Raich upheld the federal government's extensive use of the commerce clause, ruling that any action that even indirectly impacted commerce falls under the national government's implied power. The year Raich was decided, it became evident that the fight between the states and the national government was far from over.

In 2005, Montana legalized medical marijuana with 62% of the vote in a **referendum**. Still hesitant to grow due to the federal outlaw of the plant, Montana growers were encouraged by Obama's Justice Department, who stated users or growers complying with state law would not be arrested. The pot industry took off. In 2009, 3,900 patients were using the drug and there were 1,400 providers of it. By 2012, there were nearly 30,000 patients.

However, for unknown reasons, President Obama instructed his **Justice Department** to change course in 2011. Federal agents resumed arresting small-scale growers, going as far as having the **Internal Revenue Service** strictly enforce tax regulations, a sure way to destroy the industry. Despite previous reassurances that state-legal growers would be safe, the **Drug Enforcement Agency (DEA)**, **the Bureau of Alcohol, Tobacco, Firearms, and Explosives (ATF)**, and the **Federal Bureau of Investigation (FBI)** were busting marijuana growers again.

Rebecca Richman Cohen from The New York Times captured one grower's tragic story:

Consider the case of Chris Williams, who opened a marijuana grow house in Montana after the state legalized medical cannabis. Federal agents eventually arrested Mr. Williams despite Montana's medical marijuana law. He faced a mandatory minimum of more than 80 years for marijuana charges and for possessing firearms during a drug-trafficking offense.

This outcome is sad, of course — Mr. Williams will not be free to raise his teenage son — but it is also morally repugnant. Even if you think that the benefits of legalized medical marijuana do not outweigh the costs — a crucial debate, but one we can table for the moment — a coherent system of justice that claims to maintain public order must explain why one defendant is punished more harshly than the next. It must explain why a farmer who grows marijuana in compliance with state law should be punished much more harshly than some pedophiles and killers. If we cannot explain this disparity, our **political process** and **linkage institutions** lay waiting for us to change it.

Leading up to Mr. Williams's trial, federal prosecutors offered him various **plea bargains**, but he turned them all down. He believed, quixotically enough, that he deserved his day in court. He held this conviction even though prosecutors precluded him from presenting his compliance with state law as a defense to the federal charges. Without this essential context, the jury heard a deeply distorted version of Mr. Williams's story.

After Mr. Williams's conviction, the **United States Attorney General's office** came back with a new deal. If he waived his right to appeal, they would drop most of the charges so that he would face a minimum of 10 years in prison and pay a $288,000 judgment.

His response? "This is nothing more than slavery and completely disregards my rights as a citizen of the United States of America. I have declined the offer."

When asked for comment, a Department of Justice press officer said the department, like the Attorney General's office, could not discuss the facts of a pending case.

Chris Williams eventually took a deal and is now serving a 5-year federal prison sentence. Despite cases like Chris Williams's, states have gone forward with marijuana legalization.

While the federal law has not changed, Congress has used its budgetary oversight power to keep the Drug Enforcement Agency from raiding dispensaries sanctioned by state law like Chris Williams's. Instead of using its power to make laws, Congress often opts for less cumbersome methods of enacting policy. Congress has **the power of the purse** and the **oversight power** to cut funding to agencies. After William's story made headlines, Congress cut the budgets that agencies use to travel to states to arrest those operating dispensaries legally according to their state laws.

Thus, the debate continues: can the federal government pass laws as it pleases even when the laws should be left to the states, based on the 10th Amendment? Also, if the Court is on the federal government's side, who could stop it? Lastly, if states are **laboratories** for policy, how is the marijuana legalization experiment going? Make some random calls to one of the states that have legalized marijuana and ask, "How's it going?" Indeed not a scientific poll, it is fun to do with a class full of students.

Fiscal Federalism

Money is at the heart of the conflict between the federal and state governments. Who gets the power that comes with financial responsibility is known as **fiscal federalism**. While goals are easy to agree on, how to achieve them is not. For instance, we can all agree that our roads and bridges, critical components of our infrastructure, are essential. Our roads are in bad shape. World Economic Forum's Global Competitiveness Report ranks our country's infrastructure fourteenth in the world and falling. The American Society of Engineers gives our transportation system a "D" and urges Congress to spend more. In 2014, Congress spent $416 billion on transportation and water infrastructure. The engineers claimed that that number needs to jump to $1.6 trillion quick if we want to ride in style in our planes, trains, and automobiles. Historically, the federal government has increased the gas tax to pay for increased spending on roads, bridges, airports, rail lines, and harbors. However, because of political gridlock, the federal gas tax has not risen from 18 cents since 1993 and stands little chance to do so anytime soon.

So, states tack on an average of a 35-cent tax, combining for 53 cents extra at the pump per gallon. States like Iowa are raising gas taxes to fill the federal government's funding pothole to repair their roads and bridges.

When states take it upon themselves to fund their own projects, the federal government has less say. Consider how the U.S. drinking age became national policy.
In 1984 the federal government passed the National Minimum Drinking Age Act. Take a gander at the Constitution and point to the place where it mentions drinking ages or inebriating substances. Oh wait—it doesn't. So when the federal government passed a law establishing a national drinking age, it had to get creative on how to enforce it and find a constitutional basis for it. Remember, the **10th Amendment** reserves powers like setting drinking ages and speed limits to the states.

Each year, states receive money from the federal government in the form of a categorical grant that covers 25% or so of highway improvement funds. **Categorical grants** are sums of money from the central government that have many strings and stipulations attached. Under the Drinking Age Act, Congress threatened to end the federal transportation funds if states refused to increase their drinking ages from 18 to 21. States received an average $17 million from the federal government each year. After the Drinking Age Act, a string was attached: o raise in drinking age, no federal $17 million in highway funds.

All states except Louisiana increased their drinking ages. The Cajun corner of the country gambled on becoming the under-21 drinking hub of the nation. They planned to make up for the lost money by taxing the flocks of 18-20-year-olds that would come to party in the Crescent City and elsewhere. While that hardly happened, there was an increase in the number of drunk driving fatalities of 18-20-year-old drivers returning from Louisiana to their homes in Mississippi, Texas, and Arkansas. In 1996 Louisiana got on board (and started repairing their roads).

The central government will sometimes give states funding without such strings attached. Since the 1980s, the federal government has devolved power to the states—that is, states have been given more freedom from the federal government, by the federal government. During this **Devolution Revolution**, **block grants** took the place of categorical grants. Block grants are sums of money given to the states with few regulations to support broad programs in areas such as welfare.

However, the federal government does not always attach the lure of money to its mandates. Sometimes it just orders states to implement something it would like to see carried out. Such a command is known as an unfunded mandate. Such top-down orders force states and their residents to pay for federal policies.

A familiar **unfunded mandate** is **The Americans With Disabilities Act** In 1990, Congress passed a law—The Americans with Disabilities Act—that forced businesses and public places to accommodate citizens with disabilities. In addition to being barred from discriminating against those with physical or mental disabilities, businesses and local governments were instructed to build ramps, construct or remodel bathrooms, and enlarge doorways to accommodate the disabled. If businesses or local governments did not comply with the law, they would open themselves to be sued by individual plaintiffs. This unfunded mandate has given opportunities to tens of millions of mentally and physically disabled persons, and no one doubts its merits. The Labor Department looked at the costs two decades after the law was implemented and determined businesses spent an average of $500 to accommodate their disabled employees and customers.

Another high-profile unfunded mandate is the Clean Air Act of 1970. It required companies to comply with the Environmental Protection Agency's (EPA) standards. If the EPA says that passenger automobiles must get a minimum of 30 miles to the gallon, then auto companies must fund research and development towards that goal.

Latest Battle Over Federal Funding: Sanctuary Cities and the Trump Administration

Most recently, the federal government tugged at the strings of its law enforcement grants to states. States that refused to cooperate with federal immigration agencies were threatened with the prospect of fewer federal dollars. States found this to be a breach of the principle of the separation of powers and sued, claiming the federal government was using its funding role as a weapon against **state sovereignty**.

From The Associated Press (June 12, 2019):

SEATTLE — A federal appeals court on Friday gave President Trump a rare legal victory in his efforts to crack down on so-called sanctuary cities, upholding the **Justice Department's** decision to give preferential treatment in awarding community policing grants to cities that cooperate with immigration authorities.

"The Department is pleased that the Court recognized the lawful authority of the Administration to provide favorable treatment when awarding discretionary law-enforcement grants to **jurisdictions** that assist in enforcing federal immigration laws," the Justice Department said in an emailed statement.

Federal courts have blocked some efforts by the administration to withhold money from sanctuary cities, including an executive order issued by the president in 2017 that would have barred them from receiving federal grants "except as deemed necessary for law enforcement purposes."

Los Angeles applied for a grant that year, but declined to list immigration enforcement as a priority — it listed building community trust instead — or to make the certification. It failed to win the grant and sued.

The Justice Department had introduced conditions that impermissibly coerced grant applicants to enforce federal immigration law, the city said. It also said that the immigration-related conditions were contrary to the goals for which Congress had approved the grant money: to get more police officers on the beat, developing trust with the public.

The judges in the majority Friday, Sandra Ikuta and Jay Bybee, both appointed by former President George W. Bush, a Republican, rejected that argument.

Supporters of sanctuary cities say that encouraging local police departments to participate in federal immigration enforcement is counterproductive: People will be less likely to report crimes if they believe they will be deported for doing so.

But the Ninth Circuit's opinion found that to be a question of policy, not law, said David Levine, a professor at University of California Hastings College of the Law.

"What the Justice Department was doing before, they were trying to force sanctuary cities to do things, and yank money from them retroactively if they didn't," Mr. Levine said. "They've gotten a little more sophisticated now. They're saying, 'You don't have to take this money, but if you want it, it comes with strings attached.'

"That's a well-understood way the federal government gets states to do things," he added. "You don't use a stick, you use a carrot."

TRANSGENDER BATHROOMS

In 2016, the Department of Education and the Department of Justice jointly issued a directive that ordered federally funded schools—K-12 and universities—to accommodate transgender students based on their self-identified gender, rather than the gender listed on their birth certificates. The ordinance stated institutions that restrict transgender students from preferred restrooms, extracurricular organizations such as sports teams, fraternities, and sororities, and functions like school dances would lose their federal funding due to violating the 14th 'Amendment's equal protection clause.

Local school districts used arguments reminiscent of the 'Anti-Federalists' cries. They contended the federal government was reaching into areas reserved to local control by the Constitution's 10th Amendment. Such policies, they claimed, should be made on a school district by school district basis. Many localities likened Obama's order to an edict from a monarch whose word would force the 'country's 16,500 school districts to follow his dictates.

One of the first districts to push back was in Gloucester County, Virginia, which banned a transgender female who identified as a male, Gavin Grimm, from using the male bathrooms. However, the 4th **Circuit Court of Appeals** sided with the federal directive that came through the Education and Justice Departments, thereby upholding the legal basis for the mandate. This basis comes from a broad interpretation of the Education Amendments of 1972 to the Higher Education Act (1965) which include, "No person in the United States shall, on the basis of sex, be excluded from participation in, be denied the benefits of, or be subjected to discrimination under any education program or activity receiving federal financial assistance."" The act itself has been upheld on **14th Amendment equal protection grounds**.

However, at the time that the law was written, sex and gender were not considered separate. It would take several decades for courts to rule that there is a valid distinction between sexual anatomy and psychological gender. After all, the law did not plan for the protections to cover gender as well as sex. Such a legal distinction did not exist in 1972 when a ninth part, **Title IX**, was added to the 1965 Education Act.

To consider this question, let us zoom out and remember that Congress makes laws, the Executive enforces those laws, and the Judicial Branch interprets the law.

- Step 1: Congress makes the law. The Education Act is passed in 1965 and amended in 1972 to include "sex." Title IX is added as an amendment that aims to protect individuals from sex-based discrimination in schools or other federally funded programs.

- Step 2: The Executive enforces the law. The Department of Justice works with other bureaucratic **agencies** like the Department of Education to apply laws to individual cases as needs arise. Recall that a legitimate, necessary function of agencies is to fill in details of broad laws to make them more applicable and thus enforceable. This filling in of the details, this "wiggle room," is commonly called **discretionary** power.

- Step 3: The Judiciary interprets the law. After two months of Gavin Grimm using male restrooms, parents' complaints were heard. Gloucester County School Board voted 6-1 against accommodating Grimm's identification as male. The board issued a policy that students are to use the restroom that corresponds to the gender on their birth certificates. Gavin **appealed** his case to the federal district court and lost. He then appealed his case to the 4th Circuit Court. On his behalf, the American Civil Liberties Union argued for equal protection under the law per the 14th Amendment and an expanded interpretation of the Education Act to include gender as well as sex. The Circuit Court ruled in Grimm's favor on April 29, 2016.

Even with Gavin's victory, states across the nation are emulating Virginia. As of this writing, many states have or are considering passing laws restricting restroom use to the gender as listed on birth certificates.

Part 3

Government Institutions:

Congress

The Executive

The Bureaucracy

The Judiciary

Chapter 8

Congressional Elections

Congressional Districts

Congressional elections for the House of Representatives take place in 435 **districts** every two years. Elections that happen along with Presidential elections are "**on-year elections**" and those that do not are called "**midterms**." Each of the 435 districts has a single representative **(single-member-districts)** who serves as that district's legislator in the House of Representatives. All of the 435 seats are re-allotted after each **census** (a survey of the entire population conducted every ten years).

The Census

The districts members of the House are elected to represent depend on the data collected in the national **census**. The U.S. Constitution empowers the Congress to carry out the census in "such manner as they shall by Law direct" (Article I, Section 2). The plan was to count every person living in the newly created United States of America, and to use that count to determine representation in the Congress. The first census was conducted in 1790 and our country has had one every 10 years since then. Federal law does not specify which subjects or questions are to be included in the decennial census. However, it does require the Census Bureau to notify Congress of general census subjects to be addressed 3 years before the decennial census and the actual questions to be asked 2 years before the decennial census.

While it is constitutional to include questions in the decennial census beyond those concerning a simple count of the number of people, President Trump caused controversy when his Justice Department pushed the Commerce Department to include a question regarding legal citizenship status on the 2020 census.

The Supreme Court has, since 1870, consistently ruled that the Constitution's census clause (Art. 1, Sec. 2, Clause 3) is not limited to a simple headcount of the population and "does not prohibit the gathering of other statistics, if 'necessary and proper,' for the intelligent exercise of other powers enumerated in the constitution, and in such case there could be no objection to acquiring this information through the same machinery by which the population is enumerated."

President Trump's citizenship question did not pass the "necessary and proper" test according to a 2019 Supreme Court ruling. In its ruling, the court found that the federal government failed to show how such a question promotes the collection of data necessary to the purpose of the census: to count the residents in each state so a proper number of congressional seats may be allocated.

The opponents of the question argued that it would result in undercounts as undocumented residents would not participate. If a state's population is undercounted, it may be under-represented in the House. States with under-counted populations would also receive less federal funding and have less clout in the Electoral College.

Reapportionment and Redistricting

Reapportionment and redistricting congressional districts is a process. First, there must be a count of the population or a census. After the count, the state's seats in the federal Congress are reallocated, or reapportioned, based on its shifts in population. Once each state gets its fair share of the 435 House seats based on its size, it is up to the state to draw the lines of its congressional districts—to redistrict.

Section II of Article 1 of the Constitution states "The House of Representatives shall be composed of Members chosen every second year by the People of the several States.... Representatives...shall be **apportioned** among the several States which may be included within this Union, according to their respective Numbers." State legislatures use census data to create districts. They alone determine the shapes of their congressional districts and the populations they include.

The **reallocation** of congressional seats and the redrawing of district lines illustrates the complicated relationship between the federal government, state governments, and the individual rights of their citizens. The Constitution gives the job of drawing congressional boundaries to state legislatures. These legislatures re-draw the district lines (**districting**) and put the right number of people in them (apportionment) every ten years following the census.

The Constitution lays the groundwork for how **popular representation** should look as legislatures base their membership on population. Going from census data, map makers must place voters into districts in which voters will elect one representative each (**single member**). The Constitution requires that each state, no matter how small its population, gets at least one seat in the House of Representatives (currently, ten states have only one representative in the House). A federal law capped the number of congressional districts at 435, so these are split among the 50 states. Big states get more than small states.

Districts are supposed to roughly reflect the principle of "one person, one vote." That is, they should balance numbers of voters and reflect groupings of citizens as they coalesce every ten years. But, state legislatures re-draw federal congressional district lines, which often means that the party in power of a given state legislature gets to play with the crayons. And they usually use **partisan** colors. Historically, this has led to problems. To be sure, SCOTUS is currently considering cases involving the partisan drawing of district lines. To understand current redistricting cases, one must go back to 1962 and one of the most critical decisions in Supreme Court history.

Starting in 1962, the federal courts started determining the fairness and the constitutionality of redistricting practices in the states. Understanding key Supreme Court rulings will give us much insight into the practice of redrawing congressional maps.

Baker v. Carr (1962)

Baker v. Carr was such a controversial case that two justices would leave the Supreme Court because of it. One because he suffered a complete mental breakdown, and the other from a stroke. The monumental case dealt with state-drawn congressional districts and whether the federal government would extend its power into this constitutionally established state territory (elections clause). Up until Baker, states had the sole authority to draw their districts, whether they were "fair" or not.

Tennessee, by the decree in its state constitution, was supposed to redistrict every ten years, but in 1962, it had not done so since 1902. The result was a county, Shelby County, with two very uneven congressional districts. The population in the rural district was twenty times less than the population in the other urban district centered in Memphis.

Not one Supreme Court justice thought the districts had been divided fairly by the Tennessee legislature. However, many justices were hesitant to cross their federal boundaries from fear of violating state sovereignty. In cases prior to Baker, states had argued successfully that drawing district lines was a state-level power.

Two fundamental principles conflicted in this case. The immediate question of fairness (twenty black/city votes equaling one white/county vote) was pretty easy. "One person, one vote" has a gut-level, self-evident truth to it and agreed with the ethos of the **14th Amendment's Equal Protection Clause**. The second principle concerned the very nature of federalism and hinged on the vital power balance between a state government and the central government. The main question the Court had to settle was whether a state level issue like this one was justiciable. That is, was such an issue within the federal **court's jurisdiction**? States' rights proponents claimed that the Supreme Court would entangle itself in minutiae of state matters unimagined by even the Anti-Federalists; Baker would prove right Brutus's warnings of a supreme federal court trampling on state territory.

In arguments before the court, Tennessee acknowledged that the way it drew its district lines was unfair. The state's argument was staked on the principle of constitutional federalism. Redistricting had always been reserved to the states, and wholly absent from the federal government's enumerated and **expressed powers**. The state courts had ruled that voters could remedy such unfair district apportionment at the ballot box. Allowing an over powerful federal court into such matters was inviting the fox into the henhouse. Tennessee insisted that once the Court stepped over the line protecting state sovereignty from federal encroachment, it would not step back over. The Court would forever be in a position to overturn laws made democratically through state lawmaking bodies. As Brutus warned, people and their states would have no protection against the federal courts.

The justices understood the magnitude of their case. Justice Whitaker became so distressed that his decision would be immortalized that he started imagining all of his words as though they were written in stone. His strain showed when he began speaking with punctuation: "Carla comma, would you please bring me some coffee question mark." Caught between two core principles, enforcing fairness for the minority via the **14th Amendment** vs. honoring the boundaries of **federalism**, he did not decide at all in the end. When the time came to decide the case, he retreated to a cabin in the woods for three weeks. Upon his return to D.C., he was visibly unwell, and his family reported that he was suicidal. He resigned before deciding on Baker v. Carr, which would ultimately be decided 6-2 in favor of individual rights. One of the two justices on the losing side, Felix Frankfurter, was similarly broken after the decision. Seeing the relationship between the federal court and the states so "entangled," contrary to 150 years of rulings and laws, his body broke under strain. He suffered a stroke two weeks after the decision and never returned to the bench, making Baker his last case.

For the court's 150 years before Baker v Carr, the Supreme Court had not interfered in state legislative matters. The relationship between the states and the federal government shifted in 1962. Baker defined a new relationship between states and the national government. Since Baker v Carr, the court has decided on a slew of issues that would have been left to the states' jurisdiction before 1962, including abortion, gay marriage, and racial discrimination. Baker was a turning point in U.S. constitutional history. The **Warren Court** established that the 14th Amendment trumped the federalism tenet of state sovereignty. The balance of power tilted away from **states' rights** to individual rights with the federal government playing an ever-larger role in mediating the relationships between citizens and their state governments.

Gerrymandering

While Baker involved the number of members in two districts, cases like Reno v. Shaw (1990) addressed the shape of numerically equal districts and the demographic basis on which they were drawn. Besides numerical equivalence, the way state legislatures draw the lines, creating districts' shapes, is of the utmost importance when considering their fairness. The practice of **gerrymandering**—unfairly drawing district lines—could be as bad as all of the Washington sex scandals, special interests, lobbying, revolving doors, and voter fraud combined. Two vital institutions, elections and the House of Representatives, are corrupted by the practice. Most other corruptions of our system affect a single election at a time. Normal corruption is like the occasional copying of homework from a friend. Gerrymandering is cheating on the scale of hacking the teacher's grade book.

By gerrymandering districts, state legislatures win elections on behalf of their parties before they even start. It allows politicians to pick their voters instead the voters electing them. Out of 435 districts, only 40 were considered competitive in 2016. The others were "**safe seats**" in which many **incumbents** did not even have a challenger.

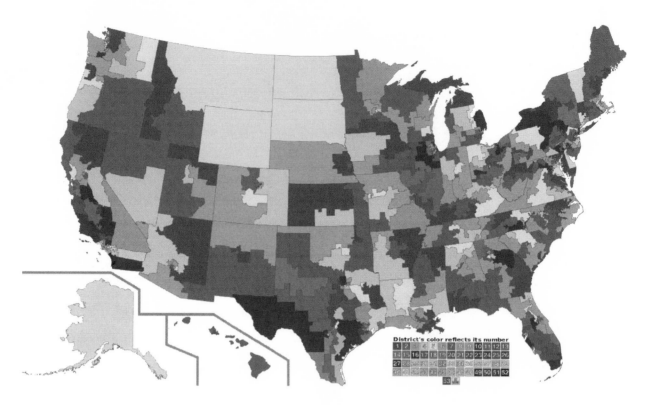

District's color reflects its number

By gerrymandering Congressional districts, partisan state legislatures seal off voters instead of blatantly stripping them of their voting rights. After each census, partisans go about reconfiguring boundaries to exclude a neighborhood here and include a neighborhood there. Exclusion and gaining an unfair advantage is the point when redistricting becomes gerrymandering. The ruling party aims to put large numbers of their supporters in each district while breaking up its opposition into districts in which they will be the minority. The Democrats have carved up California like an avocado while the Republicans have cut up Texas with the gusto they would bring to a T-bone steak.

In 2012, Democrats won in 9/10 of the nation's most gerrymandered districts, but Republicans drew 8/10 of those districts. The Republican strategy was to cram the Democrats into ten safe-seats while they spread their supporters out among more districts. Thus, they gave Democrats those ten districts but took a lot of the rest for themselves. This type of gerrymandering is called "**packing**" and assumes a racial dimension when packed districts are minorities.

How districts look in a perfect world:

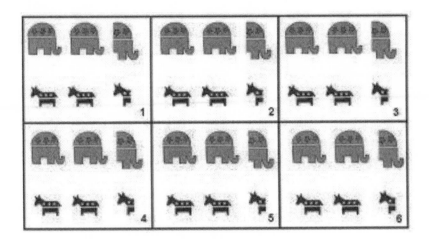

How districts look in our world:

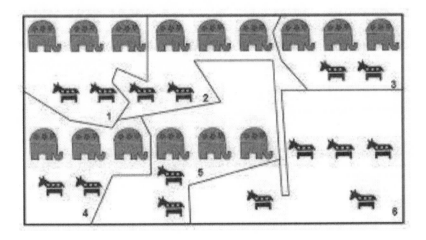

David Cohen points out that gerrymandering is worse now than ever because of big data and new computer models. Today's advanced computer modeling makes former gerrymander-ers look like they were indeed playing with crayons. Yes, they can tell how voters vote. State legislatures can draw precise lines that separate voters into blocs favorable to their party. Cohen gives a couple of scenarios that illustrate the undemocratic outcome of redistricting gone wrong.

Scenario 1: Packing

District	# of Republicans	# of Democrats
1	0	40
2	21	19
3	21	19
4	21	19
5	21	19
Districts won	4	1
Number of votes	84	116

Scenario 2: Cracking

District	# of Republicans	# of Democrats
1	21	19
2	21	19
3	21	19
4	21	19
5	21	19
Districts won	5	0
Number of votes	105	95

See North Carolina's 12th district and those surrounding it for a stellar example of partisan gerrymandering. North Carolina voters were certainly confused when the 2012 election results came in: 51% cast their ballots for a Democratic candidate, but Democrats won only 4/13 seats (31%).

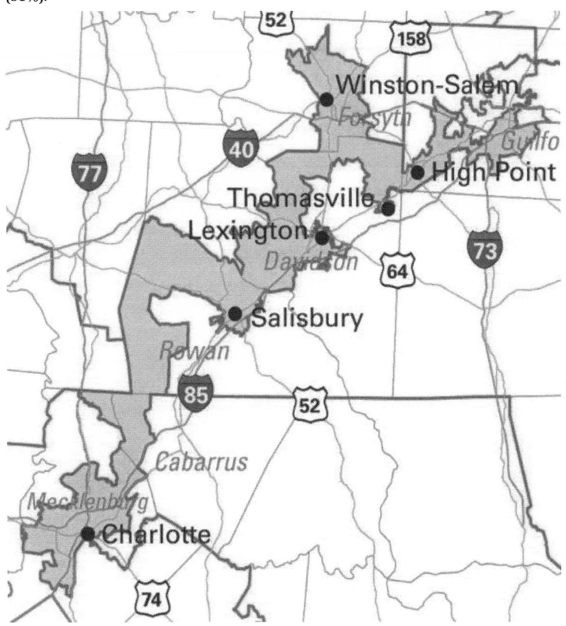

Despite examples like North Carolina's 12th District, there are rules in place that attempt to prevent gerrymandering. The federal restrictions have resulted from court cases and civil rights legislation. Baker v. Carr (1962) along with Reynolds v.

Sims (1964) produced the "one person, one vote" guideline that now applies to congressional districts.

Race and Gerrymandering: Shaw v. Reno (1992)

The Case (from Ozey.com):

Facts of the case

The U.S. Attorney General rejected a North Carolina congressional reapportionment plan because the plan created only one black-majority district. North Carolina submitted a second plan creating two black-majority districts. One of these districts was, in parts, no wider than the interstate road along which it stretched. Five North Carolina residents challenged the constitutionality of this unusually shaped district, alleging that its only purpose was to secure the election of additional black representatives. After a three-judge District Court ruled that they failed to state a constitutional claim, the residents appealed and the Supreme Court granted certiorari.

Question

Did the North Carolina residents' claim, that the State created a racially gerrymandered district, raise a valid constitutional issue under the **Fourteenth Amendment's Equal Protection Clause**?

Conclusion

5–4 DECISION FOR SHAW

Yes. The Court held that although North Carolina's reapportionment plan was racially neutral on its face, the resulting district shape was bizarre enough to suggest that it constituted an effort to separate voters into different districts based on race. The unusual district, while perhaps created by noble intentions, seemed to exceed what was reasonably necessary to avoid racial imbalances. After concluding that the residents' claim did give rise to an equal protection challenge, the Court remanded - adding that in the absence of contradictory evidence, the District Court would have to decide whether or not some **compelling governmental interest** justified North Carolina's plan.

Shaw v. Reno (1990) found race-based redistricting to be unconstitutional per the 14th Amendment Equal Protection Clause and prohibited by the **Voting Rights Act of 1965 (VRA)**. The VRA says that minorities should be given a fair chance to elect representatives of their choice, but not to be packed into a district in order to limit their broader influence. The VRA also required most Southern states to submit their redistricting plans to federal court before being enacted. This provision of the Voting Rights Act, however, was invalidated by Shelby County v. Holder (2013). In Holder, SCOTUS ruled that the submission requirement of the VRA violated the "sovereignty of the states" and transgressed the elections clause of the Constitution.

Re-Thinking the Single-Member District

At first, single member districts seemed to encourage representatives' accountability by being connected geographically and ideologically to their **constituents**. The formation of fair single-member districts has become increasingly difficult. With the use of big data and advanced computing, measures of voter behavior have become incredibly accurate, allowing **partisan** state legislatures to draw lines that guarantee their party's victory. It also raises important concerns about electoral fairness. The obvious example is the controversy over districts drawn to provide electoral opportunities for racial and ethnic minorities who have faced a history of discrimination.

Tory Mast of Fairvote.org explains:

Such districts can allow minority voters an opportunity to elect candidates of choice, yet become more problematic as our population becomes increasingly mobile and racial and ethnic minorities outside of urban areas are less concentrated in one geographic locale. In order to create some **minority majority districts**, districts must be carved out which are misshapen and incongruous, defeating the earlier notions that they be **compact and contiguous**. Similar districts of course are often drawn to protect incumbents or provide partisan advantage.

Although instituted to better represent groups in the minority, single-member districts still can consistently under-represent those in the minority, or even leave them unrepresented. Whether consciously drawn with such an intent or not, districts can consistently deny the desired representation of a permanent minority (such as blacks in most congressional districts, whites in majority black districts or Republicans in predominantly Democratic districts).

On the other hand, multi-member elections for Congress are a forgotten and overlooked part of our country's electoral history. Until thirty years ago, a majority of state legislative seats were elected from **multi-member districts**, while a majority of local officials still are elected from such districts.

When combined with proportional representation (such as cumulative voting or **preference voting**), multi-member districts would provide states with a viable method to reduce problems inherent in single-member districts. Provision for simply giving states the option to have multi-member districts requires only repeal of the single-member district requirement passed by Congress in 1967.

Incumbency Advantage: Once They're In, They're In

Political contests are supposed to be competitive. Gerrymandering ensures winners that they will continue winning. While perhaps the best insurance an incumbent has, gerrymandering is not the only advantage officeholders enjoy when seeking reelection. If gerrymandering paves the road to reelection, other **incumbency** advantages serve to smooth the path. Incumbency comes with huge perks, mainly name recognition and fundraising ability.

Advantages incumbents have over challengers include:

- Name recognition
- Connections to donors
- **Franking privilege**- (free mail for non-campaign related matters)
- **Constituent service** or **case work** (helping people back home get passports and funding for pet projects)
- Serving on seats on relevant committees- (a member of Congress whose district has a military base and sits on the Armed Forces Committee is valuable to his district and not likely to be voted out).

Perhaps their most important advantage is fundraising—special interests bet on winners, and it costs money to get one's name recognized. Some big donors are ideologically driven and want their horse to win at all costs. However, most donors have a material interest in how those in power feel about them after an election, so they give generously to both sides. They ensure that whoever the winner is will pick up the phone when called, for it is mainly access to policymakers factions want. As things are, challengers are at a considerable disadvantage, and the competitiveness of our elections is low. This lack of competition may explain our low rates of voter efficacy, high rates of voter apathy, low voter turnout, and even doubts about our government's legitimacy.

Even though the numbers show that the people elect the same Congress year after year, this does not mean Congress is popular. Only 5% of Americans rate Congress's work as "good" in a 2013 poll. Cockroaches had better approval ratings! Really, they did. However, in the subsequent 2014-**midterm elections**, 77 House seats did not even have a challenger because the incumbent's advantage was overwhelming to potential challengers. Such a lack of competition is not good! Congress, well the House, is supposed to be the political institution that most directly links the people to the government.

The lack of competition in our elections underlines the severe threat to democracy these gerrymandered "safe districts" pose. Contested elections are the platform for American citizens to become involved through educating themselves on the issues and picking a candidate who bests represents them. It is also the citizens' opportunity to "throw the bums out" of office if they have betrayed their trust or vision. To say we are sitting on the sidelines of our democracy is an exaggeration for many. For all but 40 of 435 districts, there was hardly a contest at all.

Arizona Congressional Districts are a League of their Own

Voters are growing weary from voting in gerrymandered districts. Arizona voters decided to take the job of redistricting from their partisan legislature and hired **a non-partisan** independent commission to do it instead.

To get around their legislature, full of members who got their jobs through gerrymandered districts, Arizona citizens used the **referendum**—a vote regarding a specific issue. Referendums originate from ballot **initiatives**, which are similar to petitions. Once a certain number of citizens sign an initiative saying they would like to vote on an issue, a referendum is held or put on the ballot in a **general election**. When Arizonans went to vote for their candidates, they also got to say "yes" or "no" to an independent redistricting commission.

Angry at the revoked power, the state government of Arizona challenged its constituents in the Supreme Court. Arizona argued that laws resulting from referendums were not valid. The voters won. Currently, an independent commission does the vital work of Arizona's congressional districting. With Arizona serving as a laboratory for redistricting reform, a test is underway to determine whether an "independent" commission can draw districts that foster **competitive elections**.

Chapter 10

Legislative Branch Structure

The first branch of American political institutions is the legislative branch, also referred to as Congress. The legislative branch is the subject of the first article of the Constitution and was most important to the framers. A representative body is central to having a republic, which was their aim.

As Federalist 51 explains, the framers split Congress into two parts, the House of Representatives and the Senate, reasoning that a **bicameral** legislature would internally balance its power. However, not only does the Senate have more power than the House, but it is also possible for two parties to control one Congress, creating a **divided government**.

As a result of the Great Compromise-discussed in the previous chapter- the Senate has two representatives from each state, equaling 100 in the Congress' upper house. The House currently has 435 officials, determined by each state's population, and is proportional to the population of the states. That is, if a state has 10% of the U.S. population, it will have 10% of the membership in the House of Representatives. The House's members represent their **constituencies** in the form of congressional districts. As such, there are 435 pieces in the House of Representative's pie. The representatives of these seats do **casework** for the people in their districts as well as pass laws.

Each part of the legislative branch has its own respective rules and authority, putting a check/balance mechanism within the legislative branch itself. The two halves of Congress work together in theory, but sometimes cripple each other with a checks and balances game of their own, especially when the House and the Senate are controlled by different parties.

Committees

Wherever a large group must make decisions on a wide range of specialized topics, one will find committees and subcommittees made up of members of the larger group. Small group efficiency applies to governments as small as school boards and to companies as big as Nike. Committees and their subcommittees allow policymakers to specialize by gathering information through research and hearings and hammer out their differences within a group with fewer voices.

Not surprisingly, committees in the House and Senate do most of the work in Congress. The committees are made up of members of the House and Senate, and detailed amendments, debates, and information gathering cannot happen without them. While there are different types of committees, the ones to know are the standing committees. These are the most common; they are always around and deal with the most significant policy areas. The most powerful congressmen chair standing committees. Serving on standing committees allows members of Congress to specialize in an area and better serve their constituents. It also saves time by allowing smaller groups of lawmakers to debate, **mark up**, and vote on bills. Most bills die in committee, saving time on the full floor of the House or Senate for debate.

House of Representatives	Senate	Joint
• Agriculture • Appropriations • Armed Services • Budget • Education and Labor • Energy and Commerce • Ethics • Financial Services • Foreign Affairs • Homeland Security • House Administration • Intelligence (Permanent Select) • Judiciary • Natural Resources • Oversight and Government Reform • Rules • Science, Space, and Technology • Small Business • Transportation and Infrastructure • Veterans' Affairs • Ways and Means • *(Whole)*	• Aging (Special) • Agriculture, Nutrition and Forestry • Appropriations • Armed Services • Banking, Housing, and Urban Affairs • Budget • Commerce, Science and Transportation • Energy and Natural Resources • Ethics (Select) • Environment and Public Works • Finance • Foreign Relations • Health, Education, Labor, and Pensions • Homeland Security and Governmental Affairs • Indian Affairs • Intelligence (Select) • International Narcotics Control (Special) • Judiciary • Rules and Administration • Small Business and Entrepreneurship • Veterans' Affairs	• Budget/Appropriations Reform (Select) • *(Conference)* • Economic • Library • Pensions (Select) • Printing • Taxation

Subcommittees

Standing committees each have their **subcommittees**. Subcommittee members can further focus on a bill's details and make ever more technical amendments, increasing a bill's chance for passage. Below is an example of how much **specialization** occurs on the subcommittee level of just one House Standing Committee.

Subcommittees of House Agriculture Standing Committee	Chair	Ranking Member
Agriculture	Collin Peterson (D-MN)	Mike Conaway (R-TX)
Biotechnology, Horticulture and Research	Stacey Plaskett (D-VI)	Neal Dunn (R-FL)
Commodity Exchanges, Energy and Credit	David Scott (D-GA)	Austin Scott (R-GA)
Conservation and Forestry	Abigail Spanberger (D-VA)	Doug LaMalfa (R-CA)
General Farm Commodities and Risk Management	Filemon Vela (D-TX)	Glenn Thompson (R-PA)
Livestock and Foreign Agriculture	Jim Costa (D-CA)	David Rouzer (R-NC)
Nutrition, Oversight and Department Operations	Marcia Fudge (D-OH)	Dusty Johnson (R-SD)

Oversight Function of Committees

Also, an important oversight function of Congress takes place in subcommittees: hearings. **Hearings** are public sessions in which congressmen call witnesses to answer questions. Some hearings are for information gathering, while others are for public shaming. Most importantly, hearings provide the time for members to deliberate on a given issue. Members of Congress are not specialists in the areas over which they legislate. They must get the expertise of others, and give those potentially affected by legislation a chance to come forward and testify on the real-world impacts of a given bill.

Other Committees

Other than standing committees, joint, special, select, and **conference committees** serve specific purposes other than law-making. While standing committees deal with issues of permanent legislative concern, conference committees form when different versions of the same bill pass in the House and Senate. The leaders of each chamber create a conference committee to reconcile the differences between the two versions of the bill. **Select committees** deal with temporary issues, usually investigations. Joint committees consist of members of both houses usually created to deal with a specific issue.

The House of Representatives

The House of Representatives is the lower House of Congress' bicameral legislature and the most receptive to the will of the people. Originally it was the only federal institution directly elected by the people (state legislatures chose senators until the passage of the **17th Amendment**). Just as the federal government has a specific hierarchy and structure, so does the House.

House of Representatives Basic Facts

- The "**lower house**" is another name for the House of Representatives.
- A Member of the U.S. House of Representatives is referred to as a congressman or a congresswoman.
- The House of Representatives work parallel to the Senate to pass, repeal (cancel), and amend laws.
- The House of Representatives is the larger **chamber** with 435 representatives. Each state has a number of representatives proportional to its population.
- Congressmen and Congresswomen serve in office for two years and can be re-elected as many times as the people wish (they have no **term limits**).
- The Constitution requires a **census** to be conducted every ten years. If a state's population increases, that state's number of representatives can increase too. Based on the new **demographic data**, congressional districts are **reapportioned and redistricted by state legislatures**. The corruption of this process is called **gerrymandering**.
- Qualifications: The qualifications and eligibility are that Candidates must be state residents. The Minimum Length of Citizenship to be eligible for the Senate is seven years, and the minimum age of Congressmen and Congresswomen is 25 years old.
- Congressional Record: The proceedings of each house are recorded in the Congressional Record - a significant source of **transparency**.
- The Legislative Process: Only a member of Congress may introduce a bill. The House Speaker then refers the bill to an appropriate committee.
- Upon committee approval, the bill goes to the Senate or the full House which then debates and votes on the bill. If both chambers pass the bill, it goes to the President who signs the bill into law.
- President's Veto: If a bill is vetoed (refused) by the President, it goes back to Congress, who can **override the veto** with a two-thirds vote in both houses.
- Unique Powers: The U.S. House of Representatives has the power to propose all tax bills and the power to impeach a federal official.
- The Budget: Congress has the **"power of the purse"** and must approve all government spending and appropriate the amount of money to be spent, in bills called Appropriation Bills.
- **Whips**: Whips exist in both chambers for each political party. The Whips make sure that Congressmen and Congresswomen are present for important votes and such votes result in the desired outcome for their party. They "whip" others into line for votes.

- Unlike the Senate, the U.S. House of Representatives does not permit unlimited debate. Before a bill goes to the floor for debate, it must go through the **House Rules Committee**. This committee unique to the House passes a rule to determine how much debate is permitted and how many amendments to the bill can be proposed.
- Open and Closed Rules: A **closed rule** limits or forbids any amendments. An open rule allows for anyone to propose amendments.
- The leader of the U.S. House of Representatives is the **Speaker of the House**. The Speaker of the House is second in line to succeed the President, after the Vice President.
- The Speaker of the U.S. House of Representatives is elected by the majority party (the Democratic **Party Caucus** or the Republican Party Caucus, depending on which party controls the House).

Membership and Leadership in Congress

Leading a committee comes with considerable power. Leaders make decisions about hearings, including their subject matter, witnesses, and whether a hearing will be held at all. They also set the agenda of their committee (what will be discussed) and appoint the chairpersons of its subcommittees.

Committee leadership used to be based on the **seniority rule**—the majority member with the longest record of service in a given committee becomes the chairman. While most committee chairs are still long-standing members, seniority is no longer a guarantee of a committee chairmanship. Getting a committee chairmanship now depends on a congressperson's money-raising prowess and party loyalty. In any case, committees and their memberships provide a vital source of continuity between one Congress and the next because committees are where members of Congress become relative experts in a given policy area.

Members of the majority party always fill committee leadership posts. The Speaker in the House and the Majority Leader in the Senate appoint the chairpersons. Such appointment powers give the Speaker of the House and the Majority Leader in the Senate considerable clout.

The Constitutional Leadership of the House

The Constitution specifies that the House "shall chuse their Speaker." Their spelling was so cute!

The entire house elects the **Speaker of the House**. Each of the two major parties (so, Democrats and Republicans) puts up its candidate, but the candidate of the majority party is always elected. She is the effective leader of the chamber because, more than any other Representative, she can count on majority support.

The Speaker's authority:

- Recognizes or ignores those who wish to speak
- Appoints committee chairs
- Appoints members to the **House Rules Committee**. The Rules Committee controls what is debated by placing time limits on talking time and dictating procedures for amendments.
- Refers bills to one or more committees.

The Party Leadership of the House

- Each party has its leaders who carry out virtually the same duties, just for their respective parties.
- The House majority leader is elected solely by members of the majority party. It is his job to represent the majority party, but his authority is subordinate to that of the Speaker, who is the actual head of the majority party.
- The House majority whip is the majority leader's "second in command." It is his job to gauge the opinion of the chamber and help the majority leader "whip up support" for the positions of the party.
- The Minority Caucus (minority party) has the same two officers: the House minority leader and the House minority whip. They perform the same tasks for the opposing party.

The Senate

- The "**upper house**" is another name for the Senate.
- The Senate works parallel to the House of Representatives to pass, repeal (cancel), and amend laws.
- A member of the U.S. Senate is referred to as a senator.
- The Senate is the smaller chamber having 100 members - each state has two senators.
- Senators serve in office for six years and can be re-elected as many times as the people require.
- Qualifications: The qualifications and eligibility are that Candidates must be state residents. The Minimum Length of Citizenship to be eligible for the Senate is nine years, and the minimum age of Senators is 30 years old.
- Unique Powers: The Senate has the power to approve presidential appointments, confirm all federal judicial appointments, ratify treaties and try impeached government officials.
- Senatorial proceedings are recorded in the **Congressional Record**.
- The **17th Amendment** enabled electors to vote for Senators, as opposed to the state legislatures voting, encouraging American citizens to become more involved in their government.
- The terms of one-third of the senators expire every two years.
- The Senate is presided over by the vice president of the United States.
- In the absence of **the Vice President**, his duties are assumed by a **president pro tempore**, elected by the Senate as the presiding officer.
- Leaders: The political party holding the majority in the Senate elects a majority leader, the minority party elects a minority leader.
- **Impeachment Trials**: The Senate tries cases of impeachment sent to it from the House.
- Unlike members of the House of Representatives, Senators are not subject to the **House Rules Committee** and can speak for as long as they wish and offer as many amendments as they want. This freedom makes the **filibuster** possible only in the Senate.
- Filibuster: A filibuster is a tactic employed by Senators to delay or obstruct legislation by making long speeches. Kill a bill by talking it to death.
- Whips: Whips exist in both houses for each political party. The Whips make sure that legislators are present for important votes and ensure that important votes have the desired outcome for their party on major issues.

Ranking:
- The highest-ranking member of the Senate is United States Vice President (who is called President of the Senate when he is acting in this capacity).
- The **Senate Majority Leader** is a Senator elected by the party to serve as their primary spokesperson.
- The President pro tempore presides over the Senate when the Majority Leader is absent.

The Constitutional Leadership of the Senate

The Constitution specifies two officers for the Senate.

First, the Vice President is the President of the Senate. This brief reference happens to be his only Constitutional role and has historically been a rather meager one. Until recently, the Vice Presidency was where "politicians go to die." As far as being the President of the Senate goes, the V.P. plays no regular role and rarely even appears there. However, he's the PRESIDENT of the Senate, man! You may say. There are two good reasons he has no real authority there. First, more and more governments are divided along partisan lines these days, and he is not an impartial nonpartisan. The "veep" will always be on the president's and his party's side. So, rather than being the 101st Senator, he stays out of Senate business unless there is a tie. Leading to our second reason the V.P. is an inactive president of the Senate: ties are super rare. Since 1981 veeps have broken fifteen ties.

THE TIEBREAKERS (do not wait for the movie):
Joe Biden—0
Dick Cheney—8
Dan Quayle—0
George H.W. Bush—7

The second officer of the Senate mentioned in the Constitution is the President Pro Tempore. The "Pro-Temp" holds the gavel in the Senate in the Vice President's absence. This office has always been honorary, held by the longest-serving member of the majority party.

The Party Leadership of the Senate

- The Senate majority leader is the head of the United States Senate. He is responsible for organizing the activities of the Upper House. He can always count on majority support, as he is always a member of the Majority party.
- The Senate majority whip is the majority leader's "second in command." It is his job to gauge the opinion of the chamber and help the majority leader "whip up support" for the positions of the party.
- The Senate minority leader has little power, but speaks for the minority party and strategizes on taking back the majority in the next election.
- The Senate minority whip is "Second in command" to the minority leader. It is his job to gauge the opinion of the chamber and help the majority leader "whip up support" for the positions of the party.

Chapter 11

Legislative Brach Function

Lawmaking Process

Lawmaking is a process involving certain steps. For example, watch School House Rock's, "I'm Just a Bill." The process begins when citizens see that a dangerous intersection in town needs some traffic control. A citizen calls her lawmaker with a good idea for a traffic sign. After answering on the first ring, he agrees to take on the casework. The Congressman proposes the bill; it goes to a committee and through debate there, goes to the other chamber, sees some more debate, and is finally signed by the President. However, the children's cartoon is a nice bit of elementary fiction, having little resemblance to reality.

The Steps of a Bill becoming a Law

In actuality, there are potentially 10 steps a bill can go through before becoming a law. Below is a description of each step in the process, using the Genetic Information Non-Discrimination Act of 2003, as an example.

Step 1: A Bill Is Born
Anyone may draft a bill; however, only members of Congress can **introduce legislation**, and, by doing so they become the sponsor(s). The president, a member of the cabinet, or the head of a federal agency can also propose legislation, although a member of Congress must introduce it.

On May 13, 2003, Senator Olympia Snowe (R-Maine) introduced the Genetic Information Non-Discrimination Act of 2003 (S. 1053).

S. 1053 was referred to the Senate Committee on Health, Education, Labor and Pensions (HELP).

Step 2: Committee Action
As soon as a bill is introduced, it is referred to a committee. At this point the bill is examined carefully, and its chances for passage are determined. If the committee does not act on a bill, the bill is effectively "dead."

Step 3: Subcommittee Review
Often, bills are referred to a subcommittee for study and hearings. **Hearings** provide the opportunity to put on the record the views of the executive branch, experts, other public officials and supporters, and opponents of the legislation.

*On May 21, 2003, the Senate HELP Committee held a **mark up** of S. 1053. Senator Judd Gregg (R-N.H.), chair of the HELP Committee, offered an amendment to the bill.*

Step 4: Mark up
When the hearings are completed, the subcommittee may meet to **"mark up"** the bill; that is, make changes and amendments prior to recommending the bill to the full committee. If a subcommittee votes not to report legislation to the full committee, the bill dies. If the committee votes for the bill, it is sent to the **floor**. As soon as Step 2 and through the final vote (Step 9), lawmakers agree to trade their votes on one bill they care little about in exchange for another's vote on a bill that is personally much more important to them. This practice of **logrolling** is especially common when the legislators are relatively free of control by their national party leaders and are trying to secure votes for bills that will concentrate sizable benefits on their own home districts while spreading most of the costs out over taxpayers in the rest of the

country. Local projects such as Federally funded dams, bridges, highways, housing projects, VA hospitals, job-training centers, military bases and the like are often pushed through by logrolling.

Step 5: Committee Action to Report a Bill
After receiving a subcommittee's report on a bill, the full committee votes on its recommendation to the House or Senate. This procedure is called "**ordering a bill reported**."

The Senate voted on S. 1053 on Oct. 14, 2003. It passed by a vote of 95 to 0.

Step   6:   Voting
After the debate and the approval of any amendments, the bill is passed or defeated by the members voting. Note: if the **House Rules Committee** forbids amendments of a bill, it will assuredly die in committee.

Step 7: Referral to Other Chamber
When the House or Senate passes a bill, it is referred to the other chamber, where it usually follows the same route through committee and floor action. This **chamber** may approve the bill as received, reject it, ignore it, or change it.

S. 1053 was referred to the House of Representatives where it now waits for action.

Step 8: Conference Committee Action
When the actions of the other chamber significantly alter the bill, a **conference**

committee is formed to **reconcile** the differences between the House and Senate versions. If the conferees are unable to reach agreement, the legislation dies. If agreement is reached, a conference report is prepared describing the committee members' recommendations for changes. Both the House and Senate must approve the conference report.

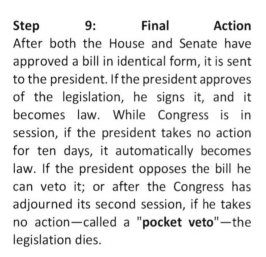

Step 9: Final Action
After both the House and Senate have approved a bill in identical form, it is sent to the president. If the president approves of the legislation, he signs it, and it becomes law. While Congress is in session, if the president takes no action for ten days, it automatically becomes law. If the president opposes the bill he can veto it; or after the Congress has adjourned its second session, if he takes no action—called a "**pocket veto**"—the legislation dies.

Step 10: Overriding a Veto
If the president vetoes a bill, Congress may attempt to "**override the veto**." If both the Senate and the House pass the bill by a two-thirds majority, the president's veto is overruled and the bill becomes a law.

How Representative are the Representatives?

Some look to the identities of officeholders and wish to see the diversity of the U.S. population reflected there. So, how representative of the U.S. population is the makeup of the current House, the most representative body in our government?

The 116th U.S. Congress took office in January, with Democrats taking control of the House while Republicans maintain an edge in the Senate.

The Pew Research Center has outlined five distinguishing characteristics of the 2018, 116th Congress:

1.   There is growing racial and ethnic diversity in Congress. The current Congress is the most racially and ethnically diverse ever. Nonwhites – including blacks, Hispanics, Asians/Pacific Islanders, and Native Americans – now account for 22% of Congress, including a quarter of the House and 9% of the Senate. By comparison, when the 79th Congress took office in 1945, nonwhites represented just 1% of the House and Senate. Despite this growing racial and ethnic diversity, Congress still lags the nation as a whole. The share of nonwhites in the United States is nearly double that of the country's legislative body (39% vs. 22%).

2.   The number of women in Congress is at an all-time high. About a century after Montana Republican Jeannette Rankin became the first woman elected to Congress, there are 127 women in the legislature, accounting for a record 24% of voting lawmakers across both chambers. There are more women in the Senate than ever (25), and in six states – Arizona, California, Minnesota, Nevada, New Hampshire, and Washington – both senators are women, up from three states in the previous Senate. The share of women in Congress remains far below the share of women in the country as a whole (24% vs. 51%).

3.   The share of immigrants in Congress has ticked up but remains well below historical highs. There are 14 foreign-born lawmakers in the 116th Congress, including 13 in the House and just one in the Senate: Mazie Hirono, a Hawaii Democrat who was born in Japan. These lawmakers account for 3% of the overall Congress, far below the shares recorded in much earlier Congresses. In the Congress of 1887-89, for example, 8% of members were born abroad. The current share of foreign-born lawmakers in Congress is also far below the foreign-born share of the U.S. as a whole, which was 13.6% as of 2017.

4.   Far fewer members of Congress now have direct military experience than in the past. In the current Congress, 96 members served in the military at some point in their lives. Between 1965 and 1975, at least 70% of lawmakers in each legislative chamber had military experience. The

share of members with military experience peaked at 75% in 1967 for the House and at 81% in 1975 for the Senate. While relatively few members of Congress today have military experience, an even smaller share of Americans do. In 2016, just 7% of U.S. adults had military experience versus 18% in 1980.

5.   Nearly all members of Congress now have college degrees. The educational attainment of Congress far outpaces that of the overall U.S. population. In 2017, around a third (34%) of American adults ages 25 and older said they had completed a bachelor's degree or more, according to U.S. Census Bureau data.

6.   Congress has become slightly more religiously diverse over time. The current Congress includes the first two Muslim women ever to serve in the House and has the fewest Christians (471) in 11 Congresses dating back to 1961. Despite this decline, Christians have still overrepresented in Congress in proportion to their share of the public: Nearly nine-in-ten congressional members are Christian (88%), compared with 71% of U.S. adults overall. By contrast, religious "nones" are underrepresented in Congress in comparison with the U.S. population. While 23% of Americans say that they are atheist, agnostic or "nothing in particular," just one congressional member, Sen. Kyrsten Sinema, D-Ariz., claims to be religiously unaffiliated.

Another way to approach the question is to ignore the **demographic data** of legislators and focus on how responsive they are to the wishes and opinions of their constituents. Under the structure of the Articles of Confederation, they acted as **delegates** who were attuned to how they were to vote on issues. **One-year terms** and the threat of **recall** kept the first congressmen on a short leash with the folks back home. The Constitution aimed to break this direct bond between the delegates and their districts. With longer terms and their pay coming from the federal government, the Constiution's structure allowed representatives to act as **trustees** of their constituents' welfare and were to vote according to how they, not the people back home, thought best. Madison explained in **Federalist 10** that representatives in the new federal legislature would be those "whose wisdom may best discern the true interest of their country, and whose patriotism and love of justice, will be least likely to sacrifice it to temporary or partial considerations. Under such a regulation, it may well happen, that the public voice, pronounced by the representatives of the people, will be more consonant to the public good, than if pronounced by the people themselves." Today, representatives use their own discretion most of the time, but the modern **politicos** understand there are times do revert to the delegate model and do exactly what their constituents want, even if they disagree.

The Senate's Power to Filibuster

Do you know who Bruce Lee was? Even if you do, watching him play Ping-Pong with nunchucks is something you should do right now. Look it up on YouTube.

There was a myth about his death that he accidentally hit himself in the head with this weapon of choice, two clubs connected by a short chain. After seeing him swat a Ping-Pong ball for point after point, I'm not sure how he died, but it sure wasn't from hitting himself. Watch the video.

However, it is no myth that Congress hits itself in the head with its preferred weapon: the filibuster. Only the Senate—the part of Congress that is supposed to be more respectable and wiser than the House—can have unlimited "debate." That is, Senators do not have to shut up until everyone is good and ready to vote. Unlike in the House, there are no rules that limit time for debate or restrict the number of possible amendments. To kill a bill through filibuster is to hold the floor of the Senate until the clock runs out. That is, talk long enough so that there is no time left to vote on a bill. No vote, no law. The only way to stop this sort of humorless stand-up is by enacting **cloture**, which requires 60/100 Senators to say, "Stop reading from the phone book and reciting recipes, STOP!" In a divided government, stopping a nomination or killing a bill is a great way the minority party can check majority power. Such protections against the tyranny of the majority is in line with Madisonian intent. Moreover, filibusters used to be dramatic, with Senators speaking for hours on end.

However, filibustering has become the drone warfare of modern politics. Members of the upper house no longer have to pilot the process from a Senate lectern reading recipes, phone books, or Bible verses. Senators merely have to say they are planning to filibuster a bill, and the bill dies through the delay. Bills that pass in the House are being killed and delayed by the Senate at a record pace, obstructing majority rule and the policymaking role of members of Congress. The number of filibusters took off in 2006 and spring-boarded after Obama took office in '08—AVERAGING TWO CLOTURE VOTES A WEEK. Yes, I'm yelling, sorry. Yell this until someone rushes in, shakes you, and asks you what kind of drug "Cloture votes" is and do they need to call an ambulance…. that just happened to me.

Not only does the filibuster gum up the gears of our bicameral legislature - the kinds of bills or nominations Senators choose to filibuster have gotten petty. In the 1950s and 1960s, hard-core racists like Strom Thurmond used the Senate as a stage to play the martyr for the racists back home. While that was a terrible use of the filibuster, the issue was at least of national importance. Since 2006, Senators in the minority party have filibustered the other side's bills and nominations solely to deny the other party a victory. Such victories are pyrrhic, however.

When political parties and their office holders forsake the public's long-term welfare for short-term gain, Madison's system has broken down. A faction runs a country like a thief drives a stolen car. So does a minority Senator filibuster a bill that is good for the country but not her party. As polarization deepens, politicians oppose ideas not on their merits but based on their authorship. When one party has a good idea, it is often shot down by the opposing party so the former cannot take credit for solving a problem. One can hardly blame the media for treating politics as a horse race when politicians act like asses, opposing good ideas because of their originators.

The obstruction within Congress gets worse. **Holds**, as in "hold up there," are the lazy man's filibuster. Originally, holds were used by senators on bills that had to do with their state or were of particular importance to them. For instance, a hold from a senator from Montana for time to study a bill that would result in an oil pipeline that cuts through his state makes sense. That same senator placing a hold on a bill to restore wetlands in Florida, not so much. In the age of party polarization and partisanship, senators are using their hold power to clog the other side's pipes rather than to give themselves time to research the pros and cons of a given bill. A cloture vote can stop a hold, but the effort and time to do so usually obstructs such action. The result is gridlock and a Congress that cannot seem to act unless a special interest turns the gears of its iron triangle.

The Problem of Madison's Minority Faction

While the outline of the lawmaking process seeks to simplify the process for the reader, the reality of policymaking is a lot more complicated than following steps like assembling Ikea furniture. The problems of the majority and **minority factions**, after all, applied to Madison's concern that special interests, or factions, would hijack Congress' policymaking role. Before the Constitution's adoption, majority factions in individual states had too much control. Especially prophetic, Brutus pointed to the downside of Madison's large-republic solution. Brutus foresaw that with a massive constituency, like a congressman's average of 750,000 constituents today, representatives could not possibly represent them all. So, of the hundreds of thousands, to whose voices would representatives listen? The few. The rich. The connected. These would be most motivated and capable of gaining access to the legislators in faraway Washington, D.C.

Brutus warned of the dangers of an elite minority faction using government for its selfish, short-term purposes. Though he did not use the word, "Iron Triangle," he foresaw that small groups with plenty of cash would capture lawmakers and law enforcers. The points of the iron triangle consist of the nexus of interest groups, members of Congress (usually on their specialized subcommittees), and agency bureaucrats who regulate special interests. These elites form a "minority faction" that makes laws disregardful of the general welfare.

Whose interest determines the policies of legislatures and regulatory agencies? Many political analysts believe it is the participants in the "Iron Triangle," especially the minority factions whose interests are served. Rather than elected officials responding to demands and interests of their constituents, policymakers have ears only for the elites, often because elected officials need money for their next campaign. In 2016, an average winning House of Representatives candidate spent over $9 million. Add to this factors such as outside spending and the cost of winning nearly doubles that $9 million average cost of winning.

According to Brutus's expression of Anti-Federalist fears, minority factions (interest groups) influence policymakers in the agencies and subcommittees that regulate their interests after the campaigning is done. Those who help fund multi-million dollar campaigns are sure to get the attention of elected policymakers and the agencies they helped elect.

Madison, in Federalist 51, acknowledged this danger of elite minorities capturing government and claimed to have offered the best solution in the Constitution's system of **checks and balances** and **separation of powers**. Moreover, federalism was to make forming a national majority unlikely and possible only in the case where general interests prevailed. This difficulty in forming national majorities would keep local majorities from dominating national policymaking, even when they could. For instance, say a majority of Christians could successfully get Congress and their states to pass an amendment guaranteeing a right to public school prayer. What might stop them from doing so? Madison would say in Federalist 51 that in a large republic, "the more powerful factions or parties be gradually induced, by a like motive, to wish for a government which will protect all parties, the weaker as well as, the more powerful." That is, a majority in a large republic would understand that it is only temporarily so. Muslim, Hindu, or atheist majorities could impose their wills on Christian minorities in smaller governments where majority coalitions form more easily. This realization would prompt temporary majorities to avoid the temptation of using their status to create permanent policies.

The Anti-Federalists argued that to prevent government oppression by a central government, constitution makers should not make any government as powerful as the Federalists had done. Brutus and his brethren would have denied the central government power to tax, raise a standing army, and regulate states' commerce. The Federalists' government was a Frankenstein's monster to Brutus: an affront against nature that would inevitably turn against its creators.

Chapter 12

The Executive Branch

The executive, the president, the Commander in Chief, and—if Alexander Hamilton had gotten his way—His Excellency is the figurehead of American politics. He is our policy leader, head military general, ultimate representative, and face of our nation. The President is often called "the most powerful person in the world." While this may be true, *Forbes* Magazine listed Obama third and Trump second on its list of "Most Powerful People in the World" in 2015 and 2016. Who got the top spot in both 2015 and 2016? I will give you a hint. He is a leader of a country whose economy is 1/10th of the United States', whose military is a fraction of the United States' but does possess more nuclear weapons (7,300 to United States' 6,970). Oh, and he is a Judo master. It is not his moves on the mat or his extra 330 nukes that pushes Vladimir Putin atop the list. Instead, it is the lack of checks and balances in the political system he is allowed to dominate. He is the type of leader our founders feared. Benjamin Franklin seems to have described him at the Constitutional Convention when the nature of the executive was being debated:

There is scarce a king in a hundred who would not....get first all the people's money, then all their lands, and then make them and their children servants for ever....there is a natural inclination in mankind to a Kingly Government. It sometimes relieves them from Aristocratic domination. They had rather have one tyrant than five hundred....I am apprehensive therefore, that the Government of these States, may in future times, end in a Monarchy...

It gets confusing, keeping straight what the framers feared. A **monarch**? The mob? An American **aristocracy**? All of the above. At the Constitutional Convention, when one branch or entity seemed to be getting too much power, another branch was given more power to keep a balance. At first, the framers intended for the Senate to appoint judges and administrators as well as negotiate treaties. Then their fear of aristocracy in the Senate prompted them to give the president these powers, contingent on the Senate's approval.

Without the power to levy taxes, regulate commerce, borrow and coin money, raise and supply an army, create courts, or declare war, the president seemed to be weak compared to rulers around the world in 1787. The "power of war" was especially meant to be off-limits to the president. In James Madison's vision, the president was to be a "man above the political fray" and unable to start as "the President would necessarily derive so much power and importance from a state of war." Madison was so fearful of the powers a war could give the president that he wanted the Senate to have the sole power to make **treaties**. He went as far to express a desire that the Senate could go behind a warmongering president's back and make a treaty without the president's consent!

Presidential Powers

Unlike Congress, the president does not have a lengthy, specific **enumerated** list of powers—which has been an advantage in the office's growth. After all, the vaguer the Constitution is about power, the more power that can be implied—recall how Congress's power grew through the vague **Elastic** and **Commerce Clauses**.

The President's Formal Powers

Even though things such as numerous checks and **divided government** have weakened the office of the President, the Executive still brings a considerable amount of power to the checks and balances tug-of-war with Congress. The president has many powers stated explicitly in the Constitution.

The Constitution calls the executive the **Commander-in-Chief** who is in charge of all things armed forces and has a number of expressed, formal powers.

The President's expressed, Article II, powers:

- Serve as commander in chief of the armed forces.
- Commission officers of the armed forces.
- Grant **reprieves and pardons** for federal offenses (except impeachment)
- Convene Congress in special sessions.
- Receive ambassadors from other nations.
- Make treaties with other nations with the **Senate's approval**.
- Appoints ambassadors with the Senate's approval.
- Veto laws passed by Congress; in order for Congress to override the veto, it must have a **supermajority** in both houses (given in Article I).

The President's Informal Powers

In addition to these expressed powers, the president has much more informal or **inherent powers** than any other branch. Keep in mind that these are based on expressed powers, but the president has taken these expressed powers a step further. For instance, the president's ability to order a bombing by the air force is an implied power because there was no air force when the Constitution was written. Many of the President's **implied powers** stem from his emergency powers. Cases like natural disasters or military conflicts require swift action from the president. For example, an implied power includes sending troops into combat without a formal declaration of war from Congress. The framers meant the president to be able to respond quickly to external, foreign threats while they were fearful of the office evolving into a monarchy. In modern times, the President has done just that. Congress has not declared war since WWII, even though we fought wars in Korea, Vietnam, Iran, and Afghanistan. Congress tried to block the president's war making power by passing the **War Powers Act** in 1973 requiring (1) president to notify Congress within 48 hours of sending troops into combat and (2) begin to remove troops after 60 days unless Congress approves of the action. Since then, the U.S has fought two wars and staged at least nine military interventions in other countries. The War Powers Act is what James Madison said the Bill of Rights would be: a **parchment barrier**.

A reading of "Federalist Paper 78" gives a good picture of the type of executive the framers had in mind. Hamilton saw the executive as a protector of the nation from internal and external threats. Internally, he could stop majority factions from enacting bad policy through the legislature with a veto. In the face of foreign threats, the president could act quickly to face an invader or put down an insurrection. Quick and decisive, the President could also act behind the scenes. Whereas the Constitution requires that Congress keep a public record of its doings, the framers gave the executive a shield of secrecy that we call **executive privilege**. They understood that some information, including the reports of spies, could not be made public but must be decisively and promptly acted upon without full transparency. While the legislature was built to move slowly, the executive was to have "energy" and the people's blessing to look out for the general welfare. While proposals were made at the Constitutional Convention for there to be more than one president or an executive council that would govern alongside the president, the convention rejected "a plurality in the executive." They wanted the voters to be able to blame one person alone for poor decisions. Knowing himself solely responsible for policy failures, the president would be mindful of popular opinion as well, making the president accountable to the people though they would not elect the officer.

The flipside of blame is praise. The president gets credit when the economy is strong and wars are won. Usually, it does not take long in office for a president's sense of a **popular mandate** to wear out. Once the **honeymoon period** is over and the president has acted on the mandate voters gave by electing him, presidents usually have until the next midterm to enact the boldest items on their agendas. Between the **honeymoon** and their inevitable **lame duck** end, the president has many tools to enact policy that do not require the cooperation of congress.

Executive Orders

Executive orders have the force of law. Unlike laws, however, they require no congressional action. Executive orders are a perfect fit for the president's emergency powers. More common since Congress has become gridlocked by hyper-partisanship, the executive's party circumvents Congress to enact its policy preferences. The proper way to make policy is for the president to get a member of Congress to write and propose a law to achieve his or her goals. The president would then use the means he has at his disposal, like the bully pulpit and his **State of the Union** Speech to pressure Congress to pass the bill. Alternatively, there is the short cut of the executive order, giving presidents the ability to order a policy into existence.

Consider when Obama issued an executive order in 2014 that changed the legal status of 5 million illegal immigrants. Know as Deferred Action for Childhood Arrivals (DACA), Obama's executive order allowed some individuals with unlawful presence in the United States after being brought to the country as children to receive a renewable two-year period of deferred action from deportation and become eligible for a work permit in the U.S. Obama's executive order prompted the Speaker of the House Paul Ryan to call him "Emperor Obama." State governments cried foul, claiming that Obama was violating the principle of separation of powers, as the Constitution gives Congress the power of naturalization (Article 1, Section 8).

In June 2016, SCOTUS voided Obama's executive order granting 5 million immigrants work permits, citing the executive order as a violation of the principle of the separation of powers. However, Obama could still prevent the deportation of the immigrants by directing the **Department of Homeland Security** not to enforce immigration law against any immigrants with work permits.

Executive orders differ from laws in one crucial way: the next president can undo and disregard them. Following President Obama's tenure, President Trump voided 138 Obama directives in his first year in office. Such sudden changes in policy leave business, other countries, and markets unsure of the rules that regulate commerce and keep domestic peace. Like the states under majorities, policies that change with election—whether its every year or four--result in disorder and long-term costs.

A history of executive orders

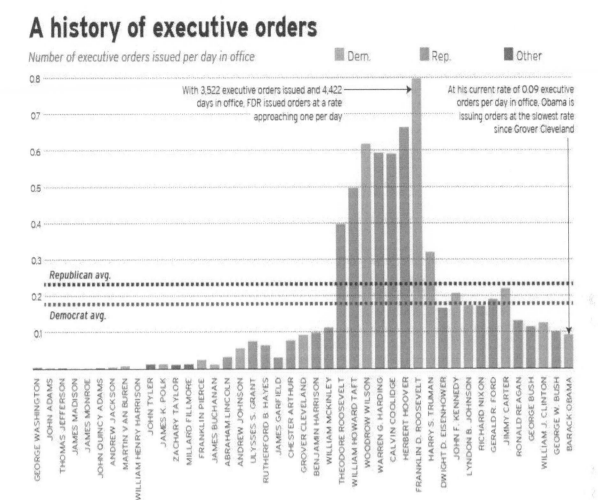

Number of executive orders issued per day in office   ■ Dem.   ■ Rep.   ■ Other

With 3,522 executive orders issued and 4,422 days in office, FDR issued orders at a rate approaching one per day

At his current rate of 0.09 executive orders per day in office, Obama is issuing orders at the slowest rate since Grover Cleveland

Republican avg.

Democrat avg.

Graphic by Christopher Ingraham. Executive order tallies from the American Presidency Project. Days served from Wikipedia.

Note: Grover Cleveland's two non-consecutive terms were merged together for the purposes of this chart.

Executive Agreements

Executive agreements are similar treaties made with foreign nations without the Senate's consent. In short, **executive agreements** give the President a way to get around the Senate to make foreign policy. The executive agreement was born in the 1930s when Franklin D. Roosevelt discovered that working around Congress was a lot easier than working with it. By merely calling deals "agreements" instead of "treaties," he was free to work with other nations without going through the trouble of getting 67 Senators to sign off on his pacts with other nations. However, just like Executive orders, the next president can undo them.

Republican Senators oddly highlighted this complexity in 2015. Obama made an agreement with Iran regarding the country's nuclear weapons program. While the deal was in the works, 47 Republican Senators sent a letter to Iran stating that "the next president could revoke such an executive agreement with the stroke of a pen." In a breach of the norm that foreign policy is executive branch turf, these Senators broke protocol in advising Iran, a U.S. adversary, to reject the president's proposal. Obama criticized Congress for violating the principle of separation of powers and made the deal. As it turns out, President Trump pulled the U.S. out of the deal in the spring of 2018. If the deal had been a treaty instead, its undoing would have required a supermajority Senate vote. Alas, **treaties** are a dying breed. Executive agreements, on the other hand, are used more and more to get around a partisan, **polarized** Congress. More than 18,500 executive agreements have been entered into since 1789: more than 17,000 of them from 1939 on. Little over 100 treaties have been made in that same timeframe.

Signing Statements

While Congress can produce policy, the final step in a bill becoming a law is the president's signature. These days, the president does a lot more than sign. The president has assumed a tradition in which he or she writes a paper explaining what the law means. He or she will then attach the paper to the law. These signing statements appear with the law in the U.S. Codebook.

Perhaps the most well-known and controversial signing statement was written by George W. Bush. It was attached to the Detainee Treatment Act of 2005, which sought to define and limit interrogation and treatment of terrorism suspects held in U.S. custody. Bush signed the anti-torture bill, but his statement practically negated it. He informed Congress that the denial of **habeas corpus** to enemies of the state is a power **inherent** to the Commander and Chief.

Executive Privilege

Presidents want their conversations, documents, and actions to be kept from public scrutiny because if we all see it, so do our enemies. So presidents have often claimed—many times unsuccessfully—that secrecy is an inherent power of the executive. Many have argued that they must have confidence that what happens in the Oval stays in the Oval. Historically, presidents enjoyed their privacy—even going so far as to have open affairs within the walls of the White House. Reporters did not hunt for presidential scandals until Nixon had the FBI spy on the Democratic Party at its campaign headquarters at The Watergate Hotel. The Supreme Court ruled in the ensuing case, Nixon v. the United States, that the executive does not have the privilege of privacy in criminal cases. The ruling forced Nixon to turn over incriminating evidence and led to his resignation. Since then, the press has been much more of a watchdog, and presidents have not had the "privilege" they once enjoyed with little interference. Since Nixon v. U.S., presidents have dusted off the old power and used it with mixed results:

• George H.W. Bush only invoked it once: In 1991, he allowed Dick Cheney, then the defense secretary, to not turn over documents **subpoenaed** during a congressional investigation into a Navy aircraft program.

• Clinton was the first president to invoke executive privilege without issuing a written order; he claimed the privilege 14 times, including to avoid having to testify before a **congressional hearing** regarding his involvement in the Whitewater scandal in 1995.

• Clinton was overruled by a federal judge three years later when he tried to avoid testifying or allowing his advisers to testify about his relationship with Monica Lewinsky. That made him the first president since Nixon to invoke the privilege and lose.

• George W. Bush invoked executive privilege to allow Karl Rove, his senior adviser at the time, to avoid testifying before Congress during its investigation into the firing of nine federal prosecutors, allegedly for partisan reasons.

Expansion of President's Power

The office of the president has extended over time for many reasons:

• MASS MEDIA. The president can use his exposure power to quickly and effectively sway public opinion through media outlets—the bully pulpit.

• ECONOMIC CRISES. In a crisis, people tend to look to an individual to have the answers, come to their rescue, and soothe feelings. As the nation's figurehead, the president fits this role perfectly.

• GLOBAL WARS. The president represents our nation, conveys information to the public after secret meetings. He has access to privileged information and distinguished people that Congressmen may never see. If a congressman from Oklahoma's 3rd district had said "the only thing we have to fear is fear itself" in response to the Japanese attack on Pearl Harbor, we probably would never have heard those brave words.

In a media-saturated, candidate-centered political culture, all eyes are on the president. Such exposure gives the offices great powers of persuasion, **agenda setting**, and action. Americans increasingly want the president free from the checks Congress and the Supreme Court impose on the offices. That is, some Americans want an unburdened President. Republicans and Democrats are perhaps never more hypocritical than when it comes to their view of presidential power. An executive order by a Democratic president has Republicans screaming "Hilter!" while Democrats suddenly forget their concern for Constitution restraint. However, let a Republican use an executive order to enact policy, and suddenly the Madisonian system becomes sacred to Democrats. Each side would do well to remember that the presidency is an institution crafted carefully in 1787 to balance power with the legislature. Like the framers, we should all fear it becoming so powerful that it breaks free of constitutional restraints no matter how much we may like a given president. It is the office, not the one holding it, that must be constrained.

The best regulators of a given executive are those within an incumbent's party. If partisans restrain those who they call their own, they will have constrained future presidents who they very well might disdain. When partisans grant a given president power, they do not give only a person power. Instead, the institution of the executive branch gains power at the expense of Congress, the Supreme Court, or state governments. A rule of law order that imposes boundaries on the executive depends on healthy institutions with enough power to check the president. The constitutional system seeks to prevent an over-powerful executive ruling by law, bending institutions to his will. So many who claim to value the Constitution cheer when a president they like takes action to thwart another party in a divided government. However, they scream tyranny when a president from the opposing party does so. This is a dangerous cycle. As the executive gains strength, the other institutions grow weaker. These are our levee system. When the flood comes, it only take one weak point for the water to breach the walls. By guarding our institutions, we keep power in its proper channels.

Chapter 13

Electing the President

The president gets his job by being elected in a specific, separate, nationwide election. It is the only branch of our government that is entirely selected by the population as a whole. The United States, along with most South American and African countries, chooses the head leader this way, in an election that is held separately from the election for Congress. Making it possible that opposing parties may control the presidency and either part of Congress opens the possibility of a **divided government**. When one party controls the executive branch while the opposing party controls one or both chambers of the legislature, the separation of powers can become a head-on conflict of powers. Divided governments are notoriously inefficient and most frustrating to executives. Putin de-fanged Russia's house, the Duma, and then got it to pass laws granting him dictatorial powers. Founders like Benjamin Franklin warned that our president would do the same if he could.

Because of these concerns, the framers were careful to keep a check on the president. The very title "president" was ignoble in itself. The title of president usually refers to one who presides over a meeting rather than titles like ruler or governor, whose will dominates an assembly. Indeed, proponents of the **New Jersey Plan** wanted to adhere to the Article's omission of the branch altogether. After ruling out ideas like an executive committee, the delegates settled on two options for the shape of the executive branch.

Option 1: The legislature would select the President who would serve only a single term that should be long enough for the executive to enact policy and gain expertise.

Option 2: The people would select the President who would be re-eligible for office but serve shorter terms.

As **Federalist 70** indicates, the founders' ideas of what the executive branch should look like varied wildly. Should there be one, two, or even four presidents in charge of different geographic regions? To keep the executive from becoming too powerful, should it be internally checked by a council?

At the **Convention**, the core of the debate was whether a national majority could choose wisely and resist the manipulation of demagogues and propagandists. Gouverneur Morris at this point in the debate referred to the future franchise as "poor reptiles" but began to see the inevitability that the new government would rest on the people's will. The ultimate goal, after all, was to have a government "of the people." After the Revolution, there would be no going back to rule by the few or the one. Despite themselves, elites like Morris were changing their minds and proposing ideas that went against their class interests.

Many at the convention favored the upper house of the legislature choosing the executive, but fear of the president and the Senate "teaming up" to "subvert the Constitution" nixed the idea. They needed an executive strong enough to balance against the people's branch but would not evolve into a monarchy. Was there a way of selecting this person without giving the "reptiles" too much of a say but enough so they would feel in charge? The riddle seemed to be unsolvable.

Then one delegate planted a seed that would become the Electoral College. On June 2, 1788, James Wilson proposed "that the Executive Magistracy shall be elected in the following manner: That the States be divided into districts: & that the persons qualified to vote in each district for members of the first branch of the national Legislature elect members for the respective districts to be electors...." So, the Electoral College was born. It would be an elite group chosen by the people in each state.

The Electoral College

The Electoral College is not a place, much less a college. Do not send your ACT scores there. It is made up of 538 electors who cast votes to decide the President and Vice-

President of the United States. The candidate who receives a majority of **electoral votes** (270) wins the Presidency. The number 538 is the sum of the nation's 435 Representatives, 100 Senators, and three **electors** given to the District of Columbia.

The Electoral College baffles Americans and stupefies foreigners. There is no electoral institution in the world like it. It is an indirect election system where the winner of the majority of the people's vote does not necessarily win. It has a strong **federalism character** in that state delegates vote for the President (and Vice President). Smaller states tend to like it while those from states with large populations increasingly feel **disenfranchised**.

In all but two states, the candidate who wins the majority of votes in a state wins all of that state's electoral votes. Nebraska and Maine award electoral votes by proportional representation, making it possible for two candidates to receive a portion of electoral votes in these states. The other 48 states grant **plurality** winners all of their electors.

SPOILER ALERT

Why not vote for a third party?

Voting for a party outside of the two-party system would make sense if our election system had a different ballot like a runoff. However, in winner-take-all elections with no runoff, voting for a party outside the Democratic and Republican parties is to waste one's vote. Voting for a third party can even help the candidate one likes the least to win. **Third parties** only spoil elections for the would-be winners, giving the victory to those who should have finished in second place. Sure, third parties, if popular enough, get the two main parties to pay attention to their issues. Is this worth consistently having voters' second choice in the White House?

Second Place Wins!

Confused how that could happen? Let us go to the food court. Imagine you and some of your friends are ordering pizza. You have three choices, and you each get to vote one time. Out of the 12 of you, 7 are vegetarians. Your choices include cheese, cheese and onion, or pepperoni. The votes play out as follows:

Cheese—4
Cheese and Onion—3
Pepperoni—5

Pepperoni it is! Never mind that the vegetarian majority is either going to have to abandon its meat-freeness or go hungry. The majority here clearly lost to a minority because the veggie majority split its vote. In U.S. elections voters know if they are the onion pizza people and choose to vote for one of the leading contenders rather than end up with their worst option.

If there were a runoff, or a second round of voting, between the top two winners, cheese and onion would not have appeared on the second ballot. Cheese would certainly win with seven votes. In ranked-choice voting, one does not go through the trouble of voting again. The voter ranks choices in order. The four vegetarians who voted for cheese would have ranked it #1 and cheese and onion for #2. They most likely would have left pepperoni blank. After the #3 choice, cheese and onion dropped from the ballot; cheese would have gotten its votes and sailed to victory.

The **spoiler effect**, which just caused our vegetarians to go hungry, is common in U.S. elections. Out of our 45 presidents, up to 9 of them would have been second-place finishers in a runoff election system.

Spoiler candidate	Election	Most popular candidate	Winning candidate
James Birney	1844	Henry Clay	James Knox Polk
Martin van Buren	1848	Lewis Cass	Zachary Taylor
Peter Cooper	1876	Samuel J. Tilden	Rutherford B. Hayes
John St. John	1884	James G. Blaine	Grover Cleveland
James B. Weaver	1892	Benjamin Harrison	Grover Cleveland
Theodore Roosevelt	1912	William Howard Taft	Woodrow Wilson
George Wallace	1968	Hubert Humphrey	Richard Nixon
Ross Perot	1992	George H. W. Bush	Bill Clinton
Ralph Nader	2000	Al Gore	George W. Bush

This trend occurs at all levels of United States political office, from Congressmen to state governors, even though third parties have little chance of winning. Instead of wasting our vote on the third party candidate we like, many choose not to vote or vote for one of the top two candidates from the established parties. Voters end up siding with "the lesser of two evils." Implementing a runoff system could remove these spoiler effect woes. A **winner-take-all**, **first-past-the-post** presidential election system has problems enough.

Add the lack of runoff elections with **plurality voting** and the most popular candidates for presidents lose even more. Consider John McCain's 2000 bid for the Republican nomination. His primary opponent, the eventual presidential race winner, was George W. Bush. Bush's journey is instructive as he was able to win the general election through the Electoral College backdoor.

How 2000's Third Most Popular Candidate Became President

First, Republican winner of the presidency George W. Bush had to knock off John McCain in the Republican primary. Since Bush had raised significantly more campaign funds, he could campaign in all state primaries, whereas McCain could afford to campaign in only a few early states. In the earliest **primary**, New Hampshire's, McCain beat Bush by 19%. Bush's campaign strategists knew he would do better. They would follow a playbook written by Bush's father's campaign guru, Lee Atwater. Atwater's playbook was simple: race bait, fear monger, and play dirty against opponents to drive voters away from him rather than try to pull them to oneself. The aim was to get more voters than one's opponent, not win over the American people.

Bush's team set to do just that before the primary season got into full swing. From somewhere, a whisper campaign began ahead of the South Carolina primary. McCain was a "fag candidate" claimed church flyers left on cars. Bob Jones University president sent out an email saying McCain "had chosen to sire children without marriage." South Carolina voters answered their phones to push polls insinuating that McCain suffered mental disorders from his time as a prisoner of war. Other push polls implied that he had an illegitimate black child. When Southern voters saw McCain and his wife posing in family photos with their dark complexioned daughter, the rumors might have seemed real. They were not. They had adopted their daughter, Bridget, from Mother Theresa's orphanage in Bangladesh. Regardless, the tactic worked, and McCain's campaign for president faltered.

Next, Bush faced Democrat Al Gore in the general election. While Gore appealed to more voters, Bush won more Electoral College votes. The plurality requirement was especially useful to the Bush strategists since Gore had a challenger within his Democratic/liberal constituency.

Ralph Nader was a long-time consumer advocate who was so popular with the left in the1960s that he was asked to be a Vice Presidential candidate. He refused. The Democrats had sold out to conservatives in his view. Nader asked to meet with Al Gore to argue that relaxing the 55 mile per hour speed limit on interstates would lead to thousands of motorists deaths. He was told, "The vice president has no time to meet with Mr. Nader." A few years later when Nader chose to run for the 2000 Democratic nomination, Gore's campaign tried to convince Nader to drop out of the race. A Nader strategist replied, "We're not going to do that." Nader wanted to punish Gore, even if his third-party run spoiled the election for Gore. The Bush campaign did not sit hopefully by and wait. They funded Nader's efforts, hoping for a spoiler effect. After honing in on the competitive counties in swing states, Bush became yet another second-place finisher to win the presidency, losing the popular vote by 543,895 votes but winning the Electoral College 271-266. To better understand such outcomes, one must grasp some intricacies about the Electoral College.

In the Electoral College, Not All Votes are Equal

First, where one votes matters. Consider this: in 2012, Obama beat Romney by 333,908 votes. But Obama got 65,915,796 votes to Romney's 60,933,500. That looks closer to 5 million.

So how can one claim that Romney came up short by just a few hundred thousand votes, not millions? Where voters cast their ballots determines their worth. A Democratic vote in California is a dime a dozen while one in Montana is considerably more prized.

The popular vote, the votes cast by the citizens, does not matter—Electoral College votes do.

So, back to those 333,908 votes mentioned above. These votes came from eight counties in eight states. Of our 50 states, only 8 were really up for grabs in 2012. The others belong to the parties they historically vote for with no surprises in store.

Electoral votes are up for grabs in the swing states: New Hampshire, Pennsylvania, Ohio, Virginia, North Carolina, Florida, Wisconsin, Iowa, Colorado, and Nevada. Most states are not competitive in presidential races. Only eight to twelve states actually have a contest between presidential candidates.

While we may see around ten swing states, electoral strategists see the voting districts within the states. Only one or two counties in these swing states are evenly divided between Democrats and Republicans and may go either way. This handful of U.S. counties, making up around 300,000 voters, is where the real race for the presidency took place in 2012.

If one lives in a safe state, and most of us do, the top two candidates have little reason to campaign nearby or run their nasty attack ads. Some states have been married to parties for so long, the magic is completely gone from the relationship. Come presidential election season, they hardly even speak. Below is a snapshot from the website Fair Vote of how little attention candidates paid to safe states in 2012, regardless of the love those states gave them:

	Money Donated to Obama and Romney Campaigns as of 10/17/12	Fundraisers attended in the state since June by a major ticket candidate	Ad Money Spent since April	Visits by major ticket candidates (9/7-10/31)
CA	$119,400,000	31	$0	0
NY	$68,700,000	23	$52,000	0
TX	$43,600,000	12	$0	0
FL	$48,600,000	16	$147,000,000	37
IL	$34,500,000	8	$15,600,000 *	0

M A	$31,400,000	13	$19,000,000 *	0
VA	$27,200,000	4	$131,000,00 0	25
PA	$23,600,000	6	$16,000,000	2

There is yet another way that not all votes are equal. The Electoral College perversely favors citizens' votes in small, rural states over populous states with big cities. A vote in Wyoming counts nearly four times as much in the Electoral College as one in Texas. Wyoming has three electoral votes for a population of 584,153, and Texas has thirty-eight electoral votes for a population of almost 27 million. By dividing the population into electoral votes, we can see that Wyoming has one "elector" for every 195,000 people, and Texas one "elector" for about every 710,525. One vote of a group of 195,000 counts more than one vote in 710,525.

Reforming the Electoral College without a Constitutional Amendment

The Electoral College not only enforces the two-party system in which voters select the "least bad" option, but it also corrupts it further. After all, even if a president does not win the popular vote, he can still be elected to office by the Electoral College. There is a way out of this. The **National Vote Plan** is a state-level reform that pledges a given state's electoral votes to the winner of the national popular vote. Eleven states have passed such a law, comprising 165 electoral votes. Once states have passed such popular vote laws that total 270, the Electoral College will matter far less. 95 to go!

Electoral College Q & A

Why are there 538 electors in the Electoral College

The number of "**electors**" a state has equals each state's number of representatives in the House and Senate. California has a bunch (2 Senators + 55 House members = 57 electors in the EC). West Virginia has a few (2 Senators + 3 House members = 5 electors in the EC).

How are the electors selected?

This process varies from state to state. Usually, political parties nominate electors at their state conventions. Sometimes that process occurs by a vote of the party's central committee. The electors are usually state-elected officials, party leaders, or people with a strong affiliation with the Presidential candidates.

Do electors have to vote for their party's candidate?

Neither the Constitution nor Federal election laws compel electors to vote for their party's candidate. That said, twenty-seven states have laws on the books that require electors to vote for their party's candidate if that candidate gets a majority of the state's popular vote. In 24 states, no such laws apply, but common practice is for electors to vote for their party's nominee.

What happens if no one gets a majority of Electoral College votes?

If no one gets a majority of electoral votes, the election goes to the U.S. House of Representatives. The top three contenders face off with each state casting one vote. Whoever wins a majority of states wins the election. The process is the same for the Vice Presidency, except that the U.S. Senate makes that selection.

When does the Electoral College cast its votes?

Each state's electors meet on the Monday following the second Wednesday of December. They cast their votes then, and the President of the Senate who reads them before both houses of Congress on January 6th.

Chapter 14

The Bureaucracy

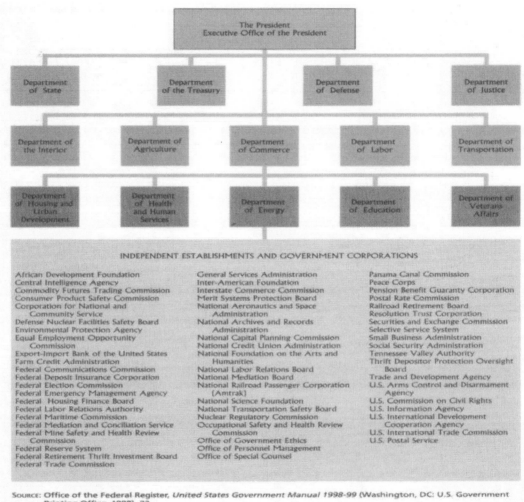

Source: Office of the Federal Register, *United States Government Manual 1998-99* (Washington, DC: U.S. Government Printing Office, 1998), 22.

Organization of the Executive Branch   T-49

© 2000 by Addison-Wesley Educational Publishers Inc.

The size of the U.S. government is daunting, and the range of areas it regulates is daunting. While Political Science 101 says that well-functioning, powerful modern nations must have a professional class of experts and **regulators**, many politicians talk as though our federal agencies are "the problem, not the solution" to our common problems. Before considering whether the executive branch bureaucracy is good or bad, take a moment to consider what it is and the functions it performs.

The President is the head of all offices under the executive branch. Many think of the "veep" as the President's right-hand man. Not so. The President's real go-to? That would be the Chief of Staff.

Hail to the Chief (Of Staff)!

The President's Chief of Staff is responsible for managing the entire **Executive Office of the President**. This organization includes everything from the residence staff that attends to the first family, to the national security adviser, to the White House communications team.

The Chief of Staff leads an inner circle of political and strategic decision makers in a White House.

The Chief also controls who gets access to the President. The Chief of Staff sees to it that only critical decisions get made by the President. The Chief puts out small fires and handles details, freeing the President to focus on the most critical priorities. The Chief of staff ultimately is an all-purpose adviser on everything from politics to policy, guiding and counseling a president on some of the toughest decisions.

The Cabinet

The Cabinet's role, inferred from the language of the Opinion Clause (Article II, Section 2, Clause 1) of the Constitution, is to serve as an advisory body to the President of the United States. Among the senior officers of the Cabinet are the Vice President and the heads of the federal executive departments (see chart). Members of the Cabinet (except for the Vice President) serve at the pleasure of the President, who can dismiss them at will for no cause. Unlike the President's staff, cabinet secretaries ("Secretary of...")--the heads of cabinet agencies—are nominated by the President and confirmed by the Senate. All federal public officials, including Cabinet members, are also subject to impeachment by the House of Representatives and trial in the Senate for "treason, bribery, and other high crimes and misdemeanors."

The Bureaucratic Agencies

It may be true that the President is one of the most powerful people in the world, but he cannot do all of the work alone. He has pack-mules, bodyguards, technocrats, scholars, and a legion of enforcers to see that the laws of Congress and rules of executive branch agencies are carried out. Counting executive agencies, the executive branch weighs in at three million employees.

The federal bureaucracy's size and increased autonomy have led some political scientists to add a dangerous fourth branch to the traditional three, "The Bureaucracy." The fourth branch argument is that it is the bureaucracy that enacts policy and engages with citizens, creating an administrative state, comprised of rules and those ruled by them. Vote as we may, we cannot affect the rules laid down behind closed doors by people who drink out of office coffee mugs. It is these people who have discretion regarding the details of the laws we follow. Critics see these pencil pushers strangle freedom's neck with their red tape. Some have even accused them of being a conspiring "deep state." Below is a typical argument from those who resent the power of regulatory agencies. Constitutional Law professor Jonathan Turley writes in the Washington Post:

The growing dominance of the federal government over the states has obscured more fundamental changes within the federal government itself: It is not just bigger, it is dangerously off kilter. Our carefully constructed system of checks and balances is being negated by the rise of a fourth branch, an administrative state of sprawling departments and agencies that govern with increasing **autonomy** and decreasing **transparency**.

When James Madison and the other Framers fashioned a new constitutional structure in the wake of the failure of the Articles of Confederation they envisioned a vastly different government. Under the **federalism** model, states would be the dominant system with most of the revenue and responsibilities of governance. The federal government was virtually microscopic by today's standards. In 1790, it had just 1,000 nonmilitary workers. In 1962, there were 2,515,000 federal employees. Today, we have 2,840,000 federal workers in 15 departments, 69 agencies and 383 nonmilitary sub-agencies.

The rise of the fourth branch has been at the expense of Congress's lawmaking authority. In fact, the vast majority of "laws" governing the United States are not passed by Congress but are issued as regulations, crafted largely by thousands of unnamed, unreachable bureaucrats. One study found that in 2007, Congress enacted 138 public laws, while federal agencies finalized 2,926 rules, including 61 major regulations.

This rulemaking comes with little accountability. It's often impossible to know, absent a major scandal, whom to blame for rules that are abusive or nonsensical. Of course, agencies owe their creation and underlying legal authority to Congress, and Congress holds the purse strings. But Capitol Hill's relatively small staff is incapable of exerting **oversight** on more than a small percentage of agency actions. And the threat of cutting funds is a blunt instrument to control a massive administrative state — like running a locomotive with an on/off switch.

The rise of the fourth branch has occurred alongside an unprecedented increase in presidential powers — from the power to determine when to go to war to the power to decide when it's reasonable to vaporize a U.S. citizen in a drone strike. In this new order, information is jealously guarded and transparency has declined sharply. That trend, in turn, has given the fourth branch even greater insularity and independence. When Congress tries to respond to cases of agency abuse, it often finds officials walled off by claims of expanding **executive privilege**.

Of course, federal agencies officially report to the White House under the umbrella of the executive branch. But in practice, the agencies have evolved into largely independent entities over which the President has very limited control. Only 1 percent of federal positions are filled by political appointees as opposed to career officials, and on average appointees serve only two years. At an individual level, career officials are insulated from political pressure by **civil service** rules. There are also entire **agencies** — including the Securities and Exchange Commission, the Federal Trade Commission and the Federal Communications Commission — that are protected from White House interference.

It's a small percentage of agency matters that rise to the level of presidential notice. The rest remain the sole concern of agency discretion.

As the power of the fourth branch has grown, conflicts between the other branches have become more acute. There is no better example than the fights over **presidential appointments**.

Wielding its power to confirm, block, or deny nominees is one of the few remaining ways Congress can influence agency policy and get a window into agency activity. Nominations now commonly trigger congressional demands for explanations of agencies' decisions and disclosures of their documents. And that commonly leads to standoffs with the White House.

The marginalization Congress feels is magnified for citizens, who are routinely pulled into the vortex of an administrative state that allows little opportunity for challenge or appeal.
In the new regulatory age, presidents and Congress can still change the government's priorities, but the agencies effectively run the show based on their interpretations and discretion. The rise of this fourth branch represents perhaps the single greatest change in our system of government since the founding.

We cannot long protect liberty if our leaders continue to act like mere bystanders to the work of government.

Corruption in the Bureaucracy

If the bureaucrats taking over was not enough, these unelected officials may be captured by special interests or given their jobs for loyalty to the President rather than their expertise and experience.

Even though George Washington promised that those working in the bureaucracy "shall be the best qualified," it only took a few decades for presidents to start treating their hiring power as a way to reward their families and friends. Starting with Andrew Jackson, whose administration warranted the famous phrase, "to the victor belongs the spoils," presidents have often used federal jobs as payments from patron to client. Giving jobs as rewards for loyalty instead of competency is often called the "**spoils system**," or **patronage**. Not only did such a practice put unqualified people into government jobs, but it also led to corruption and even the assassination of a president. One campaign volunteer shot and killed president-elect James Garfield after being denied a job in the government. In reaction, Congress passed the **Pendleton Act**, which required applicants to pass the Civil Service Exam before being hired. These policies ensured that qualified personnel staff would be working in the government.

New concerns are sprouting over the trend of bureaucrats leaving low-paying government jobs to work for the private companies they once regulated. By going through the "revolving door," former government employees and elected officials are hired by special interests for their insider knowledge and connections.

That there are corruptions in the system does not mean the agencies themselves are putrid swamps in need of draining. Government professionals are our experts, who execute the laws passed by representatives elected by the people.

For example, so many laws fall under the enumerated power of Congress to promote "science and the useful arts." The government agents fulfilling this power have performed scientific feats, from antibiotics to the Internet. Even though special interests may have hijacked parts of our agencies, there are remedies like revolving door laws. But if we cut or eliminate federal bureaucracies, we better know the areas of expertise and services we are putting on the chopping block. In a previous chapter, we discussed the gap between what we think we know and what we know. This gap tends to be very large when we consider the bureaucracy's many functions. Critics like those who decry "The Fourth Branch" applaud those who propose to cut and even eliminate whole agencies. The current head of the Department of Energy, Rick Perry, is a great example.

Michal Lewis makes this point in his 2018 book, The Fifth Risk. He tells the story of Ricky Perry, the current head of the Department of Energy. In his 2011 primary race for the Republican Party nomination for President, Perry shot himself in the foot. A "Fourth Branch," government-is-the-problem-not-the-solution candidate, Perry was for cutting government agencies, "starving the beast" that had become the federal bureaucracy. In a debate, the moderator asked Perry to list the three federal departments he would cut first. After naming the Department of Education and the Department of Commerce, Perry stumbled. "The third agency of government I would do away with...Education...the...ahhhh...ahh...Commerce, and let's see." Head lowered, he gave up. "I can't, the third one. I can't. Sorry. Oops." The Department of Energy slipped his grasp as did a nomination for President.

It will be instructive to see what such Cabinet-level agencies do. What do you think the Department of Energy does? Having answered, try to measure the gap between your answer and what follows.

Some of the things the **Department of Energy** does:

- It provides low-interest loans to innovative companies trying experimental technologies. A DOE loan allowed Tesla to build its first factory. It also funds alternative energy startups like solar panel firms.
- About half of the DOE's budget, $2.3 billion in total, in a given year maintains America's nuclear weapons arsenal and monitors nuclear threats. At events like the Super Bowl teams of DOE agents scan for radiation levels in hopes of stopping a terrorist with a dirty bomb before the worst happens.
- A quarter of its budget cleans up after the dangerous waste left behind by the manufacture and testing of nuclear weapons.
- Internationally, the DOE monitors nuclear weapon stockpiles, making sure they are not lost, stolen, or sold. Additionally, it monitors the safekeeping of nuclear weapons, watching for any indication that a weapon may detonate accidentally. The U.S.'s service to the international order is singular. No other agency on the planet performs such a task.
- The other quarter of the DOE's budget is used to maintain and increase America's access to energy.

Within these bulleted items are thousands of detailed tasks that are carried out. Lewis quotes a former head of the DOE, John MacWilliams, when describing the importance of the DOE for scientific research:

"...the sort of scientific research that requires multi-billion dollar particle accelerators. The DOE ran seventeen national labs....'The Office of Science in the DOE is not the Office of Science for DOE,' said MacWilliams. 'It's the Office of Science for all science in America. I realized pretty quickly that it was the place where you could world on the two biggest risks to human existence, nuclear weapons and climate change.'" For about half of what Americans spent on chewing gum in 2018, the DOE's protection from nuclear holocaust seems like a good deal.

If you are not horrified by the dangers of nuclear weapons, please watch the HBO miniseries Chernobyl. While it is the story of a nuclear power plant disaster and not a bomb, the effects of radiation are equally staggering. To suggest that the DOE is a superfluous agency full of "career officials" who need to be under more control of the President is laughable. As Federalist Paper 78 reiterates, such experts work apart from politician's control so "the officers of the union" can act on their expertise without worrying about pleasing a politician or voters to keep their jobs. They are so insulated because "there would be too great a disposition to consult popularity" instead of science and the best course of action. For the best policy and the most popular policy rarely are the same. Trump's pick of Rick Perry to head this agency is not hopeful. During Trump's 2016 bid for President, he said of Perry, "...he puts glasses on so people will think he looks smart" and that he "should be forced to take an IQ test." Let's hope President Trump's attacks were empty.

Chapter 15

The President and Congress Make the Federal Budget

On March 11, 2019, President Donald Trump released his budget request for 2020. Under his proposal, the federal budget would be a record $4.746 trillion. The U.S. government estimates it will receive $3.645 trillion in revenue. That creates a $1.101 trillion deficit for October 1, 2019, through September 30, 2020. As of June 18, 2019, the federal debt is $22 trillion while **national gross domestic product (GDP)** is $19.4 trillion. The debt-to-GDP ratio is around 105%. Hopefully, these numbers will make sense at the end of this chapter!

To fund the government, Congress must pass appropriations bills before the fiscal year begins on October 1, 2019. If Congress does not do so, it creates **continuing resolutions** to continue the pre-existing appropriations at the same levels as the previous year (or with minor modifications) for a set amount of time.

Government spending is in three categories:

Mandatory ($2.841 trillion)

Discretionary ($1.426 trillion)

Interest on the national debt ($479 billion)

Revenue—Taxes

Most of the taxes are paid by workers, either through income or payroll taxes.

Income taxes contribute $1.824 trillion or 50% of total receipts.

Social Security, Medicare, and other payroll taxes add $1.295 trillion or 36%.

Corporate taxes supply $255 billion or 7%.

Excise taxes and tariffs contribute $157 billion or 4%.

Estate taxes and other miscellaneous revenue supply the remaining 2%.

Spending--Appropriations

The government expects to spend $4.746 trillion. Almost 60% pays for **mandated benefits** such as Social Security, Medicare, and Medicaid.

Interest on the U.S. debt will be $479 billion. The U.S. Treasury must pay it to avoid a U.S. debt default. Interest on the approximately $22 trillion debt is already the fastest growing federal expense. From September 2018 New York Times:

The federal government could soon pay more in interest on its debt than it spends on the military, Medicaid or children's programs. The run-up in borrowing costs is a one-two punch brought on by the need to finance a fast-growing budget **deficit,** worsened by tax cuts and steadily rising interest rates that will make the debt more expensive.

With less money coming in and more going toward interest, political leaders will find it harder to address pressing needs like fixing crumbling roads and bridges or to make emergency moves like pulling the economy out of future recessions. Within a decade, more than $900 billion in interest payments will be due annually, easily outpacing spending on myriad other programs. Already the fastest-growing major government expense, the cost of interest is on track to hit $390 billion next year, nearly 50 percent more than in 2017, according to the **Congressional Budget Office**.

Setting aside money for **entitlement programs** and interest on the debt, the remaining $1.4 trillion pays for everything else. This piece of the pie is considered discretionary spending. The U.S. Congress changes this amount each year. It uses the president's budget as a starting point and can cut or increase spending in this category without passing an amendment to previous laws.

Mandatory Spending

The budget estimates mandatory spending will be $2.841 trillion in 2020. In 2018, Social Security was by far the biggest expense at $1.102 trillion. **Medicare** was next at $679 billion, followed by **Medicaid** at $418 billion.

Social Security costs are currently covered 100% by payroll taxes and interest on investments. Until 2010, there was more coming into the Social Security Trust Fund than being paid out. Thanks to its investments, the Trust Fund is still running a surplus. However, estimates indicate that this surplus will be depleted by

2032. Social Security revenue, from payroll taxes and interest earned, will cover only 77% of the benefits promised to retirees.

Medicare is already underfunded. Medicare taxes do not pay for all benefits, so this program relies on general tax dollars to pay for a portion of it. Medicaid is 100% and is presently not a source of debt.

Discretionary Spending

The discretionary budget will be $1.426 trillion. More than half goes toward military spending, including the Department of Veterans Affairs and other defense-related departments. The rest must pay for all other **domestic programs**. The largest are Health and Human Services, Education, and Housing and Urban Development. The Department of Energy falls within this category.

There is an emergency fund of $200.1 billion. Most of it goes to Overseas Contingency Operations to pay for wars. A growing portion is set aside for disaster relief for hurricanes and wildfires.

Military Spending

Military spending is the largest area of discretionary spending. The biggest expense was the Department of Defense base budget at $576 billion. Overseas Contingency Operations were estimated to cost approximately $174 billion. That pays for the war on terror costs triggered by the 9/11 attacks. These include ongoing costs from the war in Iraq and the Afghanistan war.

Military spending included $212.9 billion for defense-related departments. These include Homeland Security, the State Department, and Veterans Affairs. Add it up, and the total U.S. spending on defense is $989 billion.

The Deficit

The budget **deficit** is estimated at $1.101 trillion. That is the difference between $3.645 trillion in revenue and $4.746 trillion in spending.

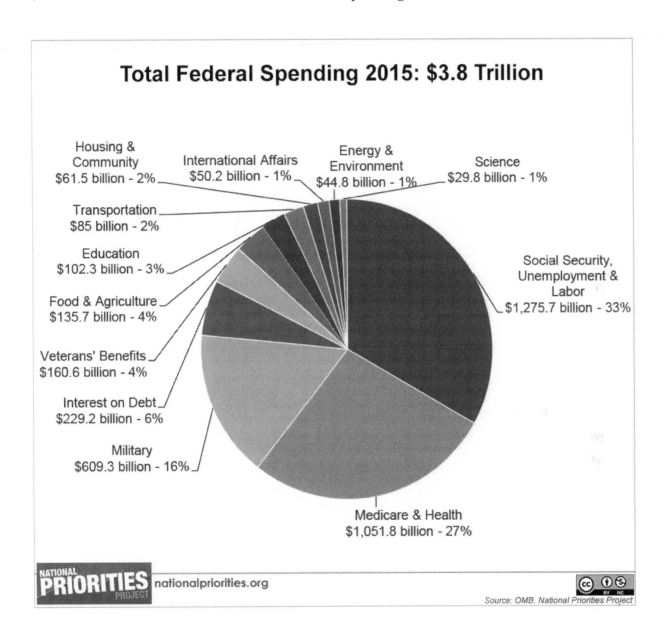

 Federal debt is on an unsustainable path

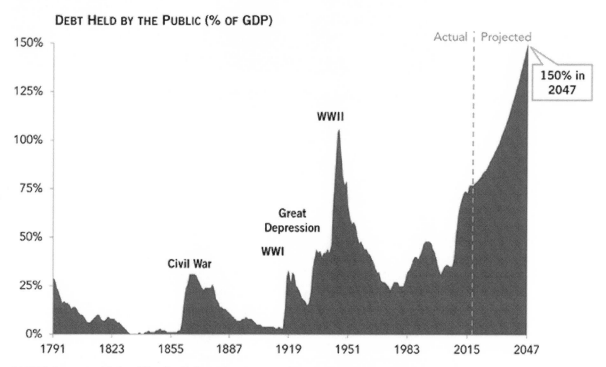

SOURCE: Congressional Budget Office, *The 2017 Long-Term Budget Outlook*, March 2017. Compiled by PGPF.

© 2017 Peter G. Peterson Foundation

PGPF.ORG

Budget Process

Congress created the budget process. It is supposed to follow these four steps:

- The Executive **Office of Management and Budget** prepares the budget.
- The president submits it to Congress on or before the first Monday in February where the **Congressional Budget Office** evaluates the president's proposed budget.
- Congress responds with spending appropriation bills that go to the president by June 30.
- The president has 10 days to reply.

Since the 2010 budget, Congress has only followed the budget process twice.

The hard deadline for budget approval is September 30. If Congress doesn't approve it by then, the government can shut down. It did just that in 2013, January 2018, and in December 2018. To avoid that, Congress usually passes continuing resolutions. These keep the government running at spending levels of the last budget. If the government does shut down, it signals a complete breakdown in the budget process.

Government Shutdown: The Power of the President's Pen

Increasingly Presidents use their signature of the budget as a power. Without a president's signature, a budget cannot go into effect. In creating a showdown with congress, the president hopes to bend the legislative branch to his will. A government shutdown dominates the news cycles as national parks close and millions of federal employees go without pay. Many times, the president loses the gamble and signs a budget or continuing resolution while not getting his way. President Trump experienced this in 2018. President Obama was more successful in his 2013 standoff with Congress.

If a government shutdown goes on long enough, the Treasury Department would have to default on the debt—fail to pay those whom we owe. A nation **defaulting** on its debt is in the category of losing a war or suffering severe depression. It is the sort of thing that marks nations as failures. Shutdowns have lasted from one day to thirty-five, the number of days the government most recently shut down. In the latest fiscal gridlock, President Trump refused to sign the annual budget bill because Congress had not included $5.7 billion for a U.S.-Mexico border wall. Trump finally relented and signed the bill. He then declared a national emergency at the border, which would have required him to show the equivalence of a Mexican invasion for the Pentagon to release some of its billions in emergency funds for a wall (it did not).

Addressing the Debt

As medical costs rise by 5.4% a year, and more people retire, Social Security, Medicare, and Medicaid are going to become more and more expensive.

Not that our **entitlement programs**--Social Security, Medicare, and Medicaid—need to go. However, fiscal conservatives argue that cutting these insurance programs is the best way to reduce the debt. It is important to remember that we all will still want to retire and get medical service when our health and the health of our loved ones fail.

While cutting spending on these programs is undoubtedly a policy option, how many of us will have saved enough to pay the medical bills for a disabled child or ourselves in the event that we develop Alzheimer's or get cancer or live to be 100? Most of us, even the wealthy, cannot pay for the accidents of our births and circumstances. Nor can we save enough to live comfortably for two or three decades without working. Whether it is a changing job market (factories move overseas) or a failing liver, most of us will need insurance to protect against the unknown. Unless one works until death while not going to the doctor--even the emergency room--he will almost certainly need insurance. The question is, can he save enough or does he need an insurer? The likely answer is that insurance will be required. Bankruptcy filings due to medical bills are down by half since the passage of the Affordable Care Act, but it is still the leading cause of bankruptcies in the U.S. Of those declaring bankruptcy because of medical bills, 78% had some form of insurance. So, it looks like we all are going to need some pretty good insurance policies as healthcare prices keep rising.

To those who say that saving for retirement and medical care are matters of personal responsibility, please consider the following scenarios. First, regarding health care, everyone is already guaranteed the most expensive form of healthcare. Since 1986's Emergency Medical Treatment Act, all hospitals that receive Medicaid payments (the vast majority of U.S. hospitals do) cannot turn away patients from emergency rooms. Before the passage of the ACA in 2012, it was common for those without insurance to go to emergency rooms for routine medical care, accounting for 17% of all emergency room visits in 2010 (the uninsured accounted for around 10%

in 2017). In a way, America has always had universal healthcare. It also happens to be the most expensive kind.

Even those with healthcare will not be able to afford medical expenses if the worst happens. Treatments of common diseases and cancers cost in the hundreds of thousands, even millions. We will all want treatments and palliative care. The question is, will we be able to pay for it? Without insurance, whether public or private, the answer is obvious.

Assuming that entitlement programs will most likely not be cut in our lifetimes, even if we wanted them to be, what are we to do about the debt? How are we going to pay for the services our elected officials made law through our beckoning?

Enter Economic Theory: Keynes v. Classical (Hayek)

Keynesian Economics

A "Keynesian" approach to the debt problem has the government as a central actor. Through monetary and fiscal policymaking, experts within the government control the money supply, interest rates, and cutting taxes and increasing government spending to stimulate the economy. Taxes would be kept higher on the wealthy, but not too burdensome to any economic class. The goal of **Keynesian economics** is to grow the economy while keeping taxes steady, even cutting them if it helps boost consumer spending. Paying off the debt is not the pressing concern—keeping the economy growing is. A thriving middle class and an economy free from toxic levels of inflation and unemployment are the main goals of government **macroeconomic policy**.

Classical Economics

The other, the classic economics approach, has the government getting out of the economy business and letting private enterprise meet consumer demand. This option would have the government step out of the way to allow goods and services to flow freely without government meddling. Paying down the debt to around 60% of GDP is the first order of business. They would cut government spending rather than raise taxes. Indeed, many in this camp would cut taxes, especially on the wealthy to give more spending power to the business and wealth creators. By allotting more money to the presumed owners and job creators of the economy, tax cuts on this group would have a "**trickle-down effect**" on the rest of the economy. That is, the rich would spend more, give raises to their employees, and create more jobs. Thereby, the GDP would grow and the government would collect more revenue by having kept taxes the same on all but the top earners.

The differences between Keynesian theory and classical economy theory affect government policies, among other things. One side believes the government should play an active role in controlling the economy, while the other school thinks the economy is better left alone to regulate itself.

From the Houston Chronicle:

Keynesian Economics and the Economy

Keynesian advocates believe capitalism is a sound system, but that it sometimes needs help. When times are good, people work, earn money and spend it on things they want. The spending stimulates the economy, and everything runs smoothly. However, when the economy goes downhill, moods change.
During tougher times, businesses start closing and firing their employees. People do not have money to spend, and they try to save what little they have left. When people quit spending, the economy loses its momentum and spirals farther down.

The Keynesian View of Government Intervention

Keynesian theory says this is exactly when government intervention makes sense. If people aren't spending, then the government has to step in and fill the void. However, there's just one problem: The government doesn't have its own money. It has to take money away from the people and companies to spend it. Higher taxes for businesses take money away that could otherwise be spent on more investments to grow the company. If the government does not tax businesses or individuals, it must borrow even more.

Classical Economics and the Free Markets

The theory of classical economics is that **free markets** will regulate themselves if they are left alone. Markets will find their own level of **equilibrium** without interference by people or the government.

In a classical economy, everyone is free to pursue their own self-interests in a market that is free and open to all competition. When people work at jobs making things, they get paid and use these wages to buy other products. In essence, workers create their own demand for goods and services.

Role of Government in the Economy

Classical economists do not like government spending, and they especially detest more government debt. They would prefer a balanced budget because they do not believe the economy benefits from higher government spending. Keynesians are okay with government borrowing, because they are convinced that government spending increases aggregate demand in the economy.

Unemployment and Inflation

Keynesian enthusiasts favor government involvement and are more concerned about people having jobs than they are about inflation. They see the role of workers as using their abilities to contribute for the good of society. Keynesians do not worry about the cost of goods or the purchasing power of the currency.

Classical economists have some concerns about unemployment but are more worried about price inflation. They see inflation as the biggest threat to a strong long-term growth of the economy. Classicists believe the economy will always seek a level of full employment. They think unemployment results from government interference in the free market or the existence of a monopoly in an industry.

Prices and Market Influences

Classical supporters want a market that is free to find its own levels of **supply and demand**. They believe that prices should fluctuate based on the wants of consumers. The market will adjust itself to any shortages and surpluses of products. Keynesians believe prices should be more rigid and that government should try to maintain price stability. They would like to see the government influence people and corporations to keep prices within specified ranges.

The Future Growth of the Economy

A key difference between Keynesians and classicists is how to predict and treat the future growth of the economy. Keynesians focus on short-term problems. They see these issues as immediate concerns that government must deal with to assure the long-term growth of the economy.

Classicists focus more on getting long-term results by letting the free market adjust to short-term problems. They believe short-term problems are just bumps in the road that the free market will eventually solve for itself.

The Economy: Machine or Organism?

Metaphorically, each has a very different view of how the economy works or what it is. Keynesians see it as a machine and economists as engineers who adjust it to operate correctly, keeping people employed and the flow of supply and demand going. In this model, the government experts and policy makers (most located in the Federal Reserve) tinker with and make adjustments to the nation's economic engine through fiscal and monetary means.

The classical model is organic. When the economy gets sick, they are not likely to have the government intervene in an economic downturn by creating jobs or increasing social welfare spending. To the free-marketer, such intervention would be akin to a doctor who operates on a patient to cure a headache or high fever. For Keynesians, the economy is mechanical; for classical economists, it is organic. One requires experts, the other self-restraint, and patience. While we have been following the Keynesian model for nearly a century, our growing debt is casting doubt on the wisdom of staying the course.

A great resource to understand these differences are the rap battles between John Maynard Keynes and Frederick Hayek, written by Stanford economist Russ Roberts (see appendix).

In conclusion, the central question is, what role is the government to play in the economy? Small-government conservatives' side with Hayek while the rest remain in the Keynesian camp, where they have been since FDR's New Deal. A federal government capable of setting monetary and fiscal policy has been a problematic issue since the Federalist v. Anti-Federalist debates and cases like McCulloch v. Maryland. Is our economy the total of private landowners and professionals like Thomas Jefferson imagined it? Alternatively, is it more like Hamilton's complex machines that require economic engineers with steady hands pulling the levers of control? Hayek would have our economy be the sum total of smart, responsible decisions made by property owners and consumers. Like the Federalists, Keynesian mindsets count on people acting selfishly and attempt to build an economic engine fueled by consumption over saving, desiring over self-regulation, material growth in the present rather than economic health in the long run. As John Maynard Keynes said, "In the long run, we're all dead!"

Chapter 16

Judicial Branch

When it came time to give shape to the Judicial Branch, the Constitutional Convention was winding down, and temperatures were peaking. The **delegates** pretty much passed the job on to Congress. The framers planned for the judiciary to grow slowly, precedent by precedent. As Federalist 78 explains, it would build, limit, and define its power through **case law** and **precedent** and follow the principle of *stare decisis*, allowing previous decisions to guide courts' rulings on current cases. When a question came before the courts, the most recent similar case would provide guidance.

Federalist 78

The framers recognized the vital need for an independent judiciary in a checks and balances system that could act independent of the constraints of politics. If judges could be fired, elected, influenced by offers of campaign cash, their independence would be practically nonexistent. So**, Article III** provides that they would get their jobs through a presidential nomination contingent on a supermajority confirmation vote by the Senate. Once the **Senate confirms** their nomination, federal judges serve life tenures.

Courts are decidedly not democratic institutions. Judges are not elected, and their decisions are final, not subject to vote or even congressional law. The only way a Supreme Court decision can be countered is through the passage of a constitutional amendment. Hamilton explains how a non-democratic body is essential in democracies in **Federalist 78**.

Without an independent judiciary, **rule *of* law** is replaced by rule *by* law, a central feature of all democracies. The "rule of law" embodies the principle that the laws apply to all equally, even to the president. Where the rule of law is absent, rulers use laws to assert their faction's interests. Vladimir Putin's Russia is a perfect example of rule by law. For instance, Putin's government routinely arrests journalists critical of his regime on falsified drug and tax evasion charges. Judges then duly convict the accused, daring not to displease an executive that can remove them. The first building block of an independent judiciary that enforces the rule of law is to have appointed judges who serve for life. In this way they are not beholden to an over-bearing president or, if elected, to popular opinion.

The most democratic institutions in the U.S. are federal Congress and state and local legislatures. In these institutions, those who serve must win reelection often. Take a member of Congress: how often or deeply can one of them afford to act in a way that sacrifices short-term for long-term gain, which ultimately displeases constituents? The answer is not at all. If a democratically elected policymaker cuts a popular program, an opponent will inevitably show up in the next election claiming what a dastardly and unnecessary thing that was. So, poof, there goes the long-term planner's job to someone who understands that he better give the people what they want now. Politicians usually act in agreement with the economist who said that "in the long run we're all dead." Presidents, too, must heed the mood of the masses, for similar reasons.

The judge, however, serves a life tenure and is appointed, not elected, and is thereby protected from political pressures. The judge, along with a few other appointed officials, can act free from political, short-term concerns and anger whomever she pleases. Only tenured university professors, heads of agencies like the Federal Reserve, and Beyonce' have such leeway in our society. As Akhil Reed Amar puts it, "elected officials cannot afford to ignore the short term" but "the Supreme Court justices have considerable **discretion** in defining their agenda. They pick the cases they want to hear, guided by their understanding that their basic mission is to correct certain kinds of mistakes that have been made by other parts of government, and especially by lower courts."

Appointed judges are more likely to be experts of the law and least likely to be those who stir up majorities for their votes. Who else knows the best legal minds than those in the most elite places of our government, the Senate and Presidency? So, the job is given to them to place judges on federal benches. In addition to having approval power, Senators have an essential, while informal, role. The president appoints all federal judges. There are currently 870 federal judgeships: nine on the Supreme Court, 179 on the courts of appeals, 673 for the district courts and nine on the Court of International Trade. When making one of 673 district court appointments, the president consults with the senior senator from the state in which the new judge will take his or her seat. While this practice of **senatorial courtesy** is not law, it is a firm custom.

Federalist 78's most difficult passages deal with the Constitution's place as "fundamental law" over human-made, legislative law. Hamilton argues that it is SCOTUS' duty "to declare all acts contrary to the manifest tenor of the Constitution void." **Judicial review** in a sentence. In striking down acts of the other federal branches, SCOTUS does its job of protecting "the intention of the people as it is enshrined in the Constitution." Wait. Around thirty men wrote this document in one summer. What makes it "the intention of the people?" How it came to be law, through state conventions solely called to vote on the ratification of the document, is the source. The people ratified it and can change it through the same state convention process. In theory, that is. The state convention method of amending the Constitution has never been used. Instead, 2/3 of Congress and 3/4 of state legislatures have voted to **amend the Constitution** 27 times.

Higher Law: Letter from a Birmingham Jail

The principle of a "higher law" frames the law by which citizens live in constitutional democracies. When it is broken, Americans have chosen to act in **civil disobedience** and break an unjust law in order to obey a higher, natural law. In his "Letter from a Birmingham Jail," Martin Luther King, Jr. appeals to his fellow white clergymen to follow such law above human laws. King showed frustration with his white brothers of the cloth: " I have almost reached the regrettable conclusion that the Negro's great stumbling block in his stride toward freedom is not the White Citizen's Councilor or the Ku Klux Klanner, but the white moderate, who is more devoted to "order" than to justice; who prefers a negative peace which is the absence of tension to a positive peace which is the presence of justice; who constantly says: 'I agree with you in the goal you seek, but I cannot agree with your methods of direct action.'" The laws of Southern state legislatures, King implored, casts shadows of inferiority over black Americans. Rule by men of state and local governments allowed "vicious mobs" to lynch at will. Rule by the laws of a planter elite had placed America's black minority into "an airtight cage of poverty" to provide a cheap labor pool. Worse even still, a minority faction of planter elites could always count on the full-throated support of a majority of white voters. King mobilized a **grass-roots** effort of defiance and the assertion that democratic principles must be applied evenly or there are none at all.

White clergy criticized King's use of the non-violent method of **direct action**: striking, boycotting, and breaking unjust laws willfully and publicly in the presence of news media. When civil rights activists were beaten, spit upon, bitten by dogs, sprayed by fire hoses, jailed, and even killed, the world would see the injustice. Even the perpetrators would see the evil in their hearts. Eventually, public opinion would change, and just laws would take the place of Jim Crow policies.
While King followed the tactic of direct action, most white clergy along with their congregations demurred from following the higher law of the Constitution or the New Testament.

The "wait" argument would have had the Civil Rights movement enact policies through local legislatures rather than the federal courts. However, legislatures in the Deep South were controlled by white majorities. If ever, it would take decades for them to pass just laws. The branch designed to act against pernicious democratic outcomes—against the tyranny of the majority--stepped up. SCOTUS acted against the majority factions behind the racist laws that were affronts to every professed democratic value. In 1954 SCOTUS's decision in Brown v. Board of Education struck down laws that gave foundation to white supremacist governments throughout the Deep South. Brown was an incredibly important and unpopular decision. In Federalist 78 Hamilton envisioned SCOTUS being able to counter laws made by the "momentary inclination of a majority" that ran counter to "the existing provisions in the constitution." The Supreme Court did so in 1954.

This only stoked the anger and fear of "states' rights" activists on the side of Jim Crow policies. They re-embodied Brutus's fears of a federal court system dominant over state courts. While the debate went back to the Federalists v. Anti-Federalist debate, those in favor of state government power staked their claim on a terrible cause.

In defeating racist policies, the federal government claimed unprecedented powers over the states. One Amendment, in particular, provided the ramrod that breached the wall between the federal government and the states. The Constitution's 14th Amendment's Equal Protection Clause with its "no state shall" language led to state legislatures and courts coming under the review of the federal courts. Under its authority, the court struck down laws passed by scores of state legislatures and reversed its precedent set in Plessy v. Ferguson in 1896, which validated future state segregation laws by establishing the precedent that Black Codes or Jim Crow laws could be "separate but equal" in their application.

Without the Constitution's Article III provisions that insulate judges from politicians and voting majorities these laws would have continued a system of legal oppression and humiliation

Nevertheless, politicians in the Deep South continued to stoop as low as majorities required. Otherwise decent men seeking office pandered to racist majorities. Politicians bragged of their KKK memberships well into the 1980s, in fact. Socially, the South resisted desegregation for decades after the **1954 Brown decision**. As Hamilton pointed out, the judicial branch has no power of enforcement, so it could not implement its decision. Finally, legislatures, governors, and Presidents backed Brown's claim that all deserve **equal protection** under the laws by enacted policies outlawing legal racism. Though it was a laborious process and increased federal power over the states, the oversight provided by SCOTUS checked majorities within southern states. Centuries after the founding, the nation finally began to remove the legal obstacles imposed on the descendants of former slaves so that majorities could maintain a cheap labor pool and feelings of white superiority.

The Structure of Federal Courts

Article III left it to Congress to determine such matters as how many federal courts there would be and how many judges would preside in each: "The Judicial Power of the United States, shall be vested in one Supreme Court, and in such **inferior courts** as the Congress may from time to time ordain and establish." Since then, Congress has come up with this:

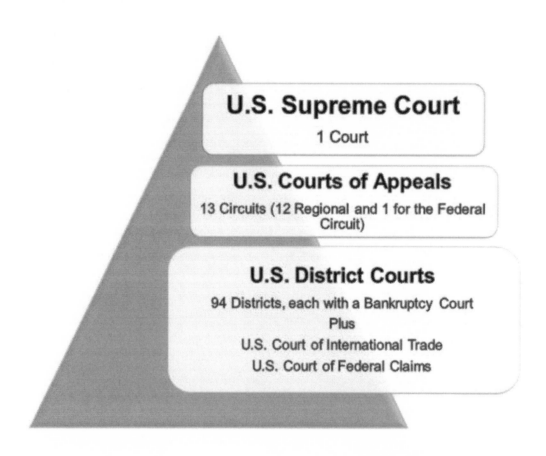

Nine judges sit on the Supreme Court bench, led by the **Chief Justice** who sits at their center when in court. Mostly a ceremonial role, he or she serves as a "first-among-equals" and is charged with running meetings of The Nine.

The judicial system of our country contains 94 district courts, 13 circuit courts, and various other specialized courts that hear a narrower range of cases. Twelve of the circuit courts are geographically based, while the thirteenth is the United States Court of Appeals for the Federal Circuit. All circuit courts are appeals only (a case that is a review of a ruling from a lower court), and cases from them can be **appealed** directly to the Supreme Court. After SCOTUS decides a case, their decision is the law of the land. The only way Congress can negate a decision by the Supreme Court is to pass an amendment to the Constitution with a 2/3 vote, which ¾ of states then have to ratify. Good luck with that, Congress.

This stipulation has caused the judicial branch's power to grow more and more over the years. Since its beginning, the Court has crawled from the Constitutional stew and evolved into an institution that can make federal, that is nation-wide, policy in a matter of hours. While Hamilton's intention was for the Court to be a constitutional referee between the legislature and the executive, he left it up to case law to influence the power of the Court. He expected the Court to vest itself with authority. It did not take long in doing so.

The Marshall Court (1801-1835) Establishes Judicial Power

Reaping its namesake from Chief Justice John Marshall, the Marshall Court ruled on cases that established the court as an equal of the other branches.

The most significant case during the period was **Marbury v. Madison** (1803). By ruling actions of the other branches unconstitutional, Marshall's Court established the principle of judicial review, the bedrock tenet of the Court's authority. Judicial review is the power of SCOTUS to invalidate a law or action of another branch.

In addition to increasing its authority, SCOTUS expanded the power of the federal government as a whole. The cases that followed Marbury v. Madison in the Marshall Court gave substance to those vague powers the Constitution granted to the legislative and executive branches. In **McCulloch v. Maryland** (1819) and Gibbons v. Ogden (1824), Marshall's court put the federal government further in control of the states through its interpretations of the necessary and proper, commerce, and supremacy clauses.

A Case's Journey to the Supreme Court

Getting to the Supreme Court is no easy matter. SCOTUS has minimal **jurisdiction** in the first place. Jurisdiction refers to the authority of courts to hear certain cases first. Most lawsuits start in the states, as states have the reserved powers to make laws regarding crime and business contracts. States have courts to hear those cases. Each state even has a supreme court to which lower courts appeal. Madison's system gave state courts the job of interpreting federal law and the ability to appeal to federal courts. **Brutus** panicked when he considered the implications of this relationship with the **Supremacy Clause**. He warned, rightfully, that state courts would become feeble before their federal counterparts.

If two or more states get into a dispute or a state's actions butt up against federal policy, the case can be taken directly to the Supreme Court. In these instances, the federal court system has **original jurisdiction**.

However, the Supreme Court hears very few cases that skip lower federal or state courts, making it primarily a court of appeals. Decisions from district courts go to circuit courts and then may go on to the Supreme Court.

To become a SCOTUS case, the appellant (that is, the applicant for an appeal) has to request a **writ of certiorari** ("writ of cert" for short). SCOTUS gets about 7,000 of these every year. The justices' clerks sift through the cases in order to narrow them down. The Nine then decide what cases to hear. If four of the justices vote to hear a case, then it is put on the **docket** (the **rule of four**). Each year, the rule of four grants around 80 of those 7,000 cases a writ of cert. The Court hears these select cases during its October-July term. (Keep that in mind—July is always a good month to be keeping up with current rulings.) Mostly all of these cases deal with issues of federal and constitutional law.

After the Court hears a case, a simple majority vote of at least five justices decides the outcome.

SCOTUS justices have much to consider before they vote. They must ask themselves if what they are ruling is consistent with case law, the Constitution, and ethics. They also must speculate on how the ruling can affect average Americans. One aid to this speculation comes in the form of **amicus curiae briefs**, which is Latin for "friend of the court." These are written explanations by citizens and interest groups detailing how the decision of the Court would impact them.

After each decision, the Court releases opinions, which summarize why justices voted one way or another. The reasoning the justices state for voting the way they did is the heart of case law. The outcome matters less than the reasons the justices give for it. In the form of dissenting opinions, even the losing side's reasoning becomes relevant sources of precedent. Indeed, some dissenting opinions turn out to be more important than that of the majority.

Types of Opinions:

- Majority opinion: Whichever side had the most votes issues a majority opinion, explaining why they ruled the way they did.
- Concurring opinion: These opinions are written separately from the majority opinion, but they agree on the outcome. Concurrences agree with the outcome of a case but for different reasons.
- Dissenting opinion: These represent the minority's reasons for disagreeing with the majority. They too become a part of case law and can be just as significant as the ruling itself. Whichever opinion a justice ultimately pens is often a reflection of his or her judicial ideology (**activist v. restraint**). Ideally, judges are supposed to be non-partisan. How many 5-4 votes along partisan lines can a body take before declaring SCOTUS of being plagued by the partisanship so characteristic of USA 2018?

By deciding cases based on precedent, judges consider case law and practice stare decisis, hopefully making purely ideological decisions less likely. Whether they do so is a question between how active or restrained a court wishes to be.

Part 4

Linkage Institutions

Chapter 17

Special Interests

The reality of policymaking is a lot more complicated than following steps like assembling Ikea furniture. The problems of the majority and minority factions, after all, applied to Madison's concern that special interests, or factions, would hijack Congress's policymaking role. Before the Constitution's adoption, majority factions in states had too much control. Especially prophetic, Brutus pointed to the downside of Madison's large-republic solution. Brutus foresaw that with a massive constituency, like a congressman's average of 750,000 **constituents** today, representatives could not possibly represent them all. So, of the hundreds of thousands, to whose voices would representatives listen? The few. The rich. The connected. These would be most motivated and capable of gaining access to the legislators in faraway Washington, D.C. Once the minority faction got into a position to rewrite the rules for itself, it could bring majorities along by false promises and outright propaganda.

Campaign Finance and Its Regulation

The final price tag for the 2016 election was $6.5 billion for the presidential and congressional elections combined. $2.4 billion of that total belongs to the Presidential election alone. The other $4 billion or so went to congressional races. To put such amounts of money in perspective, with $6.5 billion every public school teacher in America could get a $2,000 raise. Instead, Americans used that money to fuel a 596-day political contest that most of us were "disgusted" by well before it was over. At the same time that money donors reached new record highs, voter turnout hit a 20 year low at 55%.

Money pouring in while voters drain out is not a good sign for a democracy. A discussion of lawmaking would be remiss without a closer look at what Madison's factions problem might look like today. "Money in politics" is another way of stating the problem addressed in Federalist #10: how to keep our government from being the servant of interests other than the common good. How do we protect our policymakers from special interest pressure?

The framers looked to the structure of the Constitution to protect individuals from being dominated by narrow interests with short-term, selfish goals. By "pitting ambition against ambition," the framers hoped to keep those in government competing against one another for power, as local majorities did the same. Responsive to the best ideas and held accountable to the people through free and fair elections, policymakers and judges would be insulated from both majority and minority factions by being appointed by elected officials rather than elected.

A History of Trying to Reform: Money and Politics

Recognizing the corrupting influence of special interests, lawmakers have a history of fighting the influence of money on policymaking. When we put the back and forth of campaign finance regulation on a timeline, one will notice the pattern of scandal followed by reform. After Congress passes laws that have seemed to block the flow of cash from donors to public servants, money follows the hydraulic principle. Like water, money has found cracks in each dam reformers have erected. In 2010 the Supreme Court took the plug out of the dam, and each election sees record volumes of money changing hands between politicians and the interests wishing to capture them. While laws regulating campaign donations go back to the early 1900s, we will focus on the last half-century.

After the revelation of Nixon's use of campaign funds to spy on his Democratic rivals at the Watergate Hotel, Americans' trust in their government was at a low. Congress responded by passing campaign finance reforms.

Campaign Finance Regulation Since Nixon

• 1972 - President Nixon's campaign takes in $20 million in secret donations. Nixon uses some of the cash to pay for the break-in at the Watergate Hotel, using the FBI to steal campaign secrets from the Democratic Headquarters there. Nixon is also on record telling his chief of staff to tell donors that to be considered they must at least have given $200,000.

• 1974 - Responding to Watergate, Congress passes the **FECA—Federal Elections Campaign Act**. Creating the **Federal Election Commission**, the FECA is the legal basis of subsequent money-in-politics laws.

• 1975 - **Buckley v Valeo**. The Supreme Court strikes down many rules of the FEC as unconstitutional, famously asserting that the 1st Amendment protects political donations. Money = speech.

• 1980's - The rise of soft money. So far, the FEC had made rules regarding contributions to candidates, not parties. "**Soft money**" - unregulated, undisclosed, and unlimited - flowed to the parties rather than the candidates. 1988 set a fundraising height as Republicans and Democrats surpassed the $45 million mark.

• 1992 - "Soft money" balloons to $86 million, a 91% jump from the previous election.

• 1995 - Bill Clinton's team invents the "issue ad," increasing the ways donors can give their untraced, unlimited "soft money." Democrats haul in $122 million while the Republicans beat them at their own game, netting $141 million.

• 1998 - A congressional investigation reveals that Clinton stooped low to raise cash like giving big donors rides on Air Force One and sleepovers in the Lincoln Bedroom at the White House, a pleasure one guest raised $4 million in order to enjoy.

• 2002 - **The McCain-Feingold or Bipartisan Campaign Reform Act (BCRA)** is signed by George Bush, banning soft money contributions and forbidding corporations and unions from making "issue ads" about candidates in the weeks before an election. The interest group Citizens United would later violate this apart of the BCRA.

• 2005 - Republican House Majority Leader (position a rank below the highest in the House, The Speaker) Tom "The Hammer Delay" is indicted for funneling campaign donations made to the national Republican Party to state (Texas) Republican representatives. He is later convicted for money laundering.

- 2006 - Lobbyist Jack Abramoff is arrested. A Republican lobbyist close to Tom Delay, Abramoff represented Indian tribes and other clients, giving politicians money and favors to pass laws favorable to gambling interests.

- 2010 - Citizen's United v. FEC. The Supreme Court allows individuals, corporations, and unions to spend unlimited sums for or against candidates. Limits on **"independent expenditure groups"**—Political Action Committees (PACs)—are lifted. Birth of Super-PAC.

- 2012 - Combined, the Republican and Democratic candidates, parties, PACs, Super-PACS, **527's, and 501(c)'s** spend a new record - $7 billion. PACs spend $1.2 billion while Super-PACS spent $950 million. The rest goes to the candidates, their parties, issue ads (which fall under part 527 of the tax code), and single-issue advocacy groups (which fall under 501(c) section of the tax code).

- 2016 - Each candidate has parallel fund-raising groups that can accept unlimited amounts. Since Citizen's United gives "outside groups" like SuperPACs full First Amendment cover, their donors can be anonymous. The resulting lack of transparency leads to as much "dark money" as traceable funds in campaign war chests. In effect, those running for office can receive unlimited donations from corporations, individuals, and unions, and spend funds to influence elections, but are not required to disclose their donors.

The Revolving Door

With no sign of the status quo changing, **incumbents** and their challengers have seemed to have followed the axiom, "If you can't beat'em, join 'em." More and more lawmakers are becoming lobbyists after they have "served" the public. As **lobbyists**, former politicians and their staff cash in on their connections and expertise, earning significantly more than their previous government salaries.

Federalist Paper 51 lays out how to keep power from being in the sole hands of an irrational majority or a short-sited minority: create large republic with a system of checks and balances in a federal system of multiple layers of government. But the framers surely could not have anticipated our age in which multinational companies comprise over half of the world's **Gross Domestic Product (GDP)**. With such reach and economic might, companies ranging from corn production to shoe manufacturing challenge **national sovereignty** and possess the means to capture politicians. The framers were insistent that the federal government, not the states, pay legislators' and officials' salaries to secure their loyalty to the national government. However, firms like Nike or Archer Daniels Midland span the globe and generate more profits than many nation's GDPs. A fair question is, how does a member of Congress or mid-level bureaucrat withstand the mixture of pressure and temptation such firms can exert? ADM (Archer Daniels Midland), while US-based, operates in 75 countries, runs 265 processing plants converting corn and wheat into food, animal feed, and for energy. This type of "farmer" is a far cry from the Jeffersonian landowner knowing everything he needed from long walks and a reading of the family Bible. Deep-pocketed firms with narrow interests use a mixture of carrots and sticks to get their desired policy outcomes.

The biggest carrot for career politicians is a retirement to personal wealth. Firms are happy to award former policymakers with high pay for their continued service. A 2018 issue of the Atlantic Magazine gave a telling snapshot of the #1 career choice for retiring members of Congress:

"In all, more members of the House are forgoing reelection than in any year since 1992, when 65 representatives called it quits, according to the Pew Research Center. Among Republicans, it's an even bigger exodus—the most since before World War II. Some in this year's class of retirees are more junior members who've grown disenchanted with national politics...If recent history is a guide...congressional retirees won't be leaving the Beltway at all. As candidates, Republicans and Democrats alike win over voters with jeremiads against Washington, pledging to bring their hometown values to a capital city overrun by lobbyists and special interests. However, once their terms are up, a surprising number of these same politicians don't return home. They stick around town, joining law firms, **think tanks**, and **lobbying shops**. On any given day, ex-lawmakers stalk the corridors of the Capitol complex, kibitzing with their old colleagues as they prod them for votes.

Of the nearly four dozen lawmakers who left office after the 2016 election, one-fourth stayed in Washington, and one in six became lobbyists... The numbers were even higher for those who departed after the 2014 midterms: About half of those former members stuck around, and around one in four became lobbyists."

More recently, special interests' money has begun to flow to congressional staff. Congressional staff increasingly make the passage through the **revolving door**, joining their bosses in lobbying their former colleagues on behalf of special interests.

Congressional Staff and the Revolving Door

Lawmakers are generalists who spend much, if not most, of their time, asking for money and attending fundraisers. That leaves policy making to someone else who has the time and expertise to write legislation that addresses mind-numbingly technical issues.

Thus, members of Congress's staff do the heavy lifting of lawmaking. In his memoir, Senator Edward Kennedy claimed that "Ninety-five percent of the nitty-gritty work of drafting bills and negotiating their final form is now done by staff. That marks an enormous shift of responsibility over the past forty or fifty years." Good staff are those who possess "substantial expertise, sharp minds and good intuition who are not ideologically bound but who like to leave their minds free to think about good policy. They are enthusiastic about what government at its best is designed to do." They sound fantastic, don't they? Those interests that spend billions to influence policy think so.

As the money continues to flow where it can find influence, congressional staff have become highly valued targets of special interests. Since the 1980s, congressional staff has been increasingly walking through the revolving door between lobbying and lawmaking. Once long-serving and content to make $150,000 a year, congressional staff are now getting lured away from public service and going to work for those they used to regulate. In their roles as lobbyists, former regulators can make ten times their previous salaries. Lobbyist Jack Abramoff described how he laid the bait to congressional staffers in the TV program 60 Minutes:

"When we would become friendly with an office, and they were important to us, and the chief of staff was a competent person, I would say or my staff would say to him or her at some point, 'You know, when you're done working on the Hill, we'd very much like you to consider coming to work for us.' Now the moment I said that to them...that was it. We owned them. And what does that mean? Every request from our office, every request of our clients, everything we want, they're gonna do. And not only that, they're gonna think of things we can't think of to do."

The result has been an alarming decrease in the number of excellent senior staff working to craft legislation. Since the 1980s, four hundred defeated or retired members of the House and Senate and more than five thousand staff members have cashed in on their connections and insider knowledge. They have joined the expanding body of influence peddlers who flock around members of Congress, write laws, and provide expertise on behalf of special interests.

Brutus warned of the dangers of an **elite minority faction** using government for its selfish, short term purposes. Though he did not use the word, "**Iron Triangle**," he foresaw that small groups with plenty of cash would capture lawmakers and law enforcers. The points of **the iron triangle** consist of the nexus of interest groups, members of Congress (usually on their specialized **subcommittees**), and agency bureaucrats who regulate special interests.

Fill in the points of an Iron Triangle from your own research:

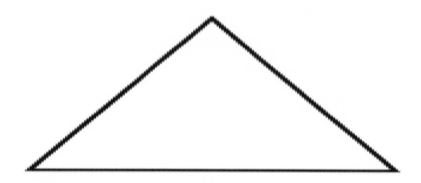

Brutus Told You So

The Anti-Federalists argued that to prevent government oppression by a central government, constitution makers should not make any government as powerful as the Federalists had done. Brutus and his brethren would have denied the central government power to tax, raise a standing army, and regulate states' commerce. The Federalists' government was a Frankenstein's monster to Brutus: an affront against nature that will inevitably turn against its creators. He might have pointed to the interests of tobacco companies entangled in government as an example of how a special interest might harness power when it is centrally located in one government.

Case in Point: The Tobacco Industry and Iron Triangles

Going back to the introduction, the framers established the Constitution's system of separation of powers and its protections of private property to foster competition. The aim of separating power vertically and horizontally is to prevent the winners-- economic and political--from rewriting the rules in their favor. Winners like the tobacco industry hate competition. Their goal is to make profits, not foster competition. Such special interests do not aim for the "greatest good for the greatest number." Tobacco companies pursue their interests at the cost of 500,000 lives a year and the ill health of millions more.

We have already discussed the tobacco industry's efforts to influence public opinion by creating their own "facts." It will be instructive to see this special interest at work in its iron triangle, creating government policies friendly to its interests. While high cigarette taxes may seem to make government enemies to tobacco companies, the latter have worked overtime to get the rules of the game written in its favor.

The latest story of how tobacco companies got the government to write the rules in its favor starts with cheap tobacco alternatives coming to market. E-cigarettes directly challenged Big Tobacco's **monopoly** on smoking products. By the

2000s, when e-Cigs began their rise in the U.S. economy, two tobacco companies controlled the entire market. The eCigarette upstarts startled "Big Tobacco." For every person who vaped instead of smoked, Big Tobacco saw a loss in revenue. To kill this upstart competitor, tobacco companies started to pull the gears of their iron triangle.

First, the lobbyists of tobacco firms contacted congressional members of subcommittees. Big Tobacco representatives pushed lawmakers to pass laws subjecting the new and much smaller vaping companies to heavy taxes and regulations. Because of past settlements, tobacco companies pay billions each year to states, compensating for state expenditures on tobacco-related illnesses. Tobacco interests wanted the government to classify e-cigarettes as tobacco products. In this way, upstart e-cigarette sellers would be responsible for paying billions of dollars in taxes as part of a 1998 settlement between cigarette companies and state governments. Imagine a beginning Uber driver having to pay for other drivers' cars before starting the first shift.

At the agency point of the iron triangle, the tobacco interest pressured the relevant regulatory agency, the Food and Drug Administration (FDA), to write and enforce the rules putting Congress' legislation into effect. The industry did this by working through members of Congress who control the regulatory agency's budgets. In this case, if the FDA did not enact rules against e-cigarette companies, they could have seen their funding cut during the next budget cycle. In a victory for the tobacco industry, the FDA now considers e-cigarettes tobacco products even if they contain no nicotine.

Odd though it may seem, Big Tobacco partnered with anti-tobacco groups and health advocates who were alarmed to see the rise in youth vaping. Tobacco companies even funded these anti-tobacco groups in their quest to regulate the budding vaping industry. Groups like the Campaign for Tobacco-Free Kids joined with their nemesis against e-cigarette companies. This years-long battle bought the tobacco product developers time to establish their vaping product lines and buy existing ones.

So, with vaping under the same regulations as tobacco now, Big Tobacco is Big Vaping as well. Presently, over 95 percent of the market for e-cigarettes is dominated by five companies: MarkTen, XL, Logic. Vuse, Blu, and JUUL. Vuse is owned by R.J. Reynolds Vapor Company, a subsidiary of Reynolds American Inc, which was acquired by British American Tobacco in 2017. Altria Group Inc owns MarkTen, and Blu is owned by Imperial Brands, which also owns Imperial Tobacco.

In 2016, e-cigarettes took in $8,610,000,000. In 2017, the market was worth more than $10 billion, and that number is projected to more than double by 2023. 2 million high school students used e-cigarettes in 2017. E-cigarettes might have provided "a less hazardous alternative to consumers who seek to break their smoking habit." But rules against advertising or that impose huge taxes "limit e-cigarette competition and evolution bring [and] with them a social cost measured in lost opportunities to improve human health." As Dr. David Abrams recently warned in the Journal of the American Medical Association: the adoption of "overly restrictive" regulations of e-cigarettes could "support the established tobacco industry" and have the perverse effect of "perpetuating the sales of conventional cigarettes well into the next century rather than speed their obsolescence." And the tobacco companies' new and improved vaping products have heavy doses of nicotine. Tobacco companies are now happy to provide a gateway to its most profitable product, cigarettes. Either way, they get to sell a highly addictive substance while the government enforces rules that make competition unlikely.

As framers like Madison knew too well, those who benefit from a fair race will change the rules after winning to benefit their factions in the next one. Tobacco companies seem to have done just that. Iron triangles and other special interest networks allow narrowness and greed to dominate our policymakers. For instance, most states depend on taxes from cigarettes and money from past settlements. If tobacco companies' revenues decrease, state budgets and politicians' campaign accounts shrink in proportion. Thus, the operations of iron triangles turn policymakers who should be legislating for the common good into Brutus's "great officers of government." Such lawmakers and bureaucrats "become above the control of the people, and abuse their power to the purpose of aggrandizing themselves." Also, the special interests of those who fund their campaigns, he might have added.

Mitch McConnel Shows How to Represent Special Interests Like Big Tobacco

Illuminating this issue, news reports from June 17, 2019 revealed that the Senate Majority Leader, Mitch McConnel, had done tobacco companies' work since he became a Kentucky senator. The report broke as McConnel's **sponsored bill** to increase the legal age to 21 was under consideration of the Congress.

From National Public Radio's Tom Dreisbach:

Senate Majority Leader Mitch McConnell, R-Ky., says one of his 'highest priorities' is to take on the leading cause of preventable death in the United States: smoking. McConnell has sponsored a bill, along with Virginia Democratic Sen. Tim Kaine, that would increase the tobacco purchase age from 18 to 21.

McConnell noted, 'I might seem like an unusual candidate to lead this charge.' For many public health advocates, that was a vast understatement. McConnell repeatedly cast doubt on the health consequences of smoking, repeated industry talking points word-for-word, attacked **federal regulators** at the industry's request and opposed bipartisan tobacco regulations going back decades.

The industry, in turn, has provided McConnell with millions of dollars in speaking fees, personal gifts, campaign contributions and charitable donations to the McConnell Center, which is home to his personal and professional archives. One lobbyist for R.J. Reynolds called McConnell a 'special friend' to the company. And, upon closer look, it appears McConnell's legislation to raise the tobacco purchase age actually followed the industry's lead.

Altria, the parent company of Philip Morris USA and a major stakeholder in the e-cigarette maker Juul, announced that it supported the measure back in 2018. Several states and localities have already raised their tobacco purchase age. NPR also found that vaping and tobacco companies are currently employing McConnell's former policy adviser, his former policy director and his former chief of staff to lobby on their behalf.

But multiple anti-smoking groups have raised concerns about McConnell's bill and the industry's support for the legislation. The Campaign For Tobacco-Free Kids called for major changes to the bill. And the Preventing Tobacco Addiction Foundation has announced its 'strenuous opposition.' One concern for these groups is that the legislation will stave off tougher regulations on vaping, particularly regulations on flavored e-cigarettes. 'It's a Jedi mind trick,' says Sharon Eubanks, who led the Justice Department's landmark racketeering case against the industry. E-cigarette companies want to avoid liability for the youth vaping epidemic, says Eubanks, and 'the industry's support for such measures gets them off the hook.' McConnell is 'covering for them,' says Dr.

David Kessler, a former commissioner of the Food and Drug Administration. Still, whatever the motivation, Kessler says he welcomes increasing the tobacco age to 21.

Soon after McConnell won a U.S. Senate seat, he was invited to the Tobacco Institute's boardroom to give a speech in January 1985. In those days, it was legal for senators to take speaking fees — called 'honoraria' — from corporations and lobbyists with business before Congress. For McConnell, that included a winter retreat to a Tobacco Institute legislative conference in Palm Springs, Calif., with 'an honorarium of $2,000, plus expenses,' according to McConnell's invite. McConnell and his Senate office frequently accepted gifts from tobacco industry lobbyists, a practice which was also legal at the time. The gifts included tickets to NFL and NBA games, a Ringo Starr concert, 'top-quality brandy,' and what McConnell called a 'beautiful ham.'

McConnell often ended his thank you notes to tobacco lobbyists with an offer: 'Please feel free to call on me whenever I may be of assistance to you.' When McConnell has sought re-election, tobacco company employees and PACs have typically donated to McConnell more than to any other member of Congress. Since 1989, he has received at least $650,000 in campaign contributions linked to the industry and solicited hundreds of thousands more in soft money donations to Republican Party committees.

Interest Groups—Their Legitimate Role

Like Madison said at the beginning of Federalist 10, interest groups—majorities and groups of elites—will always be with us. Groups centered around an issue or industry can be of great use to policymakers. After all, lawmakers have to know those whom their legislation will affect the most. Interest groups rally around an issue and promote particular policies. As linkage institutions, these groups give citizens a route to influence policy.

Groups like the **NRA, AARP, NAACP** educate and motivate voters while they provide useful services to voters like evaluating politicians based on their particular standards. For instance, the National Rifle Association grades legislators based on how they vote on gun legislation. With a glance, NRA members can see which politicians match their top policy preferences best.

Functions of Interest Groups:

Education: Interest groups educate their members and prospective members.

Motivation: Interest groups identify problems and offer a range of solutions. Some give very good discounts on hotels...

Evaluation: Interest groups, like Grover Norquist's Americans for Tax Reform and the NRA grades candidates, allowing their members to have a thumbs up or down indicator when deciding for whom to vote.

Advocacy: Interest groups will promote particular policies.

Litigation: Interest groups use the courts to promote their policy agendas.

Donations: Interest groups give money to campaigns and SuperPacs.

Recruitment: Interest groups endorse candidates.

Mobilization: Interest groups can "get out the vote" of their constituencies. In referendums and elections, interest groups and their lobbyists can join forces with other "factions" to form voting bloc majorities.

Choose an interest group and show how it: _____

Educates: Litigates:

Motivates: Donates:

Evaluates: Candidates:

Advocates: Mobilizes:

Chapter 18

Political Parties

We have already seen that voting systems create party systems and that the Constitution has no mention of them. Anytime the founders brought up the topic, it was out of a sense of foreboding and disgust. However, this did not stop them from creating them by the election of 1800.

The founders thought political parties were horrible things that would institutionalize factions. Worse than factions, political parties do not have a particular policy goal that, once achieved, compels them to call it quits. Their goal is power, and policy preferences fall second to the first imperative, which is to win elections. Each election candidates always agree on the central issue: they want to get elected.

The Problem with Parties

In theory, elected members of the government are meant to work together and leave the partisan fight of the campaign behind them. Instead of party loyalty, they are supposed to exert the prerogatives of their respective branch. In doing so, if one part of government grabs for too much power, the other branches have ways to restrain the over-reaching branch. The Constitution was built for the pilots to work together once the plane takes off. Without our elected officials compromising in government, the machine shuts down, and the plane crashes. The framers did not anticipate that a pilot and copilot may have two different destinations. Our government's capacity to solve problems and keep us safe becomes compromised when those elected refuse to work together. After elections, officials are supposed to identify more with their institutions than their parties and find solutions to the dire long-term problems that threaten the general welfare. Unfortunately, incumbents too often confuse governing with **campaigning**.

Critics of democracy point to this state of affairs and claim that all of the talk about compromise and debate is a smokescreen for the raw power that is evident in times of crisis. Like in war, there are extended periods of boredom and then short, momentous flurries of activity. In gridlocked governments, the executive acts when needed to confront a danger then recedes into the background when it is safe for us to pretend that we live in a democracy. And like war, these critics point out; two sides are lethal enemies who use any means necessary to win. Bitter conflict and any-means-necessary victory is the reality; we just tell ourselves a story of well-meaning representatives debating and compromising through a rational process under a constitutional order. The "debate" that goes on between candidates in an election seems to confirm that our elections are not about ideas or policies, but instead, rely on a more primal impulse. Real debate that would inform voters or challenge them to change their minds would not fill a bumper sticker. P.J. O'Rourke quipped that "in the American system, you're only allowed to have real ideas if it's absolutely guaranteed that you can't win an election." Instead of real ideas, political parties have a way of creating the issues they want to campaign on; that give them the best chance at looking better than the other party. Much of the time, fear works as the best tactic. H.L. Mencken observed that, "The whole aim of practical politics is to keep the populace alarmed (and hence clamorous to be led to safety) by menacing it with an endless series of hobgoblins, all of them imaginary." Mencken paints a bleak picture of "we the people" and the political system we have inherited.

Leaving aside the possibility that our entire political system is a sham, political parties have a central role to play. Perhaps most importantly, they keep the founders worse fear from materializing: the election of a **demagogue**. They also give voters clear choices by organizing issues into consistent platforms. We seem to like them. Over 90% of voters identify with the Republican and Democratic parties, with the rest claiming to be "independent." The latter are either deceiving the pollster or have violated Socrates' dictum to "know thyself."

Parties as Filtration System for Demagogues

Parties may not be great for idea-packed elections or even running governments. However, they are even worse when they are weak. Until recently, parties were strong enough to choose whom they were going to run. They weeded out dangerous populists that would otherwise skirt around them and appeal directly to voters. Demagogues, authoritarians in the peoples' clothing would use modern media to speak to the hopes and fears of voters, oversimplifying problems and "otherizing" outside groups as they laid electoral foundations. Political parties have been gatekeepers that filtered such people out, so they never showed up on a ballot come election time. Until the 1970s, parties chose candidates. **Primaries** and **caucuses** did not exist in any meaningful way. When George Wallace was getting polling numbers as high as Donald Trump's in 2015, the Republican Party did not seriously consider his nomination. Why? Because party elites would not bear his admittance into their club. Their party was too good for him.

Between the 1968 election (in which Wallace won the Deep South as a third-party candidate) and 2016 parties lost their **gate-keeping** power and gave it to the voters. The 1968 election was a disaster for the Democratic party. Party elites chose a candidate, Hubert Humphrey, that the Democratic Party voters did not want. Their candidate, Robert Kennedy, had been assassinated, which threw the nomination of a new candidate into chaos. Despite having Wallace as a potential **spoiler**, the Democrats lost the election to Republican Richard Nixon and found itself alienated from its voters. To heal the divorce between itself and the voters, the Democratic Party went to a primary system in which the voters, not party elites **in smoky backrooms**, would elect candidates. If a candidate could successfully appeal directly to voters, then the party would have no choice but get behind him or her.

The Republican Party followed suit, abdicating its gatekeeping authority to the people. The gravity of this decision would not be felt until 2015 when a true outsider ran for the Republican nomination. Donald Trump had no experience in politics and had been a Democrat for most of his life. He had the most critical assets, fame, money, and a **name recognition**. His early poll numbers were high, but established

Republicans were doubtful (and hopeful) that he would go very far in the nomination process. Articles from leading conservative think tanks and magazines fought against Trump's nomination from the beginning.

In the following, preeminent conservative scholars and commentators warn against a Trump nomination in the most respected conservative magazine, the National Review (January 22, 2016):

DAVID BOAZ

Not since George Wallace has there been a presidential candidate who made racial and religious scapegoating so central to his campaign. Trump launched his campaign talking about Mexican rapists and has gone on to rant about mass deportation, bans on Muslim immigration, shutting down mosques, and building a wall around America. America is an exceptional nation in large part because we've aspired to rise above such prejudices and guarantee life, liberty, and the pursuit of happiness to everyone.

Equally troubling is his idea of the presidency — his promise that he's the guy, the man on a white horse, who can ride into Washington, fire the stupid people, hire the best people, and fix everything. He doesn't talk about policy or working with Congress. He's effectively vowing to be an American Mussolini, concentrating power in the Trump White House and governing by fiat. It's a vision to make the last 16 years of executive abuse of power seem modest.

Without even getting into his past support for a massive wealth tax and single-payer health care, his know-nothing protectionism, or his passionate defense of eminent domain, I think we can say that this is a Republican campaign that would have appalled Buckley, Goldwater, and Reagan.

— David Boaz is the executive vice president of the Cato Institute and the author of The **Libertarian** Mind.

L. BRENT BOZELL III

Longtime conservative leader Richard Viguerie has a simple test for credentialing a conservative: Does he walk with us?

For the simple reason that he cannot win without conservatives' support, virtually every Republican presenting himself to voters swears so-help-me-God that he is a conservative. Many of these politicians are calculating, cynical charlatans, running as one thing only to govern in a completely different direction. See: McConnell, McCain, Hatch, Boehner, et al. And for decades it's worked. Conservatives look at the alternatives — Reid, Pelosi, Obama, Clinton, et al. — and bite the bullet. We so often "win" — only for nothing to come of it.

The GOP base is clearly disgusted and looking for new leadership. Enter Donald Trump, not just with policy prescriptions that challenge the cynical GOP leadership but with an attitude of disdain for that leadership — precisely in line with the sentiment of **the base**. Many conservatives are relishing this, but ah, the rub. Trump might be the greatest charlatan of them all.

A real conservative walks with us. Ronald Reagan read National Review and Human Events for intellectual sustenance; spoke annually to the Conservative Political Action Conference, Young Americans for Freedom, and other organizations to rally the troops; supported Barry Goldwater when the GOP mainstream turned its back on him; raised money for countless conservative groups; wrote hundreds of op-eds; and delivered even more speeches, everywhere championing our cause. Until he decided to run for the GOP nomination a few months ago, Trump had done none of these things, perhaps because he was too distracted publicly raising money for liberals such as the Clintons; championing Planned Parenthood, tax increases, and single-payer health coverage; and demonstrating his allegiance to the Democratic party. We conservatives should support the one candidate who walks with us.

— L. Brent Bozell III is the chairman of ForAmerica and the president of the Media Research Center. He has endorsed Ted Cruz for president.

MONA CHAREN

In December, Public Policy Polling found that 36 percent of Republican voters for whom choosing the candidate "most conservative on the issues" was the top priority said they supported Donald Trump. We can talk about whether he is a boor ("My fingers are long and beautiful, as, it has been well documented, are various other parts of my body"), a creep ("If Ivanka weren't my daughter, perhaps I'd be dating her"), or a louse (he tried to bully an elderly woman, Vera Coking, out of her house in Atlantic City because it stood on a spot he wanted to use as a garage). But one thing about which there can be no debate is that Trump is no conservative — he's simply playing one in the primaries. Call it unreality TV.

Put aside for a moment Trump's countless past departures from conservative principle on defense, racial quotas, abortion, taxes, single-payer health care, and immigration. (That's right: In 2012, he derided Mitt Romney for being too aggressive on the question, and he's made extensive use of illegal-immigrant labor in his serially bankrupt businesses.) The man has demonstrated an emotional immaturity bordering on personality disorder, and it ought to disqualify him from being a mayor, to say nothing of a commander-in-chief.

Trump has made a career out of egotism, while conservatism implies a certain modesty about government. The two cannot mix.

Who, except a pitifully insecure person, needs constantly to insult and belittle others, including, or perhaps especially, women? Where is the center of gravity in a man who in May denounces those who "needlessly provoke" Muslims and in December proposes that we ("temporarily") close our borders to all non-resident Muslims? If you don't like a Trump position, you need only wait a few months, or sometimes days. In September, he advised that we "let Russia fight ISIS." In November, after the Paris massacre, he discovered that "we're going to have to knock them out and knock them out hard." A pinball is more predictable.

Is Trump a liberal? Who knows? He played one for decades — donating to liberal causes and politicians (including Al Sharpton) and inviting Hillary Clinton to his (third) wedding. Maybe it was all a game, but voters who care about conservative ideas and principles must ask whether his recent impersonation of a conservative is just another role he's playing. When a con man swindles you, you can sue — as many embittered former Trump associates who thought themselves ill used have done. When you elect a con man, there's no recourse.

— Mona Charen is a senior fellow at the Ethics and Public Policy Center.

Donald Trump is no conservative. That's not a crime, it's just a reason to vote against him. Many fine people are not conservatives. But the reason Trump's candidacy should worry the Right runs much deeper than that: He poses a direct challenge to conservatism, because he embodies the empty promise of managerial leadership outside of politics.

Trump's diagnoses of our key problems — first and foremost, that America's elites are weak and unwilling to put the interests of Americans first — have gained him a hearing from many on the right. But when he gestures toward prescriptions, Trump reveals that even his diagnoses are not as sound as they might seem.

Conservatives incline to take the weakness of our elite institutions as an argument for recovering constitutional principles — and so for limiting the power of those institutions, reversing their centralization of authority, and recovering a vision of American life in which the chief purpose of the federal government is protective and not managerial.

Trump, on the contrary, offers himself as the alternative to our weak and foolish leaders, the guarantee of American superiority, and the cure for all that ails our society; and when pressed about how he will succeed in these ways, his answer pretty much amounts to: "great management."

The appeal of Trump's diagnoses should be instructive to conservatives. But the shallow narcissism of his prescriptions is a warning. American conservatism is an inherently skeptical political outlook. It assumes that no one can be fully trusted with public power and that self-government in a free society demands that we reject the siren song of politics-as-management.

A shortage of such skepticism is how we ended up with the problems Trump so bluntly laments. Repeating that mistake is no way to solve these problems. To address them, we need to begin by rejecting what Trump stands for, as much as what he stands against.

— Yuval Levin, a contributing editor of National Review, is the editor of National Affairs.

Alas, despite a field of over ten "establishment" Republican party stalwarts with last names like Bush and Romney, from governors to Senators, Trump was able to win through a direct appeal to voters especially through savvy use of 140 character Twitter bursts. In these, his MO was the personal attack. In a norm-breaking primary, he personally attacked fellow Republicans: "Mitt Romney had his chance to beat a failed president but he choked like a dog," the Republican nominee of 2016 wrote on Twitter about his predecessor. "Lightweight Marco Rubio was working hard last night. The problem is, he is a choker, and once a choker, always a choker! Mr. Meltdown," he wrote about his primary challenger Senator Marco Rubio (R-Florida). "Truly weird Senator Rand Paul of Kentucky reminds me of a spoiled brat without a properly functioning brain," he wrote after the first debate about another of his primary challengers. "Did Crooked Hillary help disgusting (check out sex tape and past) Alicia M become a U.S. citizen so she could use her in the debate," he asked in the middle of the night, alluding to a sex tape that does not exist. As true conservatives fled candidate Trump, conservative voters' support grew and grew. The more personal, the more insulting, the better Trump look in the polls. Good poll numbers attract donors, and Trump's campaign got the funding it needed to keep going. The Republican Party soon got on board when Trump's candidacy was assured and now seems to have no reservations about supporting President Trump's candidacy in 2020. They seem to agree on the most important issue in American politics: winning.

The Ideological Divide

Still, serious liberals and conservatives exist, though they make poor TV and require more than 140 characters and a meme to get across their ideas. They do not hate one another and communicate in paragraphs, not insulting sentence fragments. Their positions orbit policy and depend on researched solutions they determine will best serve the long-term interest of all Americans. At their best, the parties have different views on how the government should respond to a given issue.

Before attempting to detail their differences, let it be known that they agree on the bases of the Constitution and the country's principles. Neither challenges the basic tenets of democracy or capitalism, for that matter. The reasoning behind their differences is known as **ideologies**--sets of beliefs and values that guide one's thinking when considering individual issues. We will generalize and say that Republicans are **conservative** and Democrats are **liberal**. The keyword here is "generally."

As a side note, if you read or hear someone speaking as though the other party or its members are anything but well-intentioned citizens who happen to have different viewpoints from their own, walk away. A healthy, competitive party system is a key feature of democracies. The U.S. has only two. If anyone shows preference to a one-party state by demonizing the other, he is inviting **authoritarianism**. As Madison said in Federalist 51, "Ambition must be made to counteract ambition." They should be competitors, not enemies. One cannot see those with different policy positions as enemies and hold democratic values. Seeing the world as a good vs. evil fight while working within a constitutional order designed for reasoned compromise is the mayonnaise soda of political discourse.

A random list may help you understand the differences between Democrats and Republicans.

Liberals	Conservatives
Reject laissez-faire economics in favor of government regulation.	For laissez-fair economy: free markets with as little government regulation as possible.
All people should have access to basic requirements of human development necessary to assure equal opportunity.	Oppose policies like affirmative action and see education and healthcare as private goods.
Support **affirmative action** policies to correct historic injustices to minorities.	People compete for opportunities. The most capable individuals will win the most opportunity to advance in government and society.
Strong central government. Favor federal intervention when states violate individual rights	Weak central government. Favor state action regarding civil liberties like marriage.
Want a more equal distribution of wealth Pro-labor unions and for a progressive tax.	Inequality is the result of free trade. It is natural and spurs competition.
The government must be active in preventing monopolies and fostering competition. Laissez-faire is unfair in a globalized economy that is rapidly automating labor and outsourcing.	Corporations must stay competitive in a global free market. Higher wages for workers would mean increased costs to consumers.

Government should provide individuals with protections against downturns in the economy.

In a fair system, there are winners and losers. Government programs that give money to the poor or bailout failed businesses encourage unproductivity.

The government should provide workers with education, pension, and healthcare by taxing the wealthy. Healthcare, education, and pensions are public goods.

Education, healthcare, and Social Security should be privatized. People can invest for their own retirements. Education and healthcare are private goods. There is a demand for them so allow the free market supply those services.

New groups (immigrants, transgender teens) should be immediately accepted and integrated into politics and society regardless of "traditional" values or legal status of citizenship.

Those in positions of authority or power got there through being harder working and more competent than others. Church leaders, government officials, the wealthy, and parents have good reason to have more social and political clout.

The wealthy should be taxed more (progressive tax). Capitalism inevitably leads to inequalities. Redistributing wealth through taxes will support programs that serve the middle and lower classes—public education and healthcare should be among the first public investments.

Everyone should be taxed the same (flat tax) or the wealthy taxed less (regressive tax). More wealth in their hands will leader to more growth, not less, as they will invest their money, not spend it on consumer goods.
1980's: **Devolution revolution**—limited role of federal government in states and economy. Sought to undo progressive taxation of incomes and property (estate tax).

1960's: JFK, LBJ. Anti-poverty programs, Internationalism/multilateralism (Peace Corps). Pro-Civil Rights (Civil Rights Act 1964, Voting Rights Act 1965) Concerns include environmentalism and limiting spread of nuclear weapons.	**Privatization** of government services. The market will punish those products that hurt the environment. **Deregulate** markets — government regulatory agencies budgets cut.
Sharper division between church and state (*Engle v. Vitale*, 1962)—no prayer in public schools.	Less division between church and state.
Increased due process rights (5th and 14th Amendments) for criminals under 1960's **Warren Court**. Penal systems should rehabilitate, not punish.	Tough-on crime laws. War on Drugs, longer sentences, more police. Criminals should be punished to deter others.
Felons should be allowed to vote.	Felons should not have a right to vote.
The government should limit campaign contributions and generally fight the influence of money in politics.	Campaign contributions are political expressions protected by the First Amendment. Allow the free market to work.

Having listed many of the policy differences between the parties, let us not make too much of it. Increasingly, parties are **candidate-centered** rather than issue-centered, and they tend to adopt the positions of the front-runners whose ideas have already been bought by the public.

Voters Align with Parties

Between the years after the Civil War (ended in 1865) and the 1960s, southerners aligned with the Democratic Party as reliably as they drank sweet tea in the summer.

The North, the land of Lincoln, aligned with the party of Lincoln. The South, segregated and agricultural, was part of a **coalition** that went back to FDR's 1930s New Deal. Labor unions, blue-collar workers, minorities (racial, ethnic, and religious), farmers, white Southerners, people on relief, and intellectuals voted "Democrat" straight down on their ballots without even looking at the candidate, rarely **split-ticket voting** by choosing candidates from different parties. In today's candidate-centered politics, split-ticket voting is the norm, though becoming less so due to **party polarization**.

The Civil Rights Movement and the Democratic Party's adoption of its goals drove the South away, breaking up "**The New Deal Coalition**" and beginning the **realignment** of voters with the Democratic and Republican parties. Lyndon Johnson said of the Democratic Party after he signed the Voting Rights Act, "We have lost the South for a generation." It turned out to be a lot longer than a single generation. Since then, Southern black voters have been able to register but have not been able to turn their states back to blue. In most of the Deep South, "liberal" is a dirty word. Indeed, it was in the 1960s. Before then neither political party, even "the party of Lincoln," adopted a pro-civil rights plank to their **platform**. After the Democratic party adopted a pro-civil rights platform, the party of Lincoln became the party of the old Confederacy.

The party factions may seem to hate one another at levels not seen since before the Civil War, but one would be wrong to make that conclusion. Based on its surveys, the Pew Research Center concludes, "The way that the public thinks about poverty, opportunity, business, unions, religion, civic duty, foreign affairs, and many other subjects is, to a large extent, the same today as in 1987." Perhaps a media culture that thrives on conflict gives us the sense that there is more conflict than actually exists? However, there is no question that partisan animosity has increased since the 1960s' **realignments** of voters with parties. Voting coalitions are more geographically and racially determined and ideologically unified than they were before the critical elections of 1964 and 1968. After 1968 voters began a "great sorting" of themselves along racial, economic, and religious **cleavages**. With the advent of digital media, each group and subgroup has its devoted social media and cable news shows that reinforces rather than challenge their ideas.

An experiment between liberal and conservative policies seems to be underway in the laboratories of state governments. The June 22, 2019 edition of The Economist magazine highlighted Texas and California as case studies between conservative and liberal policies. How each state fares in the next decades may allow us to proclaim a winning approach to our most pressing problems.

Texafornia: The Conservative and Liberal States Case Study

From their politics one might not guess it, but Texas and California are very similar. Hispanics make up 40% of their population and they both border Mexico. Undocumented immigrants make up 6% of their populations but 8.5% of their workforce, filling jobs in agriculture and construction, especially. Whites are minorities in each state, and 46% of the entire Hispanic vote lives in "Texafornia." Together, they educate one-fourth of American students and account for the same fraction of America's GDP. If they were separate countries, Texas' economy would be larger than Canada's (10th) and California's would out-produce Germany's (5th).

Ideologically, the two could not be more different. Texas has had no Democrat elected to statewide office in twenty-five years, and California is as hospitable to Democrats as it is to Hollywood stars. Democratic presidential candidates hardly bother to campaign there and still win by over twenty percentage points. For our purposes, California uses **government regulation** to face its problems where Texas has a "small government," **laissez-faire** approach. Indeed, the Texas legislature meets only once every two years while California's legislature is full-time and had 16 referendum items on its 2018 ballot. True to form, their positions on the issues reflect the activity level of their governments.

CALIFORNIA	PROBLEM	TEXAS
Highest state income tax. Top 1% pay for 46% of income taxes. Offers earned income tax credit (aid to working poor).	**Taxes**	No state income tax. Most taxes come from sales tax. No income tax credit.
7% uninsured. Accepted ACA expansion of Medicaid.	**Healthcare**	17% uninsured. Refused ACA expansion of Medicaid.
Required family leave. Subsidized childcare. 65% of welfare recipients get cash payment. $15 minimum wage.	**Social Services**	No family leave. No subsidized childcare. 4% of welfare recipients get cash payment. $7.25 minimum wage.
	Cultural/Social Issues	
No death penalty. Withdrew national guard troops. Declared "sanctuary state." Offers in-state tuition and healthcare to undocumented children.	**Death Penalty** **Immigration**	Executes more than any other state. Spends $400 million to police boarders. Passed law barring "sanctuary cities." Police can ask for citizenship papers at their discretion. No healthcare or in-state tuition to undocumented children.

In conclusion, political parties are essential linkage institutions. They can educate voters and represent their interests in government. With offices in nearly every U.S. county, they are indispensable for candidates seeking election. However, their power has declined in recent decades. With the prevalence of television and, more recently, online advertising, campaigns are more candidate than party-centered. Individuals with **name recognition** and big war chests (lots of money) can appeal directly to voters who are willing to "**split ticket**" vote. Today, voters care less about to which party a candidate belongs. Since the 1960s, split-ticket voting has become the norm.

Increased polarization and gridlock have also become the norm. Currently, our **two-party system** rewards candidates who motivate their **bases** while suppressing the other side's turnout. With dedicated media outlets and apps, this is more effectively done than ever before. The amounts of money required to fund a "perpetual campaign" continue to rise, keeping policymakers busy raising money from special interests during on and off years. Add to this fevered grasp for money and influence each party's ability to choose their voters through gerrymandered districts and the role of the average citizen recedes further and further into the background.

There are many ideas for those who wish to confront such a bleak outlook. For those of us who wish to live in a democracy, two initial recommendations may be useful. First, on a policy level, the U.S. should go a step further in duplicating the way Australians vote. We first did so when we copied their "secret ballot" in the 1890s. Now we need to follow their lead and enact **mandatory voting**. That's right. Make everyone vote, with a fine of $15 if they do not. Required voting upped Australia's voter turnout to over 90%. How would this combat the problems of extremism and polarization? Ordinary people would vote, even in primaries! If politicians had to appeal to centrist voters instead of their base, the candidates and their messages would appeal to a more reasonable mind-set. Instead of "motivating the base," office seekers would tone down the rhetoric, stop it with the outlandish claims and proposals, and try to persuade voters who want information rather than incitement.

The second proposal is closer to home. To you, dear reader: stop being passive. Not participating in a political party or cause is not freedom. It might seem like a luxury at first to never have to engage in politics.

Take a moment to imagine your life as one who has voluntarily removed themselves from the political process. Such a life defaults to a life of being a passive spectator that just consumes stuff. With no political cause to feel a part of, no way to link yourself to the governing body, you stand no chance in being part of the process of creating the political reality you're living. Your life becomes that of a spectator, watching the world pass you by on TV screens, spending all day watching TV shows, movies and video games of fantasy worlds while you live in a fantasy world of your own, watching the soap opera of people in suits arguing about mostly insignificant. On national holidays you will be told that you should feel grateful for your life as a passive spectator. Perhaps some will argue that in the name of multiculturalism and tolerance, you should not feel so connected to a strong political identity, religious identity or national identity. Better, you should think of yourself more in terms of your identity as a global consumer. The reality of who you are is actually more connected to buying stuff than doing stuff.

Really think about how it would feel to live every day of your life utterly disconnected from the creation of the world you belong and ask yourself if that is really the kind of world that you want to be living in. While pollical parties and their media subordinates may treat you like a bystander to history, you do not have to play the part. Leave the TV-couch model behind and find a linkage institution like a political party or start one, like a Youtube channel. Use it to advocate for your idea of the best solutions to the problems one passive generation after another has handed to you. A solution with a "one-click buy" option sold by a politician is a fiction created for the politically powerless. Don't buy it.

Chapter 19

How Political Parties Choose Candidates: Primaries and Caucuses

Political parties choose their candidates using primaries and caucuses. Whichever method a party uses depends on the state, and they differ across the country.

Caucuses are like meetings that last for hours as voters debate and decide which of their party's members they will choose as congressional candidates. Party members caucus in places like church assembly halls and high school gyms. In 2016, Democrats held caucuses in 13 states, and all of the territories used them to choose their candidates (shout out to Guam!). The Republicans held caucuses in 12 states.

The rest of us register with a political party and vote in an inner-party pre-election called a **direct primary**. Only one party's candidates run in **primary election**s. There are two types of primaries:

Open Primary—A registered party member of either party can vote in Republican and Democratic primaries. They decide which primary to vote in on Election Day. Each voter can participate in only one.

Closed Primary—Only registered Republicans can vote in the Republican primary, and only registered Democrats can vote in the Democratic primary.

How Primary Elections Work

There are three key variables to the practice of holding primaries: when these primaries occur, how many delegates each party will have, and how each party gives itself a way out of going with the candidate people choose.

WHEN? Primary elections are spread out from January to June in a presidential election year. States used to move the dates of their primaries earlier to have more say in the nomination process, but that only started a **frontloading** war as all states moved their primaries up, making the election season even longer. The U.S. election cycle is abnormally long.

National Election Campaign Length (Days)

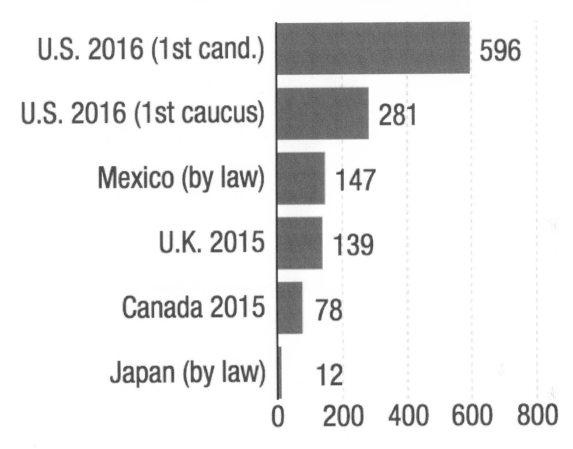

Source: NPR

U.S. parties are in a "perpetual campaign," especially considering the fundraising that is required to pay for a 596 day run for office.

Iowa holds the first caucus, and New Hampshire holds the first primary, which means candidates campaign there many months in advance. Early primary states are especially important as a good performance there gives a candidate a "winner" aura and create a **bandwagon effect** for voters and donors alike. Candidates woo primary voters in the early states with policies that are especially fit to their interests, though not necessarily anyone else's. Look no further than the corn in gasoline for evidence (Iowa is corn country).

The National Convention

After each state's Republican and Democratic caucus or primary, each state sends delegates to their party's **national convention**. National Conventions are important weeklong events because they showcase the party's **platform** as well as rising stars within the party.   For the finale, the nominee gives an acceptance speech, marking the official beginning of his presidential campaign.

Once at the convention, the delegates are "bound" by how voters in primaries and caucuses voted (more on that in a second—they are less bound than many voters think), so the winners are preordained.

In 2016, the Republicans sent 2,472 delegates (the number depends on how many Republican representatives are in a state's legislature plus a slew of other qualifying factors too numerous to list here) to their convention in Cleveland, Ohio, July 18-21. Candidates were required to win 1,237 delegates to secure the nomination.

Democrats had 4,763 delegates and required a candidate to win 2,383 of them. How states select their delegates is as confusing on the Democratic Party side of the ledger as the Republican. Each state has a different way of determining the number of delegates they will have and who will represent it at the party's convention.

Elite Party Members Get More of a Say: Superdelegates

Sometimes the parties do not approve of the candidate that receives the most delegates, so they have crafted ways to get around the **direct democracy** aspect of primary voting. Political parties are private associations that have no legal obligation to voters. When state governments have passed laws trying to make primaries more democratic and transparent, the Supreme Court has ruled in favor of the parties' freedoms of speech and assembly—that is, the parties get to choose how democratic they are.

Our nation's earliest primaries were more like polls. Parties gauged voters' opinions through the process, but did not bind themselves to a particular candidate. To appease citizens, parties have opened their doors a little wider but have still retained some elitist features that allow them to have a determining effect on candidate selection. The leading way party elites have retained the power to choose their candidates is the use of **superdelegates**. These are party elites who can vote for whomever they please, no matter the results of the primaries and caucuses. Out of the Democratic Party's 4,763 delegates, 15% are superdelegates. Halloween challenge: dress up as a superdelegate.

While they do not have superdelegates, the Republicans too dodge democratic outcomes in various ways, depending on the state. In Pennsylvania, 54 of 71 delegates are "unbound" to begin with—they can show up to the convention and vote however they please (they are pretty much superdelegates without the cool name). North Dakota's GOP did not even have a caucus or a primary—all 28 of their candidates are unbound and were chosen by a state convention.

Those Republican delegates that are "bound" by their states have to vote the way they are supposed to only once, in the first round of voting. After that, if no candidate got 1,237 votes—if there is a contested convention, all bets are off, and everybody gets to put on the unbound cape.

The perplexing details and loopholes of each party's nominating process have indeed enraged primary voters. Trump has called the system "rigged" and growled at party elites, backroom deals, and "the establishment." Bernie Sanders's supporters threatened to kill the Nevada Democratic Party **chairman** after she ruled many of Sanders's delegate votes ineligible at her party's state convention.

Even though they do not have to, parties usually follow the will of the voters when nominating candidates. If they do not, they risk a backlash (voters staying home or voting against them) or the popular candidate leaving the two-party system to form a third party. When a splinter party forms from a major party it usually has a spoiling effect on the election by splitting the disgruntled party's vote, handing the election to the other, more unified party.

Primary Voters are Primarily Extreme

Today, only 25% of registered voters even vote in primaries. Because of this small turnout, candidates have to appeal to the most extreme, most passionate constituencies to win.

Political parties have lost much control over who their candidates are. Because of campaign finance regulations, parties depend on candidates to raise money for them. Textbooks will usually say that parties recruit and nominate candidates. Increasingly, candidates can skip past their parties and appeal straight to voters. By appealing directly to donors (first) then voters (second), U.S. politics is growing more and more candidate, rather than party, centered. If a candidate is polling well and has a supply of cash, the party puts its arms around him in a prom pose and smiles for the photographer. For example, in 2016 Republican Speaker of the House Paul Ryan opposed Donald Trump's nomination but eventually supported him.

Ryan opposed Trump from the moment he entered the race. He warned fellow conservatives that Trump was using "**identity politics**" to appeal to white supremacists. He called Trump's verbal assault against a federal judge of Mexican heritage "the textbook definition of a racist comment." After reports surfaced of Trump sexually assaulting a number of women, Ryan tried to convince his party to reconsider nominating him. "I am not going to defend Donald Trump," Ryan announced. "Not now. Not in the future." Soon after the general election, Ryan became one of Trump's staunchest defenders. Such was a tale of candidate over party authority.

After firmly establishing himself in his party of choice and paying for staff, pollsters, consultants, and advertising, the candidate turns his attention to the electorate. Remembering that only 25% of voters are going to turn out for primary elections, so primary candidates must appeal to "the base" of the party. The base includes the most motivated, ideologically extreme people in the party-including the ones who thought Obama was a terrorist, or that George Bush planned 9/11. They hate the other side and are driven by intense passions easily manipulated by demagogues and their savvy political operatives. To get their votes, candidates end up endorsing these most extreme corners of their parties' platforms. After the candidates have gone through the nomination process, moderate voters are dismayed. They complain of having two bad choices and having to "choose the lesser of two evils." Never mind that they are part of the 75% who did not vote in a primary or take part in a caucus. If we are to have better candidates, "normal" people must vote in primary elections.

What is more, once these elected officials get into public office, they carry their no-compromise, extreme stances with them. Having over-simplified or even misrepresented the issues in their primary and general elections, they lack or choose not to exercise the capacity to work with others with whom they disagree. The result is a polarized, partisan government **gridlocked** by no-compromise mindsets.

Chapter 20

Voters and Voter Turnout

Many voters lack a feeling of voter efficacy. They do not think their vote matters. While the franchise has opened the door to the poor, women, and African Americans, only around half of all eligible voters turn out to vote in elections. While it is undoubtedly our civic duty to vote, there are more systemic reasons why perfectly good citizens might choose to stay at home.

Most citizens over the age of 18 have the right to vote. Not long ago, state legislatures denied African Americans the franchise. Their victory for voting rights was the last in a long line of demands for the right to vote. Different groups have won the right to vote at different times, marking milestones in American history.

15th Amendment (1868)—Granted African American men the right to vote by declaring that the "right of citizens of the United States to vote shall not be denied or abridged by the United States or by any state on account of race, color, or previous condition of servitude."

19th Amendment (1920)—Granted women's suffrage.

23rd Amendment (1961)--Washington D.C. residents can vote for president. The capital received 3 Electoral College votes but still does not have representation in Congress.

24th Amendment (1964)—No **poll taxes** required to vote. While many mistake this for a Civil Rights measure, the Amendment targeted poor white Southern voters. However, Southern Senators did not mind the smokescreen a pro-voting bill gave them to filibuster against genuine Civil Rights bills like the Voting Rights Act.

Voting Rights Act (1965)-- Forbade states from imposing discriminatory restrictions on who can vote, and provided mechanisms for the federal government to enforce its provisions. The legislation passed under pressure from protests and marches earlier that year challenging Alabama officials who injured and killed people during African American voter registration efforts. In 1964, close to a thousand civil rights workers of all races and backgrounds converged on the South to support voting rights.

26th Amendment (1971)—Granted 18 year-olds the right to vote. Eighteen-year-olds were dying in Vietnam but were unable to vote in the U.S., prompting passage of the amendment.

Motor Voter Law (part of the National Voter Registration Act) (1993)-- Intended to increase the number of eligible citizens who **register** to vote by making registration available at the Department of Motor Vehicles and public assistance and disabilities agencies.

The Right to Vote Today

I am a little facetious when I say there is not one. Most state constitutions, along with the federal Constitution, grant no affirmative right to vote. Instead, voting is a privilege that states can strip from those whom it has granted the franchise. Of course, voting is a "right." However, by not being explicitly, constitutionally guaranteed, states have an easier time taking the vote away or denying it in the first place. Who gets to vote is by no means resolved today. States, using their reserved powers, have implemented a variety of reforms/barriers that have made casting a vote either easier or harder.

Making Voting Easier

• **Online registration**: 30 states make registering to vote more accessible by simplifying the process for Internet users.
• **Election day registration**: 15 states allow voters to register on the same day they cast their ballots. The states that do not permit this close registration 25-30 days before the actual election. Millions of voters searched for "voter registration" after their states' deadlines. Researchers concluded that these citizens—5% of prospective voters—would have voted if same-day registration had been available. In states that do have election day registration, voter turnout was 10% higher in the 2012 presidential election.
• **Motor Voter Laws**: These allowed voters to register to vote at motor vehicle departments. This 1993 expansion of voting accessibility simplified registration and was designed to raise low voter turnouts, which were at 50.1% in 1988. In 1996—the

first election in which the legislation was put to the test—only 49% of registered voters appeared at the polls, calling into question the law's effectiveness. Since then, turnout rates have gone up slightly, but few credit the increase to the **Motor Voter Act**.

• Hold elections on weekends or declare election days as national holidays. People work on Tuesdays and must take a cut in wages or lose a "sick day." Having to miss one, two, even four hours of work amounts to a poll tax for many Americans.

Making Voting Harder

• **Voter ID Laws**: over 30 states have passed laws requiring voters to show an I.D. when they show up to polling locations. Advocates of this legislation aim to prevent voter fraud, in which one person impersonates another and casts a vote in his or her name. One type of deception is using a dead person's name to cast a ballot. However, the problem is not too prevalent. Between 2000 and 2013, only 31 such possible cases of voter fraud have been documented out of over a billion votes cast. To get an I.D., someone must show a Social Security Card, original birth certificate, and other official documents. Thus, these laws affect African Americans 1.8 times more than whites, and Hispanics 2.5 times more than whites.

• **Felon Disenfranchisement**: 6.1 million Americans' states prohibit felons from voting. These 12 most extreme states make up over 50 percent of the entire disenfranchised population. While it is debatable whether felony disenfranchisement laws today are intended to reduce the political clout of communities of color, this is their undeniable effect and original intent. Southern states passed such laws during Reconstruction as they sought to re-institute slavery as best as they could. Of the top ten states with the highest disenfranchised populations, eight are former slave states in the Deep South. One in every thirteen (1/13) African Americans has lost their voting rights due to **felon disenfranchisement laws** compared with one in every fifty-six (1/56) of non-minorities.

• Remove names from voter rolls:

Ohio uses a multi-step approach to take the vote away from its citizens. If someone does not vote in two consecutive years, it mails them a prepaid card the resident must fill out to verify that she lives at the same address. If the Secretary of State's office does not hear from the registered voter, her name is struck from the **voter roll** and is out of **the franchise**.

Who Are the Voters and How Do they Vote?

Who is "the electorate" or "the franchise?" First, the most faithful ones are a minority of Americans. In federal elections, 22% of adults who are eligible to vote do not even register, and another 20% report being on-again, off-again participants, depending on their interest in a given election. A steady 35% reports voting no matter the weather or poor candidate choices that may lie before them. Republican voters are more likely to vote than Democrats, making a high voter turnout good news for one party and bad for another. Advocates who "get out the vote" and urge groups, such as young people, "to just vote...it doesn't matter who you vote for, just vote!" most likely know these new recruits will likely vote for the Democratic party.

A snapshot of voter turnout:

- Republicans have a higher **voter turnout** than Democrats, as they have a more motivated base. While Democrats are cats, Republicans are canine--organized in packs.
- Educated citizens vote more than uneducated citizens.
- Whites generally vote more than minority groups. However, if one includes education levels along with color, whites vote equally to their minority counterparts.
- Those who regularly attend religious services vote more.
- Married people vote more than singles.
- Union members vote more.
- Those involved in community groups, like softball leagues, vote more than stay-at-home, Call of Duty folk.
- Those who strongly identify with a political party vote more.
- Voters in swing states vote more.

Overall, the electorate we just examined has seemingly become more apathetic, discouraged, and inactive. In 2016, the U.S. placed 26th out of 32 developed nations regarding voter turnout. Only 55% of eligible American voters use their right to do so. However, voter turnout in 2018 was a 50 year high! 47% of eligible voters turnout in 2018. Just four years earlier, in the 2014 midterm, voter turnout hit an all-time low at 36.7%. What changed? The question is more "who changed?" and the answer lies in the demographic data.

From the U.S. Census Bureau:

- Voter turnout went up more in some demographic groups than others from 2014 to 2018:
- Among 18- to 29-year-olds, voter turnout went from 20 percent in 2014 to 36 percent in 2018, the largest percentage point increase for any age group — a 79 percent jump.
- Among men and women, voter turnout increased by 11 and 12 percentage points respectively.
- Voter turnout increased among non-Hispanic Asians by 13 percentage points, a 49 percent increase.
- Among Hispanics, voter turnout increased by 13 percentage points, a 50 percent increase in Hispanic voter turnout.
- Non-Hispanic black voter turnout increased by 11 percentage points.
- Those with higher levels of education had higher levels of voter turnout in 2018. Those with less than a high school education had the smallest increase in voter turnout (5 percentage points). Those with a high school diploma or equivalent had the second-lowest increase (8 percentage points).
- Unlike the 2014 midterm election, voter turnout among those living in nonmetropolitan areas (up 8 points) was lower than for those living in metropolitan areas (up 12 points).
- A record number of women were elected to the House of Representatives in the November 2018 election. Additionally, women continued to vote at higher rates than men, just as they have in every midterm election since 1998.
- In the 2018 midterm election, 55 percent of women voted compared with 52 percent of men, a 3 percentage point gap.
- Census Bureau voting and registration data also include a detailed table package of key estimates, which allows data users to take a deeper dive into the numbers behind elections.
- Estimates in the 2018 Election table package show that the difference between male and female voter turnout varied among different demographic groups.
- In 2018, among those age 65 and older, voter turnout was 65 percent for women and 68 percent for men. In contrast, 38 percent of women 18-29 years old voted and 33 percent of men of the same age group voted.

Alternative Voting

The availability of **alternative voting methods** continues to change how voters vote. Alternative voting methods include any method other than voting in person on Election Day, such as early voting and voting by mail.

In 2018, 40 percent of voters used an alternative voting method. The percentage of voters that cast their ballot early or by mail usually declines slightly in midterm elections relative to the preceding presidential election. However, the rate in 2018 was not significantly different from the 2016 presidential election.

The use and availability of alternative voting methods varied by state. In the 2018 election, early voting was available in 39 states. Some states require that voters state a reason or excuse for mailing an absentee ballot, while others do not (no-excuse absentee voting). Three states (Washington, Oregon and Colorado) have all-mail voting systems.

The three states with the highest percentage point increases in alternative voting rates from 2014 were Utah, Texas and Georgia. Alternative voting increased by 36 percentage points in Utah, 25 points in Texas, and 21 points in Georgia.

Part 5

Individual Liberties and Rights

Chapter 21

Incorporation of the Bill of Rights Through the Fourteenth Amendment

14th Amendment (1868):

All persons born or naturalized in the United States and subject to the jurisdiction thereof, are citizens of the United States and of the State wherein they reside. No State shall make or enforce any law which shall abridge the privileges or immunities of citizens of the United States; nor shall any State deprive any person of life, liberty, or property, without due process of law; nor deny to any person within its jurisdiction the equal protection of the laws.

Bill of Rights

Amendment 1

- Freedom of Religion, Speech, and the Press

Congress shall make no law respecting an establishment of religion or prohibiting the free exercise thereof, or abridging the freedom of speech or of the press, or the right of the people peaceably to assemble and to petition the government for a redress of grievances.

Amendment 2

- The Right to Bear Arms

A well-regulated Militia being necessary to the security of a free State, the right of the people to keep and bear Arms shall not be infringed.

Amendment 3

- The Housing of Soldiers

No soldier shall, in time of peace, be quartered in any house without the consent of the owner, nor in time of war but in a manner to be prescribed by law.

Amendment 4

- Protection from Unreasonable Searches and Seizures

The right of the people to be secure in their persons, houses, papers, and effects against unreasonable searches and seizures shall not be violated, and no warrants shall issue but upon probable cause, supported by oath or affirmation, and particularly describing the place to be searched and the persons or things to be seized.

Amendment 5
- Protection of Rights to Life, Liberty, and Property

No person shall be held to answer for a capital or otherwise infamous crime unless on a presentment or indictment of a grand jury, except in cases arising in the land or naval forces, or in the militia, when in actual service in time of war or public danger; nor shall any person be subject for the same offense to be twice put in jeopardy of life or limb; nor shall be compelled in any criminal case to be a witness against himself, nor be deprived of life, liberty, or property without due process of law; nor shall private property be taken for public use without just compensation.

Amendment 6
- Rights of Accused Persons in Criminal Cases

In all criminal prosecutions, the accused shall enjoy the right to a speedy and public trial by an impartial jury of the state and district wherein the crime shall have been committed, which district shall have been previously ascertained by law, and to be informed of the nature and cause of the accusation; to be confronted with the witnesses against him; to have compulsory process for obtaining witnesses in his favor; and to have the assistance of counsel for his defense.

Amendment 7
- Rights in Civil Cases

Amendment 8
- Excessive Bail, Fines, and Punishments Forbidden

Excessive bail shall not be required, nor excessive fines imposed, nor cruel and unusual punishments inflicted.

Amendment 9
- Other Rights Kept by the People

The enumeration in the Constitution of certain rights shall not be construed to deny or disparage others retained by the people.

Amendment 10
- Undelegated Powers Kept by the States and the People

The powers not delegated to the United States by the Constitution, nor prohibited by it to the states, are reserved to the states respectively, or to the people.

The 14th Amendment turned the Constitution upside down. The difference between the phrase "Congress shall make no law" and "No State shall make or enforce any law" marks a revolution in the Constitution's meaning and application. When the Bill of Rights applied only to the actions of a federal Congress, states legally enslaved its inhabitants. Under the 14th Amendment's "No state shall" that same federal government would send federal marshals to Southern states to enforce school desegregation in 1957.

The Constitution's "Congress shall make no law" language found in the First Amendment was to apply the rights listed in the Bill to only the actions of the federal government. The Anti-Federalists wanted the assurance of a Bill of Rights to protect individual liberties from the new federal government.   As the Federalists argued when opposing the Anti-Federalists' demand for a federal Bill of Rights, the federal government did not have the police force even to do such a thing. Madison reminded the Anit-Federalists that if the federal government were to do its worst, no list of rights could stop a tyrannical government. He emphasized separation of powers in a federal system, as we saw at work in the Lopez case.

The 14th Amendment, in contrast to the Bill of Rights, was ratified in 1868 to protect individuals from their state governments, especially freemen in former slave states. Northern abolitionists penned the 14th Amendment to give the oppressed minority of former slaves full individual liberties as found in the Bill of Rights, including especially their Second Amendment right to bear arms

The 14th Amendment's import is that it made the states honor the rights listed in the Bill. Notice the irony: the Anti-Federalist wanted the Bill of Rights to protect their local governments. After the Civil War, the list in the Bill of Rights would be used by the federal government against the states. Especially for minorities, the federal government would be a shield between citizens and their state governments. The 14th Amendment and the **incorporation** of the federal Bill against state governments revolutionized the Constitution and turned its focus towards individual rights and away from the structural protections of federalism, separation of powers, and checks and balances. The post-Civil War interpretation of the Constitution would put individual rights and values like equality over structural concerns regarding the reach of federal power into that of the states. Cases like Baker v. Carr would illustrate this shift in 1962.

It would take around 75 years after the passage of the 14 Amendment before any part of the Bill of Rights would be used against state governments. It was not until 2010 that the federal government incorporated the Second Amendment against the states. SCOTUS used the 14th Amendment's due process clause to incorporate part of the 8th Amendment in 2018. The wall came down between the federal government and the states with the ratification of the 14th Amendment. It took longer than the 14th Amendment's authors ever feared. If not for a horrific civil war over slavery and the reimagining of the Constitution's meaning, the wall between the people and the Bill of Rights might still be up today. The 1960s saw the last legal supports of the wall finally come down.

Chapter 22

Student Rights of Speech, Press, and Religion Clauses of the First Amendment

To see the relevance of the incorporation doctrine in our daily lives, we can look at it through the lens of student rights. That is if they have any.

The question of students' freedom of speech loomed over the Supreme Court as it sifted through the meanings of the first two clauses of the First Amendment. It took some time before SCOTUS would issue a writ of cert for a student speech case—it waited for a good test case and lower court rulings. Two Mississippi cases would open the salvo in American students' fight for their First Amendment speech rights.

Burnside v. Byers

Kids wore buttons in the 1960s: Beatles buttons, "The Hand that Rocks the Cradle Can Rock the Boat" buttons, "Nixon Sucks Grapes" buttons, "Radiate Positive Vibes" buttons..... However, when African American students began protesting in Neshoba County, MS, principals suspended "Freedom Now" button-wearing students in fear of what would happen to them. One cannot blame them. In the summer of 1964 the KKK, in collusion with the Neshoba County police, had murdered three civil rights workers not much older than the protesting students.

One month after the bodies of James Cheney, Andrew Goodman, and Michael Schwerner were found outside Philadelphia, MS, the county seat of Neshoba, hundreds of students at the all-black Booker T. Washington High School wore "Freedom Now" and "One Person, One Vote" buttons to school that August in 1964. In the end, three refused to remove them and took their case to the federal district court. When put on the stand, fourteen-year-old Neva English explained why she refused to remove her button:

ARONSON (her lawyer): What were you trying to do with those buttons?

ENGLISH: Our rights to speech and to do the things we would like to do.

ARONSON: What kinds of things would you like to do?

ENGLISH: Go uptown and sit in the drugstores, and wherever we buy things uptown we can sit down and won't have to walk out at the time we get it.

ARONSON: What else?

ENGLISH: And to register to vote without being beat up and killed.

The federal district judge ruled against the students on the grounds that the ban on buttons was "reasonably necessary to maintain proper discipline in the school."

Blackwell vs. Issaquena Board of Education

Later that year in a similar case, 300 students were suspended from public schools in Rolling Forks, Mississippi for continuing to wear freedom buttons after several warnings and disturbances. After losing in district court as Neva English had, the NAACP appealed to the federal Fifth Circuit Court in New Orleans. In Blackwell v. Issaquena County Board of Education (1965), the students argued that their First Amendment freedom of speech rights had been violated. The justices of the Fifth Circuit Court contradicted the Burnside case in its decision that students have First Amendment rights at school. School officials would have to prove a high level of disruption before they could limit such student expression again.

The Fifth Circuit determined that while there had been "substantial disruption" in Burnside, there was none in Blackwell. When two lower federal courts contradict one another's rulings, the stage is set for the Supreme Court to make the final determination of the Constitution's meaning.

Another student protest, this time of the Vietnam War, would give SCOTUS this opportunity.

Tinker v. Des Moines (1969)

John and Mary Beth Tinker wore black armbands to school in protest of the deaths of U.S. soldiers and Vietnamese civilians in the ongoing Vietnam War. Before they showed up to school, they informed their school district of their plan to wear the armbands. On the day of the protest, December 17, John Tinker did not even go to class but instead reported directly to the principal's office. His sister was sent to the principal's office by her teacher. The school district suspended the Tinkers until they came to school without the armbands. During their suspension, false patriots threw red paint on their house (associating the color red with communism) and broke their car's windshield. A radio talk show host offered to lend someone a gun if they would kill the Tinkers' father.

In the federal district court, John Tinker gave his reason for wearing the armband: "When people are getting killed, it's important to me." That was not good enough for the district court that cited the disruption the black armbands had caused (death threats, paint, brinks, taunting).

Being a good reader, you might think, "Yes, but what about the rule set up in Burnside and Blackwell—that there had to be 'substantial and material disruption' in the normal operation of the school day?" Yes, the Tinkers' lawyer tried that, but they were in the 8th Circuit in St. Louis, MO, not the 5th Circuit in New Orleans. The 8th Circuit justices reminded the Tinkers that one circuit court's ruling is not a source of **case law/precedent/stare decisis** for another. Decisions in one lower federal court are in no way binding in another. Only SCOTUS sets the overall precedents.

SCOTUS often intervenes when circuit courts start handing out different rulings on the same issues. A writ of cert was issued, and the Supreme Court would finally answer whether students have full rights at school or not. And answer they did. Issuing one of the most quoted majority opinions in its history, SCOTUS ruled that, "...it can hardly be argued that either students or teachers shed their constitutional rights to freedom of speech or expression at the schoolhouse gate." The author of the majority's opinion, Abe Fortas, adopted the "substantial disruption" standard the 5th Circuit used when deciding Blackwell. Fortas went on: "...state operated schools may not be enclaves of totalitarianism.... Students may not be regarded as closed-circuit recipients of only that which the State chooses to communicate." Unless schools could show a "reasonable forecast of disruption," students were to be treated as full-fledged citizens at school.

As well as applying principles laid out in Barnette (called the Bill of Rights is "fixed star"), and Blackwell and Burnside (schools cannot forbid "expressions of feelings with which they do not wish to contend"), the Supreme Court reached back to 1919 for its ruling in Tinker.

In 1919, federal agents arrested Charles Schenck for distributing fliers opposing the draft during WWI. In losing his case (Schenck v. U.S.), he helped the Tinkers win theirs. In the majority opinion of Schenck, Justice Oliver Wendell Holmes reasoned that "in many places and times" Schenck could have said anything he wanted, but not during a time of war (WWI 1914-1919). Speaking against the draft in such a time created "a **clear and present danger**" that would bring about "substantive evils that Congress has a right to prevent." When applied to school, the ruckus did not have to be "dangerous" or lead to grave consequences. Instead, if students' speech clearly and immediately disrupted the educational (we will call it "pedagogical" in the future) function of the school, it could be punished. Famously, Holmes offered a clarification: "The most stringent protection of free speech would not protect a man in falsely shouting 'fire' in a theater and causing a panic."

Tinker applied the **dangerous speech test** to a school environment, requiring that those that would limit students' freedom of expression show a probability that learning would be disrupted. School officials could not limit student rights at their discretion. They now had to prove that prohibited speech had disrupted students' learning.

TYPES OF SPEECH

All speech, then, is not equal. Through many rulings, we can say the following about types of speech.

Symbolic speech: it does not have to be spoken. It can be in a pamphlet, as in Schenck's case, an expression in the Barnettes' case (refusing to say the pledge or salute the flag), or a symbol as in Tinker.

The intention of the speech in question matters. These are the most protected forms of speech:

1. Political. The free expression of political viewpoints is essential to democracy.
2. Religious. The division between church and state, public and private preserves civil society.
3. Artistic. A vibrant civil society depends on the free expression and association of creative, courageous citizens.

Moreover, there are unprotected forms of speech:

1. Subversive Advocacy. This type of speech riles people up to commit crimes and behave lawlessly.
2. **Fighting Words**. Fairly self-explanatory, this type of speech usually takes the form of pointed insults that cause the recipient to react violently.
3. True Threats. Think about bored and misguided teens who call the local school threatening to drop a bomb.
4. Obscenity. Pornography is not protected by free speech, but nude work that has artistic value is protected. This distinction is difficult to make. Justice Potter Stewart's famous "test": "I know it when I see it."
5. Child pornography. By outlawing this type of lewd behavior, the Court aimed to protect children.

Beyond the Warren Court, Back to the Future: The Burger Court

The first speech cases that came into federal courts after Tinker did not make it to SCOTUS. In the following decade, students took their school districts to court over school rules regarding hair length, protests, banned books, and the regulation of student newspapers. Tinker's "substantial and material disruption" test protected students' rights as never before.

The 1980s saw a conservative backlash against the liberal 1960s. The new Chief Justice Burger was a Nixon appointee and far less liberal than Earl Warren (Warren Court 1953-1969). Berger's Court would hear a case that put student speech on trial, just as Tinker had done, but would arrive at a very different meaning for student rights.

Bethel v. Fraser (1986)

It was election time at Bethel High School in Washington, and senior Matthew Fraser took to the podium at the student assembly to nominate his friend Jeff Kuhlman. He gave a speech that became a part of Supreme Court history:

"I know a man who is firm -- he's firm in his pants, he's firm in his shirt, his character is firm -- but most . . . of all, his belief in you, the students of Bethel, is firm.

"Jeff Kuhlman is a man who takes his point and pounds it in. If necessary, he'll take an issue and nail it to the wall. He doesn't attack things in spurts -- he drives hard, pushing and pushing until finally -- he succeeds.

"Jeff is a man who will go to the very end -- even the climax, for each and every one of you. So vote for Jeff for A. S. B. vice-president -- he'll never come (pause) between you and the best our high school can be."

Fraser ran the speech past a teacher who told him it would "raise some eyebrows" but informed him of no school rule forbidding it. After five teachers wrote letters of complaint to the principal, the school suspended Fraser for giving an "indecent, lewd, and obscene" speech and was removed from the list of possible graduation speakers. Fraser filed in federal district court on 14th Amendment and First Amendment grounds.

Because the district and federal circuit courts were going by stare decisis/precedent/case law, they both ruled in Fraser's favor. After all, Fraser hardly could have been said to have caused a disruption. He gave his political speech for an audience assembled to hear it. Moreover, it worked: the student body elected his friend Jeff Kuhlman.

When the Bethel School District argued its case before the Supreme Court, it argued that the speech was obscene (putting it on a legal level with pornography). Bethel officials declared it was within the school's authority to punish "inappropriate" speech, whether it was disruptive or not. The Court agreed that the school has the responsibility to "teach by example the shared values of a civilized social order." The

Supreme Court concluded: "Surely it is a highly appropriate function of public school education to prohibit the use of vulgar and offensive terms in public discourse." With no claim of disruption, Bethel seemed to set a new standard that favored school order over student free speech.

Student Rights Take Another Hit: TLO v. New Jersey (1985)

The reversal of the court's stand on student rights had begun a year earlier in a Fourth Amendment searches and seizures case, TLO v. New Jersey (1985). TLO, a 9th grader, was caught smoking in the girls' bathroom (the school had a smoking area for teens where smoking was allowed). When she refused to admit her guilt to the teacher who had smelled the cigarette smoke, the teacher took her to Principal Choplick's office. He seized her purse and searched it, looking for incriminating evidence that proved her guilt of smoking out-of-area (schools still had smoking areas as the tobacco industry funded its own "science" to keep the debate alive as late as the early 1990s). Upon opening TLO's purse, he saw the cigarettes and set them on his desk. He kept going, based on his "reasonable suspicion" she was hiding more than just cigarettes. Mr. Choplick would not be disappointed. TLO had in her purse a roll of small bills totaling in the hundreds, a list of people marked as "paid" and "not paid," marijuana, and a small pipe.

Mr. Choplick suspended her and turned her into police custody. TLO was convicted under state law but appealed her case to the federal courts on 4th Amendment grounds. She and her mother claimed that the search became illegal after the "probable cause" of the search had been satisfied—Choplick had cause to find cigarettes. Having found them first, that should have ended the search.

This argument was taken up in federal court. The courts, working by the light of stare decisis, ruled in accordance with Tinker and a 1961 4th Amendment incorporation case, Mapp v. Ohio. In this case, Dollree Mapp was suspected of harboring a fugitive in her home. Ohio police obtained a warrant to search her home for the fugitive. Upon searching, instead of a fugitive, they found a crate of pornography left in Mapp's rental house by a prior tenant. She was arrested, tried, and convicted. Mapp appealed to the federal courts to incorporate the 4th Amendment against her state. Her case reached the Supreme Court and confirmed the **exclusionary rule**. The exclusionary rule bars evidence obtained illegally. That is, prosecutors cannot use the findings of an illegal search in court.

TLO had reason to be confident that the Supreme Court would apply the exclusionary rule to her case since Tinker established that students possessed full constitutional rights. Surprisingly, SCOTUS ruled in the school's favor. Using Latin (you know you are in trouble when people use Latin) in explaining their decision, the Court ruled that the school acts "in place of the parent"—in loco parentis--during school hours. Acting so, school officials can search students if they have a "reasonable suspicion," a much lower standard than that of probable cause—the standard police use when initiating a search. While it may be counterintuitive, teachers and principals have more power to search students than police officers. Because of TLO, evidence these substitute parents find will be used against the students in court.

When asked about the consequences of his case 15 years later, Matthew Fraser was not optimistic about student rights in the 21st century. As a practical matter," Fraser said as an adult (and civics educator), " school administrators do what they want to do." Put together, the Fraser and TLO rulings made clear that students do not have the same rights as adults, regardless of the precedent set in Tinker.

Freedom of the Press in Schools

Tinker would be given one more chance to serve as a liberty-giving precedent in 1987 over the question of whether students possess constitutional free press rights at school. While it may not be surprising today, when Tinker was the standard, schools could not arbitrarily use the argument "because I said so." TLO made returning to such standards possible, but it was still up for debate in 1987.

However, students rested their case on the experience of the New York Times' experience with government censorship.

If the following case, America's most esteemed newspaper pressed the question, can the government stop publication (**prior restraint**) of state secrets leaked out by its trusted employees? In 1971 the standard was set for future cases of prior restraint. The central question of the matter is whether or not a government authority can keep something from being published it guesses will cause harm?

New York Times v. United States (1971)

From the Bill of Rights Institute:

Not daring to turn lights on, the researcher stood cloaked in darkness, listening to the rhythmic hum of the photocopier. He fed pages and pages of classified documents into the machine as the night wore on.

Daniel Ellsberg copied more than 7000 pages of documents that revealed the history of the government's actions in the Vietnam War. They exposed government knowledge that the war would cost more lives than the public was being told, and that the war was being escalated even as the President had said it was close to ending. They would become known as the "Pentagon Papers."

Ellsberg believed that Americans needed to know what was in the reports, and decided to make the Pentagon Papers public. To achieve his goal, he broke several laws. He gave copies to the New York Times, which began printing excerpts from the documents on June 13, 1971. The government immediately obtained a court order preventing the Times from printing more of the documents, arguing that publishing the material threatened national security. This was the first time in American history that the government had successfully ordered a prior restraint (an order that news be censored ahead of publication) on national security grounds. Historically, prior restraint has been considered the most serious form of censorship.

In response, Ellsberg released the Pentagon Papers to the Washington Post, which began printing excerpts as well. The government then sought another injunction, but this time was refused. The government appealed its case, and in less than two weeks the case—combined with the New York Times appeal—was before the Supreme Court.

The Court ruled 6-3 in New York Times v. United States that the prior restraint was unconstitutional. Though the majority justices disagreed on some critical issues, they agreed that "Only a free and unrestrained press can effectively expose deception in government...In revealing the workings of government that led to the Vietnam War, the newspapers nobly did that which the Founders hoped and trusted they would do." Dismissing the claimed threat to national security, the Court continued, "The word 'security' is a broad, vague generality whose contours should not be invoked to abrogate the fundamental law embodied in the First Amendment." New York Times v. United States remains one of the most important freedom of the press cases in American history.

Hazelwood School District v. Kuhlmeier

In the Hazelwood High School's newspaper, Student Cathy Kuhlmeier wished to publish an in-depth and personal article entitled, "Divorce's Impact on Kids May Have Lifelong Effects." Her principal prohibited its publication, saying it might upset some students and parents since the article contained interviews of their fellow classmates. If Tinker applied to the issue, then the armband case would extend to protect students at school.

Desiring to be protected as an adult would be, Kuhlmeier wanted the precedent set by New York Times v. United States (1971) to be upheld. In NYT v. US, the court ruled against the government's use of prior restraint—criminalizing a publication—towards an article about the government's cruel conduct in its involvement in Vietnam. Even though the United States government argued the article regarding "The Pentagon Papers" would do great harm to the war effort, a Warren-led SCOTUS allowed it to be printed. Would The Spectrum enjoy such protection from prior restraint?

Hazelwood East High's paper had published stories about race, dating, and drug abuse that drew from firsthand student accounts that were of a "personal" and "sensitive" matter. None of these articles had caused disruptions, and this one showed no signs of doing so. The school board's stated policy even seemed to have valued First Amendment freedoms:

"...school sponsored student publications will not restrict free expression or diverse viewpoints within the rules of responsible journalism."

After winning in district court with Tinker as the guiding case law, the students also won their case in the 8th Circuit Court of Appeals. The Hazelwood School District had one more chance and appealed to the Supreme Court. SCOTUS granted a writ of cert and heard arguments in 1988.

SCOTUS went with neither the Tinker nor the Fraser standard but chose a third. Ruling against the students, the majority opinion argued that school officials could limit student freedoms "so long as their actions are reasonably related to legitimate pedagogical [educational] concerns." The precedent the majority cited was not a student case, nor the Pentagon Papers case. Instead, it was a case involving an inmate and his fiancé who wanted to marry. The Court quoted this case in its Kuhlmeier decision. SCOTUS judged that "when a prison regulation impinges on inmates' constitutional rights, the regulation is valid if it is reasonably related to penological interests." In Kuhlmeier's case, SCOTUS just swapped out the word "penological" with "pedagogical." If you have ever felt like a prisoner at school, think of the Kuhlmeier case to remind yourself you are not crazy. And yes, "pedogogical concerns" would be defined by the pedogogues. Since Kuhlmeier, students still contest their rights in federal courts sometimes win. However, the significant cases regarding student rights lean towards order in the school and not in favor of student liberties.

Final Verdict on Student Rights: Morse v. Frederick

SCOTUS would give student speech rights at school another day in court in 2007. Twenty years after Kuhlmeier, Joseph Frederick would intentionally test the boundaries. Frederick was fascinated by hypotheticals like the ones concocted by University of Washington's Law School:

Bill O'Reilly is a nationally known conservative commentator on politics and public affairs. Mr. O'Reilly is suing defendant, Playboy Magazine, for publishing a cartoon in which Mr. O'Reilly is depicted as having drunken sex with his mother in an outhouse. The caption reads, "Mr. O'Reilly talks about his first time." The cartoon was parodying an advertisement for Vodka 1, which frequently runs ads featuring celebrities talking about the first time they tried Vodka 1. At the bottom of the cartoon, in small print, are the words, "Ad parody—not to be taken seriously." Mr. O'Reilly is furious and sues Playboy Magazine for libel and for intentional infliction of emotional distress. Is Playboy's speech protected?

One can understand Frederick's interest. In January 2002, he made his own hypothetical a reality. An Olympic Torch Relay parade was going to pass near his school, and he would use the event to stage what has become a landmark event. On the day of the parade, Frederick did not report to school. When the school dismissed students to go to the parade, they found him holding a sign that read, "Bong Hits for Jesus" on the opposite side of the street. Principal Deborah Morse was not entertained. She marched across the street, confiscated the banner and suspended him for five days. Frederick tried arguing his case, even quoting Thomas Jefferson— "Speech limited is speech lost." He did not get a good reaction. After being told by an assistant principal that the Bill of Rights did not apply to students at school, Frederick's suspension was increased to ten days. According to Frederick, his life in Juneau, Alaska changed for the worse. Rumors of him being a "druggie" abounded, and he claims to have been pulled over "sometimes twice a day" by police. He was later arrested at gunpoint for "trespassing at a city pool" while waiting in his car for his girlfriend to finish her swim. His car was impounded and "torn apart," causing "at least a thousand dollars in damage to the interior."

In the federal district court, Frederick's experiment continued to take a turn for the worse. The judge ruled that the event was a school-sponsored event, even though it was clearly off campus, and Frederick had not reported to the school. The district court judge called Frederick's speech "plainly offensive" and declared that it "directly conflicted with the school's deterrence of illegal drug use and addiction."

When SCOTUS issued a writ of cert to the school, amicus curiae briefs started to pour in. Among them, many conservative religious groups argued on Frederick's behalf. While disagreeing with whatever message Frederick was sending, religious leaders feared that students who spoke out against abortion or gay marriage would have their speech freedoms curtailed. What would stop a principal considering "Abortion is Murder" signs "offensive" and outside of "pedagogical" bounds?

The SCOTUS ruling in Morse v. Frederick confirmed the findings in TLO, Fraser, and Kuhlmeier: students are not full citizens while at school. However, the Supreme Court was careful not to bury Tinker. The justices denied that Fraser should be the last word on student speech: "We think this stretches Fraser too far; [Frederick v Morse] should not be read to encompass any speech that could fit under some definition of 'offensive.' After all, much political and religious speech might be perceived as offensive to some. The concern here is not that Frederick's speech was offensive, but that it was reasonably viewed as promoting illegal drug use." This did not seem to do much for student rights but might have been an encouragement to those behind the amicus curiae briefs.

Frederick and his lawyers then did what the Federalists recommended at the founding to individuals defending their rights: use state constitutions, laws, and courts, and leave the federal government out it. Using Alaska's guarantee of free speech rather than the federal government's, Frederick sued the school in state court and won. His settlement with the school included $45,000 and an open forum on student rights at his old high school. He, like Matthew Fraser, is now a civics educator imparting the lessons he so dearly learned.

Since Morse v. Frederick, there has not been a major student speech case to reach SCOTUS, though there have been many to reach district and circuit courts. A list to guide your interest:

Bush is a "chicken hawk" t-shirt: Guiles v Marineau (2006)

"Drugs Suck" t-shirt: Broussard v. School Board of Norfolk (1992)

Students vs. school uniforms: Jacobs v. Clark County School District (2008)

Students protest a school board policy: Lowry v. Watson Chapel School District (2008)

Student says "He's a prick" in hearing range of teacher after school: Fenton v. Stear (1976)

Student gives teacher "the finger" after school, off campus: Klein v. Smith (1986)

Student creates webpage, "Please welcome to our F*****Up High School:" Beussink v. Woodland IV School District (1998)

Student insults teachers on webpage, "Teacher Sux:" J.S. v. Bethlehem Area School District (2002)

Student calls principal a "douchebag" on blog: Doniger v. Niehoff (2008)

Student suspended for cyberbullying: United States v. Drew (2009)

Student wears anti-gay t-shirt: Harper v. Poway Unified School District (2006)

Teacher sues student for online defamation: Draker v. Schreiber (2008)

Students, then, find themselves nearly at the same place they began, uncertain of their rights when they enter the schoolhouse gates.

Religion: Free Exercise Clause and the No Establishment Clauses

Through a series of cases involving religion at school, the Court defined the difference between the two religion clauses in the First Amendment. If the activity in question is student initiated and is a school-sponsored activity, it is protected by the Free Exercise Clause. On the other hand, if the religious activity is school-sponsored and initiated by a school official, the action is prohibited under the **Establishment Clause**. Cases involving public schools and school-sponsored prayer (Engle v. Vitale, 1962), and state laws requiring school attendance until age 16 regardless of an Amish practice of finishing school at grade 8 (Wisconsin v. Yoder, 1972) bring out the meaning of the First Amendments religion clauses.

Engle v. Vitale (1962)

Facts of the Case:

The Board of Regents for the State of New York authorized a short, voluntary prayer for recitation at the start of each school day. The general prayers read as follows: "Almighty God, we acknowledge our dependence upon Thee, and beg Thy blessings upon us, our teachers, and our country."
Question:

Does the reading of a nondenominational prayer at the start of the school day violate the Establishment Clause of the First Amendment?

Outcome:
6-1 Yes. No matter how nondenominational or voluntary the prayer may be, it is still a government-sponsored religious activity and therefore violates the Establishment Clause. Despite the passage of time, the decision is still unpopular with a majority of Americans and, with school desegregation orders, created an explosion of private religious schools in the 1960s.

Wisconsin v. Yoder (1971)

Facts of the Case:

Jonas Yoder, a member of the Old Order Amish religion, was arrested under a Wisconsin law that required all children to attend public schools until age 16. The state criminalized the conduct of parents who refused to send their children to school for religious reasons. Yoder refused to send his children to the local public high school as **mandated** by state law. Yoder argued that his freedom of religion protected his church's custom of its children ending their public education upon completion of eighth grade.

Question:
Did Wisconsin's requirement that all parents send their children to school at least until age 16 violate the First Amendment's Establishment Clause?

Outcome:
7-0 Yes. In a unanimous decision, the Court held that a parent's free exercise of religion under the First Amendment outweighed the State's interests in compelling school attendance beyond the eighth grade. The possible rights of the children was not a concern of the Court.
Decision: 7 votes for Yoder...2 justices not voting

Through case law, SCOTUS has formulated a "three-pronged test" (a "test" is a question or series of questions that help determine the legality of a situation) to use when considering the relationship between religion, the government, and the citizen.

The Yoder case defined the government's role is mostly to get out of the way of the parent's liberty to practice their religion as they saw fit. The majority opinion in Wisconsin v. Yoder took a strict view of religious liberty: "the fundamental interest of parents, as contrasted with that of the State, to guide the religious future and education of their children." If the authority one is born into says that an eighth-grade education is enough, it is enough. Western "history and culture," the Chief Justice continued, "reflect a strong tradition of parental concern for the nurture and upbringing of their children." In this view, society and government are starkly separated. Views held by those with eighth-grade educations are just as good, maybe better, than a body of expert scientists. In this case, that is up to the Amish to decide.

In dissent, the minority opinion pointed to the rights of the students rather than to the liberties of the parents. William O. Douglas wrote in his dissent: "I think the children should be entitled to be heard. While the parents, absent dissent, normally speak for the entire family, the education of the child is a matter on which the child will often have decided views. He may want to be a pianist or an astronaut or an oceanographer. It is the future of the students, not the future of the parents, that is imperiled by today's decision. If a parent keeps his child out of school beyond the grade school, then the child will be forever barred from entry into the new and amazing world of diversity that we have today. The child may decide that that is the preferred course, or he may rebel. It is the student's judgment, not his parents', that is essential if we are to give full meaning to what we have said about the Bill of Rights and of the right of students to be masters of their own destiny."

The Difference Between Civil Rights and Civil Liberties

Civil rights concern the basic right to be free from unequal treatment in settings such as employment, education, housing, and access to public facilities. Most civil rights laws are established through the federal government via federal legislation or case law rather than the Constitution. While we use the word "rights" more than "liberties," it should be the other way around. The Bill of Rights is a list of liberties. There are only a few rights. The government providing a lawyer is a "right" while being free from unreasonable searches or undue interference with speech or religious practice is a liberty. Liberties can be understood as freedoms from government while rights are freedoms to do or access something.

In American political culture, rights are relatively scarce. Other countries grant citizens rights to things like healthcare and education in their constitutions. Not so in the U.S. In a liberty centered political culture, the government provides the space (or liberty) for citizens to acquire these things themselves. In this view, when government leaves everyone alone equally, fairness is achieved. Where the government ends, individual responsibility and initiative begin.

Referring to the $100 race we discussed in the Introduction, there are problems with a liberty conception of freedom and equality. As we saw, people born with advantages were unequal and were unfairly close to the finish line before the sprint even began. Consider the argument that the government has a positive roll to play in recreating a fair race for each generation, especially in providing a good education and adequate healthcare. The reasoning goes, how equal or free can one be when born and raised in disadvantageous conditions? Some high school students took the idea that freedom and equality depend on the fulfillment of rights to federal court.

From the Atlantic Magazine (July 6, 2018)

What to do when a school is infested with vermin, when textbooks are outdated, when students can't even read? Perhaps the answer is sue the government.

That's what seven students in Detroit have done. Their class-action suit filed against the state of Michigan asserts that education is a basic right, and that they have been denied it.

Usually, such education-equity cases wend their way through state courts, as all 50 state constitutions mandate public-education systems, while the country's guiding document doesn't even include the word education. But this case, *Gary B. v. Snyder*, was filed in federal court, and thus seeks to invoke the Constitution. And as of this week, it's headed to the federal appeals court in Cincinnati.

The lawyers filing the suit contend that the students (who attend five of Detroit's lowest-performing schools) are receiving an education so inferior and underfunded that it's as if they're not attending school at all. The 100-page-plus complaint alleges that the state of Michigan (which has overseen Detroit's public schools for nearly two decades) is depriving these children—97 percent of whom are students of color—of their constitutional rights to liberty and nondiscrimination by denying them access to basic literacy. Almost all the students at these schools perform well below grade level in reading and writing, and, the suit argues, those skills are necessary to function properly in society. It's the first case to argue that the U.S. Constitution guarantees the right to become literate (and thus to be educated) because other rights in the Constitution necessarily require the ability to read.

Education Week Magazine reported on the outcome:

A federal district court has dismissed a legal challenge asserting that Michigan policymakers deprived Detroit students of a constitutional right to literacy. The case, *Gary B. v. Snyder*, based its claims in the U.S. Constitution rather than in state laws—the basis of most education-equity lawsuits—arguing that students in the Detroit schools were so ill-served by Michigan policymakers that their failure to learn how to read ran afoul of their due process and equal protection rights under the 14th Amendment.

While sympathizing with the students who brought the lawsuit, Judge Stephen J. Murphy III wrote that despite the well-documented problems of vermin-filled classrooms, outdated textbooks, and dysfunctional leadership in Detroit, the U.S. Constitution doesn't guarantee literacy.

"The conditions and outcomes of Plaintiffs' schools, as alleged, are nothing short of devastating. When a child who could be taught to read goes untaught, the child suffers a lasting injury—and so does society," Murphy wrote. "But the Court is faced with a discrete question: does the due process clause demand that a state affirmatively provide each child with a defined, minimum level of education by which the child can attain literacy? Based on the foregoing analysis, the answer to the question is no."

Such freedom-as-liberty judgements seem to agree with Anatole France when he recognized how "the law, in its majestic equality, forbids the rich as well as the poor to sleep under bridges, to beg in the streets and to steal bread." In its federal structure, the United States has 50 chances to decide this question for its citizens starting the race behind before they even learn to run.

Chapter 23

The Second Amendment's Right to Bear Arms

The 2nd Amendment (1791) reads as follows:

A well-regulated Militia, being necessary to the security of a free State, the right of the people, to keep and bear Arms, shall not be infringed.

The 14th Amendment (1868) reads as follows:

All persons born or naturalized in the United States and subject to the jurisdiction thereof, are citizens of the United States and of the State wherein they reside. No State shall make or enforce any law which shall abridge the privileges or immunities of citizens of the United States; nor shall any State deprive any person of life, liberty, or property, without due process of law; nor deny to any person within its jurisdiction the equal protection of the laws.

No other amendment shows us the way the meaning of the Constitution has changed more than the Second Amendment. SCOTUS and lower federal courts (and state courts for that matter) did not pay the Second Amendment much attention until 2008. In 1939 the Supreme Court affirmed that the Second Amendment was about militias and belonged to a bygone era. The Amendment was treated as if it had gone the way of the state militia.

In the past few decades, however, constitutional law has made an about-face. The purpose of a constitutional protection of gun ownership went from a militiaman's responsibility to serve in a militia to an individual's right to own a gun to protect his or her home. Heck, in Mississippi, one does not have to even be in their home to legally kill someone, due to the "stand your ground" law.

While we may skip over the histories of other provisions in the Bill of Rights, to understand the landmark cases regarding the Second Amendment, we must go through some history. For in no other area has the Supreme Court "done history" so thoroughly or with as much import as in Heller v. D.C (2008). Consequently, in McDonald v. Chicago (2010), the Supreme Court's reading of history would incorporate a private right to gun ownership against every state, offering protection to the ownership of AR-15s everywhere.

Bearing Arms in State Militias: The Second Amendment in 1791

"A well regulated Militia, being necessary to the security of a free State…"

The sacredness of state **militias** and fears of a standing army dominated discussion surrounding the passage of the Second Amendment during Congress' first session in 1791. Anti-Federalists like Brutus feared that the new over-powerful central government would use a standing army to crush local militias: "They have always proved the destruction of liberty, and are abhorrent to the spirit of a free republic…they have always been complained of as oppressive and unconstitutional" (Brutus I). Citizens under a standing army, Brutus continued, would obey their leaders out of fear while citizen soldiers serving in small-republic militias would have confidence in their rulers because the soldiers would know them and would have the power to remove them in local elections. That's right, local militias electing their own officers. In contrast, a people living in fear of their rulers can hardly be said to have a social compact with their government. To the Anti-Federalists like Brutus, a large republic would be too distant for the people to feel loyalty towards it and too powerful for the people to resist it. As such, the framers had created an American monarchy and handed the king-president a standing army to rule his subjects. Anti-Federalists had ratified the Constitution on the condition that a Bill of Rights would be added to protect the state governments. Anti-Federalists especially wanted to protect the militia system of citizen-soldiers and local control. In short, Anti-Federalist fear of a **standing army** and their desire to protect local militias is the thrust of the Second Amendment.

From the Federalist perspective, the states began to ignore and resist federal actions altogether and had nearly cost the new nation victory through their stinginess with arms and men. The breaking point came when most of the militia who were called on to put down Shays Rebellion, instead joined the violent protesters after taking a vote among themselves. It became clear to the Federalists that the nation could not be held together by local citizen militias. One-third of the 55 delegates to the Constitutional Convention had served in the national army and knew all too well the danger of relying on state militias for national purposes. As the national army had been scaled back to 700 men following the war, the Articles left its head commander a mockery of a modern army.

As early as 1776 Washington complained bitterly about the state militias he was tasked with commanding: "I am wearied to death all day with a variety of perplexing circumstances, disturbed at the conduct of the militia, whose behavior and want of discipline has done great injury to the other troops, who never had officers, except in a few instances, worth the bread they eat." Out of such frustrations, he and other Federalists formed a central government that would break its dependence on state militias once and for all.

A constitutional compromise was the result of this vast difference in opinion, a "cooperative federalism" blend of federal and state power. The compromise determined that militias would remain the primary military unit and be based on an armed citizenry, but these militias would fall under the command of the president when Congress called them into federal service. Congress would regulate or set the rules for militias, and the state militias would dutifully follow the central government's lead. Additionally, the federal government could now impose taxes to raise its own army, though the Constitution imposed a two-year limit on army funding. The Constitution provisions for a standing army in Article I's list of powers, "but no Appropriation of Money to that Use shall be for a longer Term than two Years." A two-year funding limit ensured that if the federal standing army became oppressive, voters could reject the offending incumbents in the next congressional elections in favor of new legislators who would carry out the will of the people.

A separation of military powers between the president, Congress, and the states would check the danger of a standing army. Even if the worst happened and a president led his national army against the states, the federal structure of governments would offer protection. Madison reminded Anti-Federalists that state militias would still be the basic military unit. He estimated that 30,000 federal troops would face 500,000 state militiamen in the unlikely event of a federal standing army invasion of the states. Madison added since states would appoint officers, those commanding troops would show more loyalty to their states and protect those against a tyrannical, distant federal government. Splitting the roles of state and federal governments in the military was yet another cure found in the separation of powers. And the Second Amendment was the shield that protected the state militias' ability to rebel if the federal government broke the **social contract**. The Second Amendment protected the militias' armories. Private, individual ownership of guns would not become part of the conversation until nearly a hundred years later. It simply was not a part of the discussion at the founding.

"...the right of the people to keep and bear Arms, shall not be infringed."

"Arms" were muskets in 1791, and there was no difference between the one over the fireplace and the one used in the local militia. They were single shot and, by today's standards, inaccurate. These fired one round and reloading required a multistep process which required training to do. Under the state militia systems, guns were not seen as personal possessions so much as the possessions of the local militia. Some colonies had even required that muskets be stored in a common area to protect them from rust and to keep gunpowder dry. Anyone who has used such a weapon to deer hunt can attest that the rust problem is real! Men aged 16-60 were required to have a musket. State laws mandated that all eligible men purchase muskets and train when called. The Articles of Confederation (1781) required "Every State...keep up a well-regulated and disciplined militia....and shall provide and constantly have ready for use, in public stores, a due number of field pieces and tents, and proper quantity of arms, ammunition and camp equipage."

Laws regulating gun ownership and use abounded in the states under the Articles. In Boston, it was illegal to keep a loaded gun in one's home. Most cities made it illegal to fire guns within their limits, and people deemed dangerous were barred from owning weapons. Rhode Island even had a state gun registry. To enforce registry laws, officials went house-to-house cataloging gun owners' weapons. Pennsylvania even recalled all of the guns in the state to be inspected and cleaned. The regulation of privately held firearms was a reserved power of states that allowed local governments to regulate firearm possession without question or interference from the federal government. To the Federalists and Anti-Federalists alike, such laws were not controversial. Private gun ownership, apart from militia service, was alien to the founding generation, Federalists and Anti-Federalists alike. When arguing for a Bill of Rights, Thomas Jefferson wrote Madison from Paris: "I will now add what I do not like. First the omission of a bill of rights providing" stipulations for "freedom of religion, freedom of the press, protection against standing armies...." Absent from his list was any concern over an individual right to bear arms for any purpose beyond militia service.

No citizen, until 1939's U.S. v. Miller, challenged the constitutionality of such state laws. In U.S. v. Miller, SCOTUS upheld the militia-purpose interpretation of the Second Amendment in a 9-0 vote. There was not even a dissenting opinion on the matter until SCOTUS overturned centuries of Second Amendment interpretations in Heller v. D.C. (2008).

U.S. v. Miller (1939) backgrounder from Cornell Legal Information Institute:

An Arkansas federal district court charged Jack Miller and Frank Layton with violating the National Firearms Act of 1934 ("NFA") when they transported a sawed-off double-barrel 12-gauge shotgun in interstate commerce. Miller and Layton argued that the NFA violated their Second Amendment right to keep and bear arms. The government argued against the men that the Second Amendment does not guarantee an individual the right to keep and bear a sawed-off double-barrel shotgun. The unanimous Court reasoned that because possessing a sawed-off double barrel shotgun does not have a reasonable relationship to the preservation or efficiency of a well-regulated militia, the Second Amendment does not protect the possession of such an instrument.

Second Amendment, Meet the Fourteenth!

Between the founding (1879) and the end of the Civil War (1865), the state militias system outlined in the Constitution failed the test of war. After conflicts on the high seas, Britain sent a land force to confront the U.S. and bring it to heel. That was 1812 and the war that resulted ended with the White House in ashes and the Brits leaving, satisfied that they had taught their former colonies a lesson. Before the White House burned, members of Congress saw the need for a stronger federal army. Pro-militia legislators like Daniel Webster defeated bills proposing a military draft into a standing federal army. Webster cried to fellow legislators from the floor, "Where is it written in the Constitution,...that you may take children from their parents, and parents from their children...?" The militia would remain the backbone of the nation's military and the heart of local communities for decades to come.

The Civil War (1861-1865) and Amendments 13, 14, and 15 would fundamentally change the relationship between the central and state governments and alter the meaning of the Constitution. The **14th Amendment** especially changed the meaning and application of the Constitution.

The document would no longer be about structure and principles like separation of powers. Instead, rights and liberties would come to the forefront. After the Civil War, the central government would begin to fulfill every Anti-Federalist's nightmare of a powerful national government.

The nature of militias also significantly changed after the Civil War. They were a source of chaos and even terror. Some were for self-protection. Black militias formed to fight against re-entering slavery while white militias like the KKK aimed to re-enslave them. This report is indicative of the low gauge warfare that continued in the south after the Civil War:

"On July 24, 1868, The Tennessean(newspaper) reported that a group of approximately 50 black men were found to be conducting military drills on the flat land at the bottom of St. Cloud Hill, near the Franklin Turnpike. The next day, the same group of men, who reportedly conducted a daily fatigue march at the hill, purchased a keg of gunpowder ..."

The 14th Amendment was passed in 1868 to protect the rights of newly freed slaves, keeping them armed in the face of laws--Black Codes--that forbade them to possess guns. The 14th Amendment provided "equal protection" under the law, and this was meant to include gun possession as protection against racist mobs trying to steal the North's defeat of the slave system. In doing so, the "founders" of the 14th Amendment abandoned the Anti-Federalists fears of a central army. Militias had become sources of tyranny, and only the federal government could protect minorities in the South from them. The authors of the 14th Amendment, abolitionists victorious in their cause, were not concerned with the power of a federal government trampling on state militias. After all, state militias had made up the bulk of the Southern fighting force the Northern army had defeated. The victors now sought to put firearms into the hands of former slaves so they could protect themselves from terror and re-enslavement. For the first time in its history, the 2nd Amendment was read to give a personal, individual right to bear arms apart from militia service. This interpretation would gain mainstream appeal through conservative groups like the National Riffle Association in the 1980s.

The aim of the 14th Amendment remained the same from 1868 to 1968. Senator Jacob M. Howard of Michigan introduced the proposal, explaining that the "great object" of the amendment is to "restrain the power of the states and compel them in all times to respect these great fundamental guarantees. ... Secured by the first eight amendments of the Constitution [including] the right to keep and bear arms." The 14th Amendment's protection of these fundamental rights would provide "all persons," including non-citizens, the protections listed in the Bill of Rights. That included guns. Southern Senators and a reluctant Supreme Court would delay the realization of the 14th Amendment's purpose for decades to come, selectively incorporating provisions of the Bill, one at a time. In 2018 the last of the personal liberty protections of the Bill of Rights was finally incorporated against the states (8th Amendment protection against excessive fines and bails).

Case Summaries of D.C. v. Heller (2008) and McDonald v. Chicago (2010)

DISTRICT OF COLUMBIA v. HELLER (2008)

Facts of the Case

For the first time in seventy years, the Court heard a case regarding the central meaning of the Second Amendment and its relation to gun control laws. After the District of Columbia passed legislation barring the registration of handguns, requiring licenses for all pistols, and mandating that all legal firearms must be kept unloaded and disassembled or trigger locked, a group of private gun-owners brought suit claiming the laws violated their Second Amendment right to bear arms. The federal trial court in Washington D.C. held that the Second Amendment applies only to militias, such as the National Guard, and not to private gun ownership.

The U.S. Court of Appeals for the District of Columbia Circuit disagreed, voting two to one that the Second Amendment does in fact protect private gun owners. The federal city of Washington, D.C. appealed to the Supreme Court, asking the Court to review the case in order to clearly define the relationship between federal gun control laws and the Second Amendment.

Question

Do provisions of the D.C. Code generally barring the registration of handguns, prohibiting carrying a pistol without a license, and requiring all lawful firearms to be kept unloaded and either disassembled or trigger locked violate the Second Amendment rights of individuals who are not affiliated with any state-regulated militia, but who wish to keep handguns and other firearms for private use for self-protection in their homes?

Outcome

In a 5-4 decision, the Court held that the Second Amendment protects an individual right to possess a firearm unconnected with service in a militia, and to use that firearm for traditionally lawful purposes, such as self- defense within the home. The Court based its holding on the text of the Second Amendment, as well as applicable language in state constitutions adopted soon after the Second Amendment

MCDONALD v. CHICAGO (2010)

Facts of the Case

Several suits were filed against Chicago challenging their gun bans after the Supreme Court issued its opinion in District of Columbia v. Heller. Here, plaintiffs argued that the Second Amendment should also apply to the states—that the Second Amendment should be incorporated against the states

Question

Does the Second Amendment apply to the states because it is incorporated by the Fourteenth Amendment's Due Process clause and thereby made applicable to the states?

Outcome

Incorporating the Second Amendment against the states, the Court reasoned that rights that are "fundamental to the Nation's scheme of ordered liberty" or that are "deeply rooted in this Nation's history and tradition" are appropriately applied to the states through the Fourteenth Amendment. The Court recognized in Heller that the right to self-defense was one such "fundamental" and "deeply rooted" right. The Court reasoned that because of its holding in Heller, the Second Amendment applied to the states.

The four dissenting justices argued that there is nothing in the Second Amendment's "text, history, or underlying rationale" that characterizes it as a "fundamental right" warranting incorporation through the Fourteenth Amendment. After McDonald, gun possession in America is as sacred a right as is freedom of religion, speech, or press.

Chapter 24

Incorporation of Due Process Rights

Due process rights are the crown jewels of the rule of law. If those in government try to rule by law, the legal protections guarding citizens' rights to life, liberty, and property keep them from doing so. The rule of law places everyone, even the president, under the same legal code. No one is above the law. Earlier we saw how the founders feared the president gaining king-like powers who would act above the law to "get first all the peoples' money, then all their lands, and then make them and their children servants forever," as Benjamin Franklin phrased it. To prevent this Congress included a due process provision in the Bill of Rights. Couched within the Fifth Amendment, the due process clause reads that no person shall "be deprived of life, liberty, or property, without due process of law." As we have seen, before incorporation this and all other protections and liberties offered in the Bill protected citizens from the federal government only. The authors of the 14th Amendment used the exact language of the Fifth Amendment's due process clause with the critical preface "No state shall." The combined impact of the words "No state shall" with the due process clauses, and equal protection clauses transformed the relationships between state and federal governments. The words "no state shall" reversed the role of the Bill of Rights. Before the 14th Amendment, the Bill protected state governments and their citizens from the federal government. After the 14th, the Bill protected citizens from their state governments using federal enforcement power if necessary.

Because of mainly former slave state resistance, the Bill of Rights did not apply all at once. A constitutional war commenced when the Civil War ended. One at a time, battles waged over almost every clause in the Bill. Freedom of speech became the first clause to claim a victory over state power. In 1925, Gitlow v. New York marked the first case in which the federal government intervened between a state and one of its citizens to protect individual freedom against state power. Since then, the Bill's key provisions have been "**selectively incorporated**." The latest clause to make it into the list of incorporated rights won its battle against Indiana's state power in 2019. We will begin there, on the Eighth Amendment.

Due Process and Punishments: 8th Amendment:

Bails and Fines

"Excessive bail shall not be required, nor excessive fines imposed, nor cruel and unusual punishments inflicted."

In 2019 Tyson Timbs's case resulted in the protection of all citizens from the type of excessive fine he received as part of a drug conviction.

From the Associated Press:
"Tyson Timbs made a mistake, but not one as important as Indiana's Supreme Court made in allowing to stand the punishment the state inflicted on him.
He was a drug addict — first with opioids prescribed for a work-related injury, then heroin — when his father died. He blew the $73,000 insurance payout on drugs and a $41,558 Land Rover, which he drove when selling $225 worth of drugs — two grams of heroin — to undercover police officers. Timbs's vehicle was seized and kept, which amounted to a fine more than 184 times larger than the sum involved in his offense.
The question before the Court was whether this violated the Eighth Amendment, which says: 'Excessive bail shall not be required, nor excessive fines imposed, nor cruel and unusual punishments inflicted.'
(AP-Lucrative Law Enforcement Will Become Lawless. November 28, 2018)

Timbs won his case. Once the federal government enforces a protection against state power under the 14th Amendment's "No state shall" language, the protection applies to all states and their citizens. We can all thank Tyson Timbs for the federal protection of our right against unreasonable fines if one of us ever gets into trouble.

Due Process to Life: The Death Penalty

Since 1972's Gregg v. Georgia, SCOTUS has stepped between citizens of states and the death penalty. SCOTUS judged the death penalty a cruel punishment in Gregg after seeing that it had been unequally applied to African Americans. In a reversal, SCOTUS reinstated the punishment in 1976 provided that states not use it in a discriminatory or arbitrary manner. Since then, SCOTUS has heard cases challenging states giving death sentences to minors (Roper v. Simmons, 2005) and their use of lethal injections (Glossop v. Gross, 2015). In Roper, the court outlawed those under 18 from receiving the sentence.

Protection Against Unreasonable Searches and Seizures

The Fourth Amendment:
"The right of the people to be secure in their persons, houses, papers, and effects, against unreasonable searches and seizures, shall not be violated, and no warrants shall issue, but upon probable cause, supported by oath or affirmation, and particularly describing the place to be searched, and the persons or things to be seized."

We have already examined some cases that invoked the Fourth Amendment regarding "persons, houses, and papers," such as Mapp v. Ohio. These taught us that authority figures must adhere to the 4th Amendment and perform searches only when they have a warrant. No warrant, no search. A judge will sign a warrant only if the police can show a probable cause that justifies the search. The **exclusionary rule** applies in an unwarranted search, making illegally obtained evidence inadmissible in court.

In recent years, the Fourth Amendment has been to court often. Recent SCOTUS 4th Amendment rulings:

2012: Police placing a GPS tracker on a suspect's car must get a warrant to do so.
2013: The use of drug-sniffing dogs without a warrant is a violation of the 4th Amendment.
2015: Requiring a convict to wear a GPS tracking device is an unreasonable search.
2018: The Fourth Amendment protects cell phone location information.

Due Process: The Steps the Government Must Take Upon Arrest, At Trial, and When Taking Land.

The Fifth Amendment:

"No person shall be held to answer for a capital, or otherwise infamous crime, unless on a presentment or indictment of a grand jury, except in cases arising in the land or naval forces, or in the militia, when in actual service in time of war or public danger; nor shall any person be subject for the same offense to be twice put in jeopardy of life or limb; nor shall be compelled in any criminal case to be a witness against himself, nor be deprived of life, liberty, or property, without due process of law; nor shall private property be taken for public use, without just compensation."

The Fifth Amendment has four separate due process provisions, three of which involve pre-trial criminal rights and pertain to liberty due process rights. The last part of the Fifth, the Takings Clause, concerns property rights.

DOUBLE JEOPARDY: nor shall any person be subject for the same offense to be twice put in jeopardy of life or limb;

The **double jeopardy** clause applies to those found innocent in their first trial. The government gets one chance to put the accused through the stress of a trial. However, if the accused is found guilty, more trials remain possible pending appeals and newly discovered evidence.

RIGHT AGAINST SELF-INCRIMINATION:

Nor shall be compelled in any criminal case to be a witness against himself,

"You have the right to remain silent...." and "I plead the Fifth" come from this clause that protects individuals from being forced to tell on themselves—like being put in prison until someone fesses up. Being informed of this right upon arrest was mandated after the Miranda v. Arizona (1966) decision. In that case, SCOTUS listed the due process rights of those being arrested:

"You have the right to remain silent and refuse to answer questions. Anything you say may be used against you in a court of law. You have the right to consult an attorney before speaking to the police and to have an attorney present during questioning now or in the future. If you cannot afford an attorney, one will be appointed for you before any questioning if you wish. If you decide to answer questions now without an attorney present, you will still have the right to stop answering at any time until you talk to an attorney. Knowing and understanding your rights as I have explained them to you, are you willing to answer my questions without an attorney present?"

RIGHT TO A GRAND JURY:

No person shall be held to answer for a capital, or otherwise infamous crime, unless on a presentment or indictment of a grand jury, except in cases arising in the land or naval forces, or in the militia, when in actual service in time of war or public danger.... Grand juries are usually made up of 18-23 people and are used to examine evidence and determine whether an arrest (indictment) should be made or not (acquittal). They often evaluate the evidence in complicated, technical matters.

TAKINGS CLAUSE:

Nor shall private property be taken for public use, without just compensation.

The "Takings Clause" of the 5th Amendment, also known as "**eminent domain**," prohibits the government from seizing private property unless for public use (libraries, schools, roads) and the owner is paid the market price ("just compensation"). Recent interpretations of "public use" have caused many states to pass laws better defining the purposes for which the government—state or federal--can seize privately held land.

Kelo v. City of New London, CT, asked whether the government could take private land and give it to another private person or company. In New London, a woman's house was taken so that the city council could develop her neighborhood into an economic and urban zone. They gave her land to a drug company, claiming the job creation and increased tax base met the definition of "public use." SCOTUS upheld this confiscation, stretching the concept of "public use" to lengths that seemed to enrage both sides of the ideological and political spectrum.

Due Process at Trial and Upon Arrest

The Sixth Amendment:
In all criminal prosecutions, the accused shall enjoy the right to a speedy and public trial, by an impartial jury of the state and district wherein the crime shall have been committed, which district shall have been previously ascertained by law, and to be informed of the nature and cause of the accusation; to be confronted with the witnesses against him; to have compulsory process for obtaining witnesses in his favor, and to have the assistance of counsel for his defense.

The Sixth Amendment's due process provisions:

- In all criminal prosecutions, the accused shall enjoy **the right to a speedy and public trial**

- an **impartial jury** of the state and district wherein the crime shall have been committed, which district shall have been previously ascertained by law.

In 1974, Rebecca Machetti of Georgia hired a hit man to kill her ex-husband and his new wife so that she could collect a $20,000 insurance claim. When she was taken to trial, she became the only woman on Georgia's death row—sentenced by a jury of eleven men and one woman. However, around the same time as Machetti's case, SCOTUS ruled that the provision of the 6th Amendment that states, "of the state and district" should be taken to mean that juries should represent a fair cross-section of the population of the accused's peers. Machetti claimed that eleven "Georgia good old boys" and "one bitch" who praised the death penalty during voir dire were not her peers. After years on death row, Machetti was granted a new trial with a jury that contained five women. She got a life sentence from this jury. She was released in 2010 and is now a free woman.

- To **be informed of the nature and cause of the accusation**. We find this provision included in the Miranda warning.

- to be **confronted with the witnesses against him**;

One cannot stand accused under arrest and tried without the accuser coming to court and making the charge publicly. This part of the 6th Amendment is the "look me in the eye and say I did it" provision for the accused. Without it, people could accuse one another, send them off to trial after the arrest, and stay on their couches comfortably. However, enforcing this right for those accused of domestic or sexual abuse proves difficult as the witnesses in such cases are often traumatized and unable to face an abuser or rapist.

- To have **compulsory process for obtaining witnesses** in his favor...

A subpoena will be issued for witnesses the accused wishes to use at trial. They have to come.

- To have the **assistance of counsel** for his defense.

Gideon v. Wainwright (1962)

Consider the case of Clarence Earl Gideon. He was an unlikely hero. Gideon was a man with an eighth-grade education who ran away from home when he was in middle school. He spent much of his early adult life in and out of prisons for petty crimes. Charged with breaking and entering into the Bay Harbor Pool Room, a bar Gideon frequented, he faced up to five years in prison under Florida law. At trial, Gideon appeared in court without an attorney. In open court, he asked the judge to appoint counsel for him because he could not afford an attorney. The trial judge denied Gideon's request because Florida law only permitted the appointment of counsel for defendants charged with capital offenses who could not afford lawyers.

At trial, Gideon represented himself. Despite his efforts, the jury found Gideon guilty. The state court of Florida sentenced him to five years imprisonment.

Gideon filed a handwritten appeal (a **writ of certiorari**) in the Supreme Court of the United States. The Court agreed to hear the case to resolve the question of whether the right to counsel guaranteed under the Sixth Amendment of the Constitution applies to defendants in state court.

Before being incorporated, Florida paid for defense lawyers sparingly—only in capital cases. The uneducated, illiterate, and poor had to defend themselves. Clarence Earl Gideon challenged that practice from a prison cell. Written in pencil on a notebook sheet of paper, he applied for a writ of cert, and the rest became part of SCOTUS history. Because of *Gideon v. Wainwright* (1962 everyone who cannot afford counsel—a lawyer--is entitled to one for free, even for the smallest of crimes.

PRIVACY RIGHTS: Roe v. Wade (1972)

We cannot leave our discussion of liberty rights without addressing privacy. It is a "right" we all feel that we have, but it makes no appearance in the Constitution.
The discussion of privacy rights in America began with a birth control case in 1965. Until that year, birth control was illegal in Connecticut. Well, it was illegal to use but not to buy. Figure that one out! Griswold, a birth control advocate, arranged for herself to be arrested so she could take part in a test case.

Griswold v. Connecticut (1965)

In *Griswold v. Connecticut* (1965) SCOTUS ruled that the "penumbra" of the Bill of Rights included privacy rights. That is, it is in the shadows of the other amendments, namely the First, Third, Fourth, and Fifth Amendments. The Court pointed to various indirect references to the protection of privacy in each amendment, especially the First and Fourth Amendments. SCOTUS declared privacy was a right held by each citizen that state governments could not violate because of the due processes liberty protections of the 14th Amendment. In this case, birth control was a matter of a woman's privacy. For the first time, the Ninth Amendment got a shout-out from the Court. The Ninth was where the Anti-Federalists addressed the Federalist argument that a list of rights could be used against individuals like

Griswold. Privacy is not listed, so a judge could deny the existence of the right when going by a list. The Ninth Amendment makes it clear that not all rights are listed. Some, it says, are un-enumerated like the right to privacy.

The right to privacy, as defined in Griswold, has been used in several controversial cases since. The most notable *is Roe v. Wade* (1973), in which abortion was legalized for the sake of a woman's right to privacy. A woman's decision to abort a pregnancy, the Court reasoned, is too personal and technical for a single ruling or law to regulate. The Roe ruling left the decision to abort between a woman and her doctor. It barred states from making blanket laws outlawing the practice. States and the federal courts have been in perennial conflict ever since the Roe ruling. As recently as November 2018, the state with the most restrictive laws, Mississippi, had a law invalidated by the 14th Amendment's due process right to liberty a federal district court.

From CNN, November 21, 2018:

A federal judge blocked a Mississippi state law that sought to forbid most abortions after 15 weeks of pregnancy, writing a sharply worded opinion with implications for states weighing similar measures.

Gov. Phil Bryant signed H.B. 1510, also known as the Gestational Age Act, in March, pledging his "commitment to making Mississippi the safest place in America for an unborn child."

The law made exceptions only for medical emergencies or cases in which there's a "severe fetal abnormality." There were no exceptions for incidents of rape or incest.

The next day, the sole facility providing abortion services in Mississippi sued to prevent the law from taking effect, setting off months of legal challenges culminating in the district court's ruling. US District Judge Carlton Reeves of Mississippi's Southern District, who was appointed by President Obama, wrote that the law "unequivocally" infringes upon a woman's 14th Amendment due process rights and defies Supreme Court precedents.

Most rights Americans hold dear are due process rights, thanks to the Fourteenth Amendment. As most protections in the Bill now apply against the states as well as the Federal government, conflicts abound. Freedom of speech and religious liberties exist within the tense federal system of multiple governments presiding over the same land and people. One current battle is between state majorities who want the religious freedom to deny services to legally married couples.

Gay marriage became a nationally legal 14th Amendment right in 2015 Obergefell v. Hodges. Here the Court held that the Due Process Clause of the Fourteenth Amendment guarantees the right to marry as one of the fundamental due process rights protected by the Constitution. The exclusion of same-sex couples from the right to marry violates the Due Process Clause of the Fourteenth Amendment and the Equal Protection Clause of the Fourteenth Amendment. Same-sex couples now have the right to marry on the same terms as those of opposite-sex couples.

In dissent of the 5-4 ruling, the minority argued that the Constitution does not address it, and therefore it is a reserved power of the states and up to them to recognize or license such unions. Thus, such an issue should be left to state legislatures based on the will of their voting majorities.

Whereas the federal government protects the rights of the minority of gay couples within states like Mississippi, states have advocated for a different set of individual rights. States like Mississippi have large conservative Christian voting blocs that seek the protection of their religious freedom not to recognize gay marriage as legitimate.

In response to voting majorities, the Mississippi legislature passed a law that affirmed the rights of those who believe marriage is between a man and a woman, and that an individual's gender is determined at birth.

The state law protects organizations or people that make decisions based on moral and religious beliefs about sexuality. Among the decisions covered are hiring, adoption or foster care, provision of gender reassignment health care, and providing personal services such as baking or photography. If a photographer thinks gay marriage is a sin, she can decline to take family portraits of same-sex families. Bakers can deny them their services, and so on. Without state law, the 14th Amendment's Equal Protection clause would usually bar such actions. Eventually, federal courts will have the last say as long as the Constitution remains "the Supreme law of the land."

CONCLUSION

The founders defined freedom as liberty from government control. The Bill of Rights should be called "The Bill of Liberties." Its provisions keep the government at a safe distance. Apart from government, individuals are supposed to pursue their selfish goals. In doing so, they will naturally form groups, or factions, with others seeking the same goals. In groups, a plurality of interests will compete for dominance. Madison recognized that factions were a matter of free speech and were bound to exist in a free country. Yet, their nature would use that freedom to limit that of others.

The art of Madison's system was to create a government that could not be held by one interest without another checking its power through a separate institution or level of government. **Keynesians**, **liberals**, **conservatives**, and **classical economists** like F.A. Hayek endorse this view. On one end of the belief in limited government, the classical economist would say there is something to be said for the idea of the survival of the fittest. Even education, healthcare, and clean water are goods that reasonable people will want. The government's role is not to ensure such things, making them "rights." If people want these things, they will provide and purchase these goods and services from one another. The government's role is to give people the liberty to do so without burdening them with many laws and heavy taxes. To the "small government" minded, individuals will provide such goods to one another in a free market unfettered by government control. If a group is hungry in a city, good people will provide soup kitchens and food pantries. More importantly, the hungry people will be pushed by their hunger to find a way to provide a good or service for which others will pay. "Necessity is the mother of all invention," they say. This view rests on faith that individuals have enough information and goodwill to make right decisions and that, having good information, they will act accordingly. It presupposes that individuals know what their interests are and will actively pursue them. Critics like Walter Lippman have mocked this view, and current behavioral economists debunk it. Nevertheless, this vision of America as a collection of self-reliant communities goes back to Jefferson's imagining of America in 1776. With dirt on their hands cleaned with homemade soap and water from the well, citizens would operate democratically in local governments. The larger the sphere of government, the less democratic it became and the more sinister it seemed.

If this picture of agrarian communities running their local affairs was ever accurate, it is a distant reality now. Only 2% of Americans work on farms. Today's "farmers" are employees of one of a handful of global agriculture conglomerates. Instead of following the "laws of nature," modern food producers have fought against and molded natural processes through genetic modification and chemical enhancement of every agricultural product. Indeed, without scientific victories over nature since the founding, the global population would be a fraction of what it is today. Modern agriculture is one of thousands of technical systems no single individual or group can grasp. Yet citizens are called upon to vote on policies ranging from healthcare systems and economic plans to foreign policy concerns with nations most of us could not place on a map. Voters must discern whether or not genetically modified crops are a blessing or a curse while considering the question of whether vaccines cause autism. As we noted in the Media chapter, the gulf between the world we know and the complex realities beyond our small spheres of experience is vast. That the average voter might be expected to "be an informed citizen" on such a range of topics for which the mass media is his source of information circles us back to the oldest question about democracy. Is the average citizen of a society the right person to be making the decisions about who should be making the decisions for that society? From Plato to the framers, the answer was an obvious "No." Anti-Federalists like Brutus answered, "Yes," as long as those decisions were made in small republics on mostly local issues. Living in a globalized world, the food we eat travels an average of 2,000 miles from its sources to our forks. Geography lessons can be taught from the "Made in..." tags on our clothing. Bodies of experts in every imaginable field have conflicting views among themselves. No issue, and barely any item we consume, is purely local or simple.

The average citizen imagines that he learns about such a world through the media. However, our sources of information have goals that run counter to informing the electorate. Media must grab the attention of the consumer and make money while conveying "news." If news consumers do not seek out information that challenges what they think they know, their biases will be confirmed within echo chambers in which tailor-made information suits their preconceived notions.

Such an outlook dooms the student to a pessimistic view of democracy. It paints a picture of democracy as nothing more than occasional elections in which voters are herded into voting blocs by information technocrats doing the work of the highest bidders.

Democracy is Social, Not Only Political

A more hopeful view, and the one shared by your author, is that democracy is more than a mechanical system of electing leaders through majorities of "informed citizens." In addition to our occasional vote, we are members of a free society, not only a political party or special interest faction. In this view, "democracy" is a set of values and a way of interacting with others and within groups that is more of a relationship than a transaction or conflict between self-interested parties. Cut-throat competing interests are not the basic model of social interactions like a theory of factions would have you imagine. In a social view of democracy, a view of democracy that happens more in society and less in governments, social connections and cooperation rather than political affiliations and conflicting interests become the context in which a common good is achieved. Such a society's members value democratic ideals like inclusion of varied perspectives, debate, deliberation, and reflection. Such a view departs from the win-at-all-cost ethos of special interests and political parties.

A democratic personality becomes unconfined by echo chambers and lazy of habits of thought that stem from her socialization, not her free choices. She resents those who would manipulate her emotions and determines to educate herself to guard against those who would prey on her weakest impulses. As Henry David Theroux advised, she intends to live a deliberate life based on ideals and intelligence. She understands that the enemy lies within, not in boogeymen about whom she learns from those who want her money, her vote, and then her silence.

Sure, there are too many facts for any one person or group to grasp. Instead of grasping for certainty, the democratic character seeks better and better questions in the face of practical problems. An experimental attitude rejects filtering things through ideologies that answer all questions but ask none. One who holds democracy dear resists that tendency of the powerful to impose their false certainties on themselves or others.

In a democracy that is more than a voting system with interest groups fighting for what they want, citizens consciously play a role in creating the social conditions that lead to the freedom of others as well as their own. They do not delegate that freedom to the central government. This vision does not require voting, a protest movement, or a digital media campaign. A democratic mindset can be fostered wherever one finds himself. Classrooms can be democratic. In these, teachers encourage students to reflect on their historical context and identify the range of choices that were before previous generations and those currently before them. Students are given questions and problems instead of "objective facts" and answers to closed questions. Students are encouraged to deliberate with one another, question the teacher's conclusions, and debate various points of view. Language and information are accorded value. Imprecision and oversimplification do not stand. Listeners reject emotional appeals but respond when a fact is made self-evident. Voting need not happen, but an open exchange of ideas does.

An appreciation of the complexity embedded in every issue requires consideration of multiple points of view through discussion as well as fact gathering. Teachers, then, have a larger role than imparting facts; they must facilitate the expression of various perspectives and aid students in judging the validity of arguments and claims. Public classrooms especially can be incubators of democracy where students first grasp that what they think they know about the world is limited to their experience and if they rely solely on their perceptions, they will be misled. In contrast to a good teacher, partisan faction operatives will assure their audience that they are normal, that the "other" is bad, that their side is fighting the good fight and that they are the "real America." Those who think truth is simple and can be received instead of earned become more and more certain of the righteousness of their cause.

Algorithms and news channels give them the "news" they want to hear, confirming their every bias. They fail to sense the daily insults to their intelligence and their tragic departure from democratic values as they allow distant personalities behind cameras to demonize their neighbors and coworkers. A thoughtful classroom might foster a counter-attitude that sees difference as good and complication as the norm.

Democracy is Our Responsibility

So, what to do? Join groups—personal and professional--preferably with those who come from different backgrounds and have different ideas. Hold yourself and your group to democratic standards of fairness, transparency, and equal regard to the value of each member. Every group has a government, hierarchy, or ruling class. Take a sports team, for instance. What does "All men are created equal look like" there? Surely not everyone has equal talent? Surely players do not vote on who starts and in what positions. The coach is in charge and everyone else passively receives his instruction. Right? Not if you apply democratic values like fulfilling one's potential (a legitimate interpretation of "the pursuit of happiness") and striving for a common good over individual success. One holding democratic values will ask questions like, do the best players ball hog and blame others or find ways to be useful in helping others improve? Do coaches threaten and punish when they could listen and persuade? Do players reflect on their mistakes and work to improve? Are habits like hard work and smart play valued over winning at all costs? Do those who sit on the bench go 100% at practice to help the starters get up to game speed? Do players and coaches have a spirit of experimentation as they seek to improve? Is being on a team a way each individual can focus on their individual greatness? Is a game the time to showcase this greatness? Most great coaches create democratic habits among their players. They value them as individuals, not part of the equipment they need for a winning season. If the best players fail to make those around them better, their teams rarely succeed.

While coaches should not go overboard with discussion and debate, other social groups are perfectly suited for them. Churches, classrooms, and even workplaces can be small democratic communities. Between elections is when true democracy happens

Vote. Run for office. Join a political party. Most importantly, act on democratic values like being fair and humble, understanding that no one has possession of the whole truth and that, even if he did, having full power to act on it would still be disastrous. If there is democratic behavior in local communities, at school and in workplaces, an authoritarian government cannot possibly take root in such soil. Madison's system works. On the local level, citizens are able to participate democratically in their local communities while they send delegates to the higher offices of government. In a democratic society each and every person is unique and thus brings a unique perspective to the problems society is facing. Any and all good ideas are welcome. In such a political culture, why would citizens elect a panel of oligarchs or a single dictator? However, for this to work we must do as much as we can to ensure that people are not only as educated as possible, but also are taught how to think critically and adapt with changing environments. True democracy is not people just voting for what they want. It is especially not special interest groups vying for influence and the power to write the rules in their favor. True democracy should allow every citizen within it to realize their full potential, to achieve happiness. Each time someone reaches his or her potential, the nation is made better because of it. Helping others reach theirs is the highest civic duty.

Sure, certain people are going to demonize others and simplify complex problems, even reducing them to conspiracies. These examples should cause us to re-up on our commitment to gain the skills to avoid the traps of simplified thinking. As America's current citizens, we have the same problems as the founding generation. We still puzzle over how to remain free under a government so powerful and whether the average group of citizens can appoint excellent leaders. And when voters get it wrong and elect bad people, we still have to wonder if our government's structure is strong enough to resist them? How many bad choices can voters make before democracy ends and tyranny begins? We serve our country well to remember that democracy and tyranny begin in the home, the school, and the workplace. A society of individuals who join groups and value democratic ideals will not stand for injustice and tyranny when it comes from the federal government. However, a society of atomized individuals, heads down in their cell phones' news feeds, allowing news personalities, forwarded snatches of opinions, and memes to shape their view of reality will have no defense when tyranny comes to town. Fairness, justice, and equality are values that people, not governments, best embody. James Madison and the framers did their job in creating a government that is guarded against selfish, short-sighted actors. However, the government does not protect us from demagoguery. It falls to each of us to become men and women who likewise cannot be swayed by the designs of the selfish and ambitious. If we live by democratic principles, the policies that our elected delegates enact will rest on them. Finally, in our pursuit these ideals we may share in Rabandranath Tagore's realization:

I slept and dreamt that life was joy. I awoke and saw that life was service. I acted and behold, service was joy.

Bibliography

Introduction

The Great Upheaval by Jay Wink

Madison's Notes at the Constitutional Convention by James Madison

Freedom's Power by Paul Starr

All Out War: The Story of Brexit by Tim Shipman

It's Even Worse Than It Looks by Thomas E. Mann and Norman J. Ornstein

What's the Matter with Kansas by Thomas Frank

The Declaration of Independence: A Revolutionary Beginning

Original Meanings by Jack Rakove

Jefferson's Pillow by Roger W. Wilkins

The American Soul: Rediscovering the Wisdom of the Founders by Jacob Needleman

The American Revolution by Gordon Wood

The Creation of the American Republic by Gordon Wood

The Radicalism of the American Revolution by Gordon Wood

Media

Amusing Ourselves to Death by Neil Postman

Lies, Incorporated by Ari Rabin-Havt

Public Opinion by Walter Lippman

How Democracies Die by Steven Levitsky and Daniel Ziblatt

The Future of Freedom: Illiberal Democracy at Home and Abroad by Fareed Zakaria

The Technological Society by Jacques Ellul

Autonomous Technology by Landon Winner

The Making of the President 1968 by Theodore White

Shaping Public Opinion

Public Opinion by Walter Lippman

How Democracies Die by Steven Levitsky and Daniel Ziblatt

Lies, Incorporated by Ari Rabin-Havt

The Future of Freedom: Illiberal Democracy at Home and Abroad by Fareed Zakaria

The Technological Society by Jacques Ellul

Autonomous Technology by Landon Winner

Making One Nation Out of Independent States

Novus Ordo Seclorum by Forrest McDonald

Original Meanings by Jack Rakove

The Crisis of the Middle-Class Constitution by Ganesh Sitaraman

The Constitution: A Biography by Akhil Reed Amar

The Great Debate: Anti-Federalists vs. Federalists

Origins of the Bill of Rights by Leonard W. Levy

The Great Upheaval by Jay Wink

Founding Brothers by Joseph J. Ellis

A People's History of the Supreme Court by Peter Irons

Federalist 10

Federalist 51

Brutus I

The Constitution: A Network of Compromises

Creating the Constitution by Thorton Anderson

Madison's Notes at the Constitutional Convention by James Madison

The Constitution Today by Akhil Reed Amar

America's Constitution by Akhil Reed Amar

The Creation of the American Republic by Gordon S. Wood

Origins of the Bill of Rights by Leonard Levy

Original Meanings by Jack N. Rakove

Federalism: The Power Flow Between Federal and State Governments

Uncertain Justice by Laurence Tribe and Joshua Matz

A People's History of the Supreme Court by Peter Irons

The Constitution Today by Akhil Reed Amar

A People's History of the Supreme Court by Peter Irons

Original Meanings by Jack N. Rakove

The Fractured Republic by Yuval Levin

Federalist Papers 10 and 51

Congressional Elections

It's Even Worse Than It Looks by Thomas E. Mann and Norman J. Ornstein

America's Unwritten Constitution by Akhil Reed Amar

The Fractured Republic by Yuval Levin

Gaming the Vote by William Poundstone

Madison's Notes at the Constitutional Convention by James Madison

Legislative Branch Structure

Original Meanings by Jack Rakove

Notes on the Constitutional Convention by James Madison

Creating the Constitution by Thorton Anderson

Madison's Notes at the Constitutional Convention by James Madison

Federalist Papers 10 and 51

Brutus I

Legislative Brach Function

Act of Congress by Robert G. Kaiser

Original Meanings by Jack Rakove

Notes on the Constitutional Convention by James Madison

It's Even Worse Than It Looks by Thomas E. Mann and Norman J. Ornstein

Federalist Papers 10 and 51

Brutus I

The Executive Branch

White House Burning by Simon Johnson and James Kwak

Mr. President: How and Why the Founders Created a Chief Executive by Ray Raphael

Creating the Constitution by Thorton Anderson

Federalist Paper 70

Brutus I

Electing the President

Gaming the Vote by William Poundstone

The Constitution Today by Akhil Reed Amar

Madison's Notes at the Constitutional Convention by James Madison

The Bureaucracy

The Fifth Risk by Michael Lewis

The President and Congress Make the Federal Budget

Keynes Hayek: The Clash That Defined Modern Economics

White House Burning by Simon Johnson and James Kwak

America's Constitution: A Biography by Akhil Reed Amar

Federalist Paper 78

Judicial Branch

Uncertain Justice by Laurence Tribe and Joshua Matz

The Constitution Today by Akhil Reed Amar

A People's History of the Supreme Court Peter Irons

Madison's Notes at the Constitutional Convention by James Madison

Federalist Paper 78

Special Interests

Act of Congress: How America's Essential Institution Works, and How It Doesn't by Robert G. Kaiser

The Second Civil War: How Extreme Partisanship Has Paralyzed Washington and Polarized America by Ronald Brownstein

It's Even Worse Than It Looks by Thomas E. Mann and Norman J. Ornstein

https://www.washingtonpost.com/news/wonk/wp/2017/04/14/somebody-just-put-a-price-tag-on-the-2016-election-its-a-doozy/?utm_term=.a91f8c6fc890

https://www.theatlantic.com/politics/archive/2018/05/lobbying-the-job-of-choice-for-retired-members-of-congress/558851/

Baptists, Bootleggers & Electronic Cigarettes by Jonathan H. Adler

Political Parties

Parties and Elections in America by Sandy Maisel and Kara Buckley

The Future of Freedom by Fareed Zakaria

The Fractured Republic by Yuval Levin

Keynes Hayek by Nicholas Wapshott

Freedom's Power by Paul Starr

The American Soul: Rediscovering the Wisdom of the Founders by Jacob Needleman

Federalist Papers 10 and 51

How Political Parties Choose Candidates: Primaries and Caucuses

Parties and Elections in America by Sandy Maisel and Kara Buckley

The Future of Freedom by Fareed Zakaria

The Fractured Republic by Yuval Levin

Give Us the Ballot by Ari Berman

Voters and Voter Turnout

The Crisis of the Middle Class Constitution by Ganesh Sitaraman

Give Us The Ballot by Ari Berman

Gaming the Vote by William Poundstone

Incorporation of the Bill of Rights Through the Fourteenth Amendment

The Constitution Today by Akhil Reed Amar

A People's History of the Supreme Court Peter Irons

The Origins of the Bill of Rights by Leonard Levy

Student Rights of Speech, Press, and Religion Clauses of the First Amendment

The Constitution Today by Akhil Reed Amar

A People's History of the Supreme Court Peter Irons

Origins of the Bill of Rights by Leonard Levy

Give Us the Ballot by Ari Berman

The Second Amendment's Right to Bear Arms

The Second Amendment: A Biography by Michael Waldman

The American Revolution by Gordon S. Wood

The Constitution Today by Akhil Reed Amar

The Bill of Rights by Akhil Reed Amar

The Great Upheaval by Jay Wink

A People's History of the Supreme Court by Peter Irons

Origins of the Bill of Rights by Leonard Levy

Uncertain Justice by Laurence Tribe and Joshua Matz

Incorporation of Due Process Rights

The Constitution Today by Akhil Reed Amar

A People's History of the Supreme Court Peter Irons

Origins of the Bill of Rights by Leonard Levy

Gideon's Trumpet by Anthony Lewis

The Bill of Rights by Akhil Reed Amar

Conclusion

Public Opinion by Walter Lippman

The Public and Its Problems by John Dewey

The Ethics of Ambiguity by Simone De Beauvoir

The Rebel by Albert Camus

Freedom's Power by Paul Starr

The Human Condition by Hannah Arendt

The Concept of the Political by Carl Schmitt

APPENDIX

Declaration of Independence

In Congress, July 4, 1776.

The unanimous Declaration of the thirteen united States of America,
When in the Course of human events, it becomes necessary for one people to dissolve the political bands which have connected them with another, and to assume among the powers of the earth, the separate and equal station to which the Laws of Nature and of Nature's God entitle them, a decent respect to the opinions of mankind requires that they should declare the causes which impel them to the separation.

We hold these truths to be self-evident, that all men are created equal, that they are endowed by their Creator with certain unalienable Rights, that among these are Life, Liberty and the pursuit of Happiness.--That to secure these rights, Governments are instituted among Men, deriving their just powers from the consent of the governed, --That whenever any Form of Government becomes destructive of these ends, it is the Right of the People to alter or to abolish it, and to institute new Government, laying its foundation on such principles and organizing its powers in such form, as to them shall seem most likely to effect their Safety and Happiness. Prudence, indeed, will dictate that Governments long established should not be changed for light and transient causes; and accordingly all experience hath shewn, that mankind are more disposed to suffer, while evils are sufferable, than to right themselves by abolishing the forms to which they are accustomed. But when a long train of abuses and usurpations, pursuing invariably the same Object evinces a design to reduce them under absolute Despotism, it is their right, it is their duty, to throw off such Government, and to provide new Guards for their future security.--Such has been the patient sufferance of these Colonies; and such is now the necessity which constrains them to alter their former Systems of Government. The history of the present King of Great Britain is a history of repeated injuries and usurpations, all having in direct object the establishment of an absolute Tyranny over these States. To prove this, let Facts be submitted to a candid world.

He has refused his Assent to Laws, the most wholesome and necessary for the public good.

He has forbidden his Governors to pass Laws of immediate and pressing importance, unless suspended in their operation till his Assent should be obtained; and when so suspended, he has utterly neglected to attend to them.

He has refused to pass other Laws for the accommodation of large districts of people, unless those people would relinquish the right of Representation in the Legislature, a right inestimable to them and formidable to tyrants only.

He has called together legislative bodies at places unusual, uncomfortable, and distant from the depository of their public Records, for the sole purpose of fatiguing them into compliance with his measures.

He has dissolved Representative Houses repeatedly, for opposing with manly firmness his invasions on the rights of the people.

He has refused for a long time, after such dissolutions, to cause others to be elected; whereby the Legislative powers, incapable of Annihilation, have returned to the People at large for their exercise; the State remaining in the mean time exposed to all the dangers of invasion from without, and convulsions within.

He has endeavoured to prevent the population of these States; for that purpose obstructing the Laws for Naturalization of Foreigners; refusing to pass others to encourage their migrations hither, and raising the conditions of new Appropriations of Lands.

He has obstructed the Administration of Justice, by refusing his Assent to Laws for establishing Judiciary powers.

He has made Judges dependent on his Will alone, for the tenure of their offices, and the amount and payment of their salaries.

He has erected a multitude of New Offices, and sent hither swarms of Officers to harrass our people, and eat out their substance.

He has kept among us, in times of peace, Standing Armies without the Consent of our legislatures.

He has affected to render the Military independent of and superior to the Civil power.

He has combined with others to subject us to a jurisdiction foreign to our constitution, and unacknowledged by our laws; giving his Assent to their Acts of pretended Legislation:

For Quartering large bodies of armed troops among us:

For protecting them, by a mock Trial, from punishment for any Murders which they should commit on the Inhabitants of these States:

For cutting off our Trade with all parts of the world:

For imposing Taxes on us without our Consent:

For depriving us in many cases, of the benefits of Trial by Jury:

For transporting us beyond Seas to be tried for pretended offences

For abolishing the free System of English Laws in a neighbouring Province, establishing therein an Arbitrary government, and enlarging its Boundaries so as to render it at once an example and fit instrument for introducing the same absolute rule into these Colonies:

For taking away our Charters, abolishing our most valuable Laws, and altering fundamentally the Forms of our Governments:

For suspending our own Legislatures, and declaring themselves invested with power to legislate for us in all cases whatsoever.

He has abdicated Government here, by declaring us out of his Protection and waging War against us.

He has plundered our seas, ravaged our Coasts, burnt our towns, and destroyed the lives of our people.

He is at this time transporting large Armies of foreign Mercenaries to compleat the works of death, desolation and tyranny, already begun with circumstances of Cruelty & perfidy scarcely paralleled in the most barbarous ages, and totally unworthy the Head of a civilized nation.

He has constrained our fellow Citizens taken Captive on the high Seas to bear Arms against their Country, to become the executioners of their friends and Brethren, or to fall themselves by their Hands.

He has excited domestic insurrections amongst us, and has endeavoured to bring on the inhabitants of our frontiers, the merciless Indian Savages, whose known rule of warfare, is an undistinguished destruction of all ages, sexes and conditions.

In every stage of these Oppressions We have Petitioned for Redress in the most humble terms: Our repeated Petitions have been answered only by repeated injury. A Prince whose character is thus marked by every act which may define a Tyrant, is unfit to be the ruler of a free people.

Nor have We been wanting in attentions to our Brittish brethren. We have warned them from time to time of attempts by their legislature to extend an unwarrantable jurisdiction over us. We have reminded them of the circumstances of our emigration and settlement here. We have appealed to their native justice and magnanimity, and we have conjured them by the ties of our common kindred to disavow these usurpations, which, would inevitably interrupt our connections and correspondence. They too have been deaf to the voice of justice and of consanguinity. We must, therefore, acquiesce in the necessity, which denounces our Separation, and hold them, as we hold the rest of mankind, Enemies in War, in Peace Friends.

We, therefore, the Representatives of the united States of America, in General Congress, Assembled, appealing to the Supreme Judge of the world for the rectitude of our intentions, do, in the Name, and by Authority of the good People of these Colonies, solemnly publish and declare, That these United Colonies are, and of Right ought to be Free and Independent States; that they are Absolved from all Allegiance to the British Crown, and that all political connection between them and the State of Great Britain, is and ought to be totally dissolved; and that as Free and Independent States, they have full Power to levy War, conclude Peace, contract Alliances, establish Commerce, and to do all other Acts and Things which Independent States may of right do. And for the support of this Declaration, with a firm reliance on the protection of divine Providence, we mutually pledge to each other our Lives, our Fortunes and our sacred Honor.

Articles of Confederation

The Articles of Confederation and Perpetual Union — 1777

To all to whom these Presents shall come, we the undersigned Delegates of the States affixed to our Names, send greeting.

Whereas the Delegates of the United States of America, in Congress assembled, did, on the 15th day of November, in the Year of Our Lord One thousand Seven Hundred and Seventy seven, and in the Second Year of the Independence of America, agree to certain articles of Confederation and perpetual Union between the States of New-hampshire, Massachusetts-bay, Rhodeisland and Providence Plantations, Connecticut, New York, New Jersey, Pennsylvania, Delaware, Maryland, Virginia, North-Carolina, South-Carolina, and Georgia in the words following, viz. "Articles of Confederation and perpetual Union between the states of New-hampshire, Massachusetts-bay, Rhodeisland and Providence Plantations, Connecticut, New-York, New-Jersey, Pennsylvania, Delaware, Maryland, Virginia, North-Carolina, South-Carolina and Georgia".

Article I.

The Stile of this confederacy shall be "The United States of America."

Article II.

Each state retains its sovereignty, freedom, and independence, and every Power, Jurisdiction and right, which is not by this confederation expressly delegated to the United States, in Congress assembled.

Article III.

The said states hereby severally enter into a firm league of friendship with each other, for their common defence, the security of their Liberties, and their mutual and general welfare, binding themselves to assist each other, against all force offered to, or attacks made upon them, or any of them, on account of religion, sovereignty, trade, or any other pretence whatever.

Article IV.

The better to secure and perpetuate mutual friendship and intercourse among the people of the different states in this union, the free inhabitants of each of these states, paupers, vagabonds and fugitives from justice excepted, shall be entitled to all privileges and immunities of free citizens in the several states; and the people of each state shall have free ingress and regress to and from any other state, and shall enjoy therein all the privileges of trade and commerce, subject to the same duties impositions and restrictions as the inhabitants thereof respectively, provided that such restriction shall not extend so far as to prevent the removal of property imported into any state, to any other state, of which the Owner is an inhabitant; provided also that no imposition, duties or restriction shall be laid by any state, on the property of the united states, or either of them. If any Person guilty of, or charged with treason, felony, — or other high misdemeanor in any state, shall flee from Justice, and be found in any of the united states, he shall, upon demand of the Governor or executive power, of the state from which he fled, be delivered up and removed to the state having jurisdiction of his offence. Full faith and credit shall be given in each of these states to the records, acts and judicial proceedings of the courts and magistrates of every other state.

Article V.

For the more convenient management of the general interests of the united states, delegates shall be annually appointed in such manner as the legislature of each state shall direct, to meet in Congress on the first Monday in November, in every year, with a power reserved to each state, to recal its delegates, or any of them, at any time within the year, and to send others in their stead, for the remainder of the Year.

No state shall be represented in Congress by less than two, nor by more than seven Members; and no person shall be capable of being a delegate for more than three years in any term of six years; nor shall any person, being a delegate, be capable of holding any office under the united states, for which he, or another for his benefit receives any salary, fees or emolument of any kind.

Each state shall maintain its own delegates in a meeting of the states, and while they act as members of the committee of the states. In determining questions in the united states in Congress assembled, each state shall have one vote.

Freedom of speech and debate in Congress shall not be impeached or questioned in any Court, or place out of Congress, and the members of congress shall be protected in their persons from arrests and imprisonments, during the time of their going to and from, and attendance on congress, except for treason, felony, or breach of the peace.

Article VI.

No state, without the Consent of the united states in congress assembled, shall send any embassy to, or receive any embassy from, or enter into any conference agreement, alliance or treaty with any King prince or state; nor shall any person holding any office of profit or trust under the united states, or any of them, accept of any present, emolument, office or title of any kind whatever from any king, prince or foreign state; nor shall the united states in congress assembled, or any of them, grant any title of nobility.

No two or more states shall enter into any treaty, confederation or alliance whatever between them, without the consent of the united states in congress assembled, specifying accurately the purposes for which the same is to be entered into, and how long it shall continue.

No state shall lay any imposts or duties, which may interfere with any stipulations in treaties, entered into by the united states in congress assembled, with any king, prince or state, in pursuance of any treaties already proposed by congress, to the courts of France and Spain.

No vessels of war shall be kept up in time of peace by any state, except such number only, as shall be deemed necessary by the united states in congress assembled, for the defence of such state, or its trade; nor shall any body of forces be kept up by any state, in time of peace, except such number only, as in the judgment of the united states, in congress assembled, shall be deemed requisite to garrison the forts necessary for the defence of such state; but every state shall always keep up a well regulated and disciplined militia, sufficiently armed and accoutered, and shall provide and constantly have ready for use, in public stores, a due number of field pieces and tents, and a proper quantity of arms, ammunition and camp equipage. No state shall engage in any war without the consent of the united states in congress assembled, unless such state be actually invaded by enemies, or shall have received certain advice of a resolution being formed by some nation of Indians to invade such state, and the danger is so imminent as not to admit of a delay till the united states in congress assembled can be consulted: nor shall any state grant commissions to any ships or vessels of war, nor letters of marque or reprisal, except it be after a declaration of war by the united states in congress assembled, and then only against the kingdom or state and the subjects thereof, against which war has been so declared, and under such regulations as shall be established by the united states in congress assembled, unless such state be infested by pirates, in which case vessels of war may be fitted out for that occasion, and kept so long as the danger shall continue, or until the united states in congress assembled, shall determine otherwise.

Article VII.
When land-forces are raised by any state for the common defence, all officers of or under the rank of colonel, shall be appointed by the legislature of each state respectively, by whom such forces shall be raised, or in such manner as such state shall direct, and all vacancies shall be filled up by the State which first made the appointment.

Article VIII.
All charges of war, and all other expences that shall be incurred for the common defence or general welfare, and allowed by the united states in congress assembled, shall be defrayed out of a common treasury, which shall be supplied by the several states in proportion to the value of all land within each state, granted to or surveyed for any Person, as such land and the buildings and improvements thereon shall be estimated according to such mode as the united states in congress assembled, shall from time to time direct and appoint.

The taxes for paying that proportion shall be laid and levied by the authority and direction of the legislatures of the several states within the time agreed upon by the united states in congress assembled.

Article IX.

The united states in congress assembled, shall have the sole and exclusive right and power of determining on peace and war, except in the cases mentioned in the sixth article — of sending and receiving ambassadors — entering into treaties and alliances, provided that no treaty of commerce shall be made whereby the legislative power of the respective states shall be restrained from imposing such imposts and duties on foreigners as their own people are subjected to, or from prohibiting the exportation or importation of any species of goods or commodities, whatsoever — of establishing rules for deciding in all cases, what captures on land or water shall be legal, and in what manner prizes taken by land or naval forces in the service of the united states shall be divided or appropriated — of granting letters of marque and reprisal in times of peace — appointing courts for the trial of piracies and felonies committed on the high seas and establishing courts for receiving and determining finally appeals in all cases of captures, provided that no member of congress shall be appointed a judge of any of the said courts.

The united states in congress assembled shall also be the last resort on appeal in all disputes and differences now subsisting or that hereafter may arise between two or more states concerning boundary, jurisdiction or any other cause whatever; which authority shall always be exercised in the manner following. Whenever the legislative or executive authority or lawful agent of any state in controversy with another shall present a petition to congress stating the matter in question and praying for a hearing, notice thereof shall be given by order of congress to the legislative or executive authority of the other state in controversy, and a day assigned for the appearance of the parties by their lawful agents, who shall then be directed to appoint by joint consent, commissioners or judges to constitute a court for hearing and determining the matter in question: but if they cannot agree, congress shall name three persons out of each of the united states, and from the list of such persons each party shall alternately strike out one, the petitioners beginning, until the number shall be reduced to thirteen; and from that number not less than seven, nor more than nine names as congress shall direct, shall in the presence of congress be drawn out by lot, and the persons whose names shall be so drawn or any five of them, shall be commissioners or judges, to hear and finally determine the controversy, so always as a major part of the judges who shall hear the cause shall agree in the determination: and if either party shall neglect to attend at the day appointed, without showing reasons, which congress shall judge sufficient, or being present shall refuse to strike, the congress shall proceed to nominate three persons out of each state, and the secretary of congress shall strike in behalf of such party absent or refusing; and the judgment and sentence of the court to be appointed, in the manner before prescribed, shall be final and conclusive; and if any of the parties shall refuse to submit to the authority of such court, or to appear or defend their claim or cause, the court shall nevertheless proceed to pronounce sentence, or judgment, which shall in like manner be final and decisive, the judgment or sentence and other proceedings being in either case transmitted to congress, and lodged among the acts of congress for the security of the parties concerned: provided that every commissioner, before he sits in judgment, shall take an oath to be administered by one of the judges of the supreme or superior court of the state, where the cause shall be tried, "well and truly to hear and determine the matter in question, according to the best of his judgment, without favour, affection or hope of reward:" provided also, that no state shall be deprived of territory for the benefit of the united states.

All controversies concerning the private right of soil claimed under different grants of two or more states, whose jurisdictions as they may respect such lands, and the states which passed such grants are adjusted, the said grants or either of them being at the same time claimed to have originated antecedent to such settlement of jurisdiction, shall on the petition of either party to the congress of the united states, be finally determined as near as may be in the same manner as is before prescribed for deciding disputes respecting territorial jurisdiction between different states.

The united states in congress assembled shall also have the sole and exclusive right and power of regulating the alloy and value of coin struck by their own authority, or by that of the respective states — fixing the standard of weights and measures throughout the united states — regulating the trade and managing all affairs with the Indians, not members of any of the states, provided that the legislative right of any state within its own limits be not infringed or violated — establishing or regulating post offices from one state to another, throughout all the united states, and exacting such postage on the papers passing thro' the same as may be requisite to defray the expences of the said office — appointing all officers of the land forces, in the service of the united states, excepting regimental officers — appointing all the officers of the naval forces, and commissioning all officers whatever in the service of the united states — making rules for the government and regulation of the said land and naval forces, and directing their operations.

The united states in congress assembled shall have authority to appoint a committee, to sit in the recess of congress, to be denominated "A Committee of the States," and to consist of one delegate from each state; and to appoint such other committees and civil officers as may be necessary for managing the general affairs of the united states under their direction — to appoint one of their number to preside, provided that no person be allowed to serve in the office of president more than one year in any term of three years; to ascertain the necessary sums of money to be raised for the service of the united states, and to appropriate and apply the same for defraying the public expences to borrow money, or emit bills on the credit of the united states, transmitting every half year to the respective states an account of the sums of money so borrowed or emitted, — to build and equip a navy — to agree upon the number of land forces, and to make requisitions from each state for its quota, in proportion to the number of white inhabitants in such state; which requisition shall be binding, and thereupon the legislature of each state shall appoint the regimental officers, raise the men and cloth, arm and equip them in a soldier like manner, at the expence of the united states; and the officers and men so cloathed, armed and quipped shall march to the place appointed, and within the time agreed on by the united states in congress assembled: But if the united states in congress assembled shall, on consideration of circumstances judge proper that any state should not raise men, or should raise a smaller number than its quota, and that any other state should raise a greater number of men than the quota thereof, such extra number shall be raised, officered, cloathed, armed and equipped in the same manner as the quota of such state, unless the legislature of such sta te shall judge that such extra number cannot be safely spared out of the same, in which case they shall raise officer, cloath, arm and equip as many of such extra number as they judge can be safely spared. And the officers and men so cloathed, armed and equipped, shall march to the place appointed, and within the time agreed on by the united states in congress assembled.

The united states in congress assembled shall never engage in a war, nor grant letters of marque and reprisal in time of peace, nor enter into any treaties or alliances, nor coin money, nor regulate the value thereof, nor ascertain the sums and expences necessary for the defence and welfare of the united states, or any of them, nor emit bills, nor borrow money on the credit of the united states, nor appropriate money, nor agree upon the number of vessels of war, to be built or purchased, or the number of land or sea forces to be raised, nor appoint a commander in chief of the army or navy, unless nine states assent to the same: nor shall a question on any other point, except for adjourning from day to day be determined, unless by the votes of a majority of the united states in congress assembled.

The congress of the united states shall have power to adjourn to any time within the year, and to any place within the united states, so that no period of adjournment be for a longer duration than the space of six Months, and shall publish the Journal of their proceedings monthly, except such parts thereof relating to treaties, alliances or military operations, as in their judgment require secrecy; and the yeas and nays of the delegates of each state on any question shall be entered on the Journal, when it is desired by any delegate; and the delegates of a state, or any of them, at his or their request shall be furnished with a transcript of the said Journal, except such parts as are above excepted, to lay before the legislatures of the several states.

Article X.

The committee of the states, or any nine of them, shall be authorized to execute, in the recess of congress, such of the powers of congress as the united states in congress assembled, by the consent of nine states, shall from time to time think expedient to vest them with; provided that no power be delegated to the said committee, for the exercise of which, by the articles of confederation, the voice of nine states in the congress of the united states assembled is requisite.

Article XI.

Canada acceding to this confederation, and joining in the measures of the united states, shall be admitted into, and entitled to all the advantages of this union: but no other colony shall be admitted into the same, unless such admission be agreed to by nine states.

Article XII.

All bills of credit emitted, monies borrowed and debts contracted by, or under the authority of congress, before the assembling of the united states, in pursuance of the present confederation, shall be deemed and considered as a charge against the united states, for payment and satisfaction whereof the said united states, and the public faith are hereby solemnly pledged.

Article XIII.

Every state shall abide by the determinations of the united states in congress assembled, on all questions which by this confederation are submitted to them. And the Articles of this confederation shall be inviolably observed by every state, and the union shall be perpetual; nor shall any alteration at any time hereafter be made in any of them; unless such alteration be agreed to in a congress of the united states, and be afterwards confirmed by the legislatures of every state.

And Whereas it hath pleased the Great Governor of the World to incline the hearts of the legislatures we respectively represent in congress, to approve of, and to authorize us to ratify the said articles of confederation and perpetual union. Know Ye that we the undersigned delegates, by virtue of the power and authority to us given for that pur pose, do by these presents, in the name and in behalf of our respective constituents, fully and entirely ratify and confirm each and every of the said articles of confederation and perpetual union, and all and singular the matters and things therein contained: And we do further solemnly plight and engage the faith of our respective constituents, that they shall abide by the determinations of the united states in congress assembled, on all questions, which by the said confederation are submitted to them. And that the articles thereof shall be inviolably observed by the states we respectively represent, and that the union shall be perpetual.

In Witness whereof we have hereunto set our hands in Congress. Done at Philadelphia in the state of Pennsylvania the ninth day of July in the Year of our Lord one Thousand seven Hundred and Seventy-eight, and in the third year of the independence of America.

Federalist 10

Among the numerous advantages promised by a well constructed union, none deserves to be more accurately developed, than its tendency to break and control the violence of faction. The friend of popular governments, never finds himself so much alarmed for their character and fate, as when he contemplates their propensity to this dangerous vice. He will not fail, therefore, to set a due value on any plan which, without violating the principles to which he is attached, provides a proper cure for it. The instability, injustice, and confusion, introduced into the public councils, have, in truth, been the mortal diseases under which popular governments have every where perished; as they continue to be the favourite and fruitful topics from which the adversaries to liberty derive their most specious declamations. The valuable improvements made by the American constitutions on the popular models, both ancient and modern, cannot certainly be too much admired; but it would be an unwarrantable partiality, to contend that they have as effectually obviated the danger on this side, as was wished and expected. Complaints are every where heard from our most considerate and virtuous citizens, equally the friends of public and private faith, and of public and personal liberty, that our governments are too unstable; that the public good is disregarded in the conflicts of rival parties; and that measures are too often decided, not according to the rules of justice, and the rights of the minor party, but by the superior force of an interested and overbearing majority. However anxiously we may wish that these complaints had no foundation, the evidence of known facts will not permit us to deny that they are in some degree true. It will be found, indeed, on a candid review of our situation, that some of the distresses under which we labour, have been erroneously charged on the operation of our governments; but it will be found, at the same time, that other causes will not alone account for many of our heaviest misfortunes; and, particularly, for that prevailing and increasing distrust of public engagements, and alarm for private rights, which are echoed from one end of the continent to the other. These must be chiefly, if not wholly, effects of the unsteadiness and injustice, with which a factious spirit has tainted our public administrations.

By a faction, I understand a number of citizens, whether amounting to a majority or minority of the whole, who are united and actuated by some common impulse of passion, or of interest, adverse to the rights of other citizens, or to the permanent and aggregate interests of the community.

There are two methods of curing the mischiefs of faction: The one, by removing its causes; the other, by controling its effects.

There are again two methods of removing the causes of faction: The one, by destroying the liberty which is essential to its existence; the other, by giving to every citizen the same opinions, the same passions, and the same interests.

It could never be more truly said, than of the first remedy, that it is worse than the disease. Liberty is to faction, what air is to fire, an aliment, without which it instantly expires. But it could not be a less folly to abolish liberty, which is essential to political life, because it nourishes faction, than it would be to wish the annihilation of air, which is essential to animal life, because it imparts to fire its destructive agency.

The second expedient is as impracticable, as the first would be unwise. As long as the reason of man continues fallible, and he is at liberty to exercise it, different opinions will be formed. As long as the connection subsists between his reason and his self-love, his opinions and his passions will have a reciprocal influence on each other; and the former will be objects to which the latter will attach themselves. The diversity in the faculties of men, from which the rights of property originate, is not less an insuperable obstacle to an uniformity of interests. The protection of these faculties, is the first object of government. From the protection of different and unequal faculties of acquiring property, the possession of different degrees and kinds of property immediately results; and from the influence of these on the sentiments and views of the respective proprietors, ensues a division of the society into different interests and parties.

The latent causes of faction are thus sown in the nature of man; and we see them every where brought into different degrees of activity, according to the different circumstances of civil society. A zeal for different opinions concerning religion, concerning government, and many other points, as well of speculation as of practice; an attachment to different leaders, ambitiously contending for pre-eminence and power; or to persons of other descriptions, whose fortunes have been interesting to the human passions, have, in turn, divided mankind into parties, inflamed them with mutual animosity, and rendered them much more disposed to vex and oppress each other, than to co-operate for their common good. So strong is this propensity of mankind, to fall into mutual animosities, that where no substantial occasion presents itself, the most frivolous and fanciful distinctions have been sufficient to kindle their unfriendly passions, and excite their most violent conflicts. But the most common and durable source of factions, has been the various and unequal distribution of property. Those who hold, and those who are without property, have ever formed distinct interests in society. Those who are creditors, and those who are debtors, fall under a like discrimination. A landed interest, a manufacturing interest, a mercantile interest, a monied interest, with many lesser interests, grow up of necessity in civilized nations, and divide them into different classes, actuated by different sentiments and views. The regulation of these various and interfering interests, forms the principal task of modern legislation, and involves the spirit of party and faction in the necessary and ordinary operations of government.

No man is allowed to be a judge in his own cause; because his interest would certainly bias his judgment, and, not improbably, corrupt his integrity. With equal, nay, with greater reason, a body of men are unfit to be both judges and parties, at the same time; yet, what are many of the most important acts of legislation, but so many judicial determinations, not indeed concerning the rights of single persons, but concerning the rights of large bodies of citizens? and what are the different classes of legislators, but advocates and parties to the causes which they determine? Is a law proposed concerning private debts? It is a question to which the creditors are parties on one side, and the debtors on the other. Justice ought to hold the balance between them. Yet the parties are, and must be, themselves the judges; and the most numerous party, or, in other words, the most powerful faction, must be expected to prevail. Shall domestic manufactures be encouraged, and in what degree, by restrictions on foreign manufactures? are questions which would be differently decided by the landed and the manufacturing classes; and probably by neither with a sole regard to justice and the public good. The apportionment of taxes, on the various descriptions of property, is an act which seems to require the most exact impartiality; yet there is, perhaps, no legislative act in which greater opportunity and temptation are given to a predominant party, to trample on the rules of justice. Every shilling with which they over-burden the inferior number, is a shilling saved to their own pockets.

It is in vain to say, that enlightened statesmen will be able to adjust these clashing interests, and render them all subservient to the public good. Enlightened statesmen will not always be at the helm: nor, in many cases, can such an adjustment be made at all, without taking into view indirect and remote considerations, which will rarely prevail over the immediate interest which one party may find in disregarding the rights of another, or the good of the whole.

The inference to which we are brought, is, that the *causes* of faction cannot be removed; and that relief is only to be sought in the means of controlling its *effects*.

If a faction consists of less than a majority, relief is supplied by the republican principle, which enables the majority to defeat its sinister views, by regular vote. It may clog the administration, it may convulse the society; but it will be unable to execute and mask its violence under the forms of the constitution. When a majority is included in a faction, the form of popular government, on the other hand, enables it to sacrifice to its ruling passion or interest, both the public good and the rights of other citizens. To secure the public good, and private rights, against the danger of such a faction, and at the same time to preserve the spirit and the form of popular government, is then the great object to which our inquiries are directed. Let me add, that it is the great desideratum, by which alone this form of government can be rescued from the opprobrium under which it has so long laboured, and be recommended to the esteem and adoption of mankind.

By what means is this object attainable? Evidently by one of two only. Either the existence of the same passion or interest in a majority, at the same time, must be prevented; or the majority, having such co-existent passion or interest, must be rendered, by their number and local situation, unable to concert and carry into effect schemes of oppression. If the impulse and the opportunity be suffered to coincide, we well know, that neither moral nor religious motives can be relied on as an adequate control. They are not found to be such on the injustice and violence of individuals, and lose their efficacy in proportion to the number combined together; that is, in proportion as their efficacy becomes needful.

From this view of the subject, it may be concluded, that a pure democracy, by which I mean, a society consisting of a small number of citizens, who assemble and administer the government in person, can admit of no cure for the mischiefs of faction. A common passion or interest will, in almost every case, be felt by a majority of the whole; a communication and concert, results from the form of government itself; and there is nothing to check the inducements to sacrifice the weaker party, or an obnoxious individual. Hence it is, that such democracies have ever been spectacles of turbulence and contention; have ever been found incompatible with personal security, or the rights of property; and have, in general, been as short in their lives, as they have been violent in their deaths. Theoretic politicians, who have patronised this species of government, have erroneously supposed, that, by reducing mankind to a perfect equality in their political rights, they would, at the same time, be perfectly equalized and assimilated in their possessions, their opinions, and their passions.

A republic, by which I mean a government in which the scheme of representation takes place, opens a different prospect, and promises the cure for which we are seeking. Let us examine the points in which it varies from pure democracy, and we shall comprehend both the nature of the cure and the efficacy which it must derive from the union.

The two great points of difference, between a democracy and a republic, are, first, the delegation of the government, in the latter, to a small number of citizens elected by the rest; secondly, the greater number of citizens, and greater sphere of country, over which the latter may be extended.

The effect of the first difference is, on the one hand, to refine and enlarge the public views, by passing them through the medium of a chosen body of citizens, whose wisdom may best discern the true interest of their country, and whose patriotism and love of justice, will be least likely to sacrifice it to temporary or partial considerations. Under such a regulation, it may well happen, that the public voice, pronounced by the representatives of the people, will be more consonant to the public good, than if pronounced by the people themselves, convened for the purpose. On the other hand, the effect may be inverted. Men of factious tempers, of local prejudices, or of sinister designs, may by intrigue, by corruption, or by other means, first obtain the suffrages, and then betray the interests of the people. The question resulting is, whether small or extensive republics are most favourable to the election of proper guardians of the public weal; and it is clearly decided in favour of the latter by two obvious considerations.

In the first place, it is to be remarked, that however small the republic may be, the representatives must be raised to a certain number, in order to guard against the cabals of a few; and that, however large it may be, they must be limited to a certain number, in order to guard against the confusion of a multitude. Hence, the number of representatives in the two cases not being in proportion to that of the constituents, and being proportionally greatest in the small republic, it follows, that if the proportion of fit characters be not less in the large than in the small republic, the former will present a greater option, and consequently a greater probability of a fit choice.

In the next place, as each representative will be chosen by a greater number of citizens in the large than in the small republic, it will be more difficult for unworthy candidates to practise with success the vicious arts, by which elections are too often carried; and the suffrages of the people being more free, will be more likely to centre in men who possess the most attractive merit, and the most diffusive and established characters.

It must be confessed, that in this, as in most other cases, there is a mean, on both sides of which inconveniences will be found to lie. By enlarging too much the number of electors, you render the representative too little acquainted with all their local circumstances and lesser interests; as by reducing it too much, you render him unduly attached to these, and too little fit to comprehend and pursue great and national objects. The federal constitution forms a happy combination in this respect; the great and aggregate interests, being referred to the national, the local and particular to the state legislatures.

The other point of difference is, the greater number of citizens, and extent of territory, which may be brought within the compass of republican, than of democratic government; and it is this circumstance principally which renders factious combinations less to be dreaded in the former, than in the latter. The smaller the society, the fewer probably will be the distinct parties and interests composing it; the fewer the distinct parties and interests, the more frequently will a majority be found of the same party; and the smaller the number of individuals composing a majority, and the smaller the compass within which they are placed, the more easily will they concert and execute their plans of oppression. Extend the sphere, and you take in a greater variety of parties and interests; you make it less probable that a majority of the whole will have a common motive to invade the rights of other citizens; or if such a common motive exists, it will be more difficult for all who feel it to discover their own strength, and to act in unison with each other. Besides other impediments, it may be remarked, that where there is a consciousness of unjust or dishonourable purposes, communication is always checked by distrust, in proportion to the number whose concurrence is necessary.

Hence it clearly appears, that the same advantage, which a republic has over a democracy, in controling the effects of faction, is enjoyed by a large over a small republic . . . is enjoyed by the union over the states composing it. Does this advantage consist in the substitution of representatives, whose enlightened views and virtuous sentiments render them superior to local prejudices, and to schemes of injustice? It will not be denied, that the representation of the union will be most likely to possess these requisite endowments. Does it consist in the greater security afforded by a greater variety of parties, against the event of any one party being able to outnumber and oppress the rest? In an equal degree does the increased variety of parties, comprised within the union, increase this security. Does it, in fine, consist in the greater obstacles opposed to the concert and accomplishment of the secret wishes of an unjust and interested majority? Here, again, the extent of the union gives it the most palpable advantage.

The influence of factious leaders may kindle a flame within their particular states, but will be unable to spread a general conflagration through the other states: a religious sect may degenerate into a political faction in a part of the confederacy; but the variety of sects dispersed over the entire face of it, must secure the national councils against any danger from that source: a rage for paper money, for an abolition of debts, for an equal division of property, or for any other improper or wicked project, will be less apt to pervade the whole body of the union, than a particular member of it; in the same proportion as such a malady is more likely to taint a particular county or district, than an entire state.

In the extent and proper structure of the union, therefore, we behold a republican remedy for the diseases most incident to republican government. And according to the degree of pleasure and pride we feel in being republicans, ought to be our zeal in cherishing the spirit, and supporting the character of federalists.

PUBLIUS

Brutus 1

To the Citizens of the State of New-York.

When the public is called to investigate and decide upon a question in which not only the present members of the community are deeply interested, but upon which the happiness and misery of generations yet unborn is in great measure suspended, the benevolent mind cannot help feeling itself peculiarly interested in the result.

In this situation, I trust the feeble efforts of an individual, to lead the minds of the people to a wise and prudent determination, cannot fail of being acceptable to the candid and dispassionate part of the community. Encouraged by this consideration, I have been induced to offer my thoughts upon the present important crisis of our public affairs.

Perhaps this country never saw so critical a period in their political concerns. We have felt the feebleness of the ties by which these United-States are held together, and the want of sufficient energy in our present confederation, to manage, in some instances, our general concerns. Various expedients have been proposed to remedy these evils, but none have succeeded. At length a Convention of the states has been assembled, they have formed a constitution which will now, probably, be submitted to the people to ratify or reject, who are the fountain of all power, to whom alone it of right belongs to make or unmake constitutions, or forms of government, at their pleasure. The most important question that was ever proposed to your decision, or to the decision of any people under heaven, is before you, and you are to decide upon it by men of your own election, chosen specially for this purpose. If the constitution, offered to [your acceptance], be a wise one, calculated to preserve the invaluable blessings of liberty, to secure the inestimable rights of mankind, and promote human happiness, then, if you accept it, you will lay a lasting foundation of happiness for millions yet unborn; generations to come will rise up and call you blessed. You may rejoice in the prospects of this vast extended continent becoming filled with freemen, who will assert the dignity of human nature. You may solace yourselves with the idea, that society, in this favoured land, will fast advance to the highest point of perfection; the human mind will expand in knowledge and virtue, and the golden age be, in some measure, realised. But if, on the other hand, this form of government contains principles that will lead to the subversion of liberty — if it tends to establish a despotism, or, what is worse, a tyrannic aristocracy; then, if you adopt it, this only remaining assylum for liberty will be [shut] up, and posterity will execrate your memory.

Momentous then is the question you have to determine, and you are called upon by every motive which should influence a noble and virtuous mind, to examine it well, and to make up a wise judgment. It is insisted, indeed, that this constitution must be received, be it ever so imperfect. If it has its defects, it is said, they can be best amended when they are experienced. But remember, when the people once part with power, they can seldom or never resume it again but by force. Many instances can be produced in which the people have voluntarily increased the powers of their rulers; but few, if any, in which rulers have willingly abridged their authority. This is a sufficient reason to induce you to be careful, in the first instance, how you deposit the powers of government.

With these few introductory remarks I shall proceed to a consideration of this constitution:

The first question that presents itself on the subject is, whether a confederated government be the best for the United States or not? Or in other words, whether the thirteen United States should be reduced to one great republic, governed by one legislature, and under the direction of one executive and judicial; or whether they should continue thirteen confederated republics, under the direction and controul of a supreme federal head for certain defined national purposes only?

This enquiry is important, because, although the government reported by the convention does not go to a perfect and entire consolidation, yet it approaches so near to it, that it must, if executed, certainly and infallibly terminate in it.

This government is to possess absolute and uncontroulable power, legislative, executive and judicial, with respect to every object to which it extends, for by the last clause of section 8th, article Ist, it is declared "that the Congress shall have power to make all laws which shall be necessary and proper for carrying into execution the foregoing powers, and all other powers vested by this constitution, in the government of the United States; or in any department or office thereof." And by the 6th article, it is declared "that this constitution, and the laws of the United States, which shall be made in pursuance thereof, and the treaties made, or which shall be made, under the authority of the United States, shall be the supreme law of the land; and the judges in every state shall be bound thereby, any thing in the constitution, or law of any state to the contrary notwithstanding." It appears from these articles that there is no need of any intervention of the state governments, between the Congress and the people, to execute any one power vested in the general government, and that the constitution and laws of every state are nullified and declared void, so far as they are or shall be inconsistent with this constitution, or the laws made in pursuance of it, or with treaties made under the authority of the United States. — The government then, so far as it extends, is a complete one, and not a confederation. It is as much one complete government as that of New-York or Massachusetts, has as absolute and perfect powers to make and execute all laws, to appoint officers, institute courts, declare offences, and annex penalties, with respect to every object to which it extends, as any other in the world. So far therefore as its powers reach, all ideas of confederation are given up and lost. It is true this government is limited to certain objects, or to speak more properly, some small degree of power is still left to the states, but a little attention to the powers vested in the general government, will convince every candid man, that if it is capable of being executed, all that is reserved for the individual states must very soon be annihilated, except so far as they are barely necessary to the organization of the general government. The powers of the general legislature extend to every case that is of the least importance — there is nothing valuable to human nature, nothing dear to freemen, but what is within its power. It has authority to make laws which will affect the lives, the liberty, and property of every man in the United States; nor can the constitution or laws of any state, in any way prevent or impede the full and complete execution of every power given. The legislative power is competent to lay taxes, duties, imposts, and excises; — there is no limitation to this power, unless it be said that the clause which directs the use to which those taxes, and duties shall be applied, may be said to be a limitation; but this is no restriction of the power at all, for by this clause they are to be applied to pay the debts and provide for the common defence and general welfare of the United States; but the legislature have authority to contract debts at their discretion; they are the sole judges of what is necessary to provide for the common defence, and they only are to determine what is for the general welfare: this power therefore is neither more nor less, than a power to lay and collect taxes, imposts, and excises, at their pleasure; not only the power to lay taxes unlimited, as to the amount they may require, but it is perfect and absolute to raise them in any mode they please. No state legislature, or any power in the state governments, have any more to do in carrying this into effect, than the authority of one state has to do with that of another. In the business therefore of laying and collecting taxes, the idea of confederation is totally lost, and that of one entire republic is embraced. It is proper here to remark, that the authority to lay and collect taxes is the most important of any power that can be granted; it connects with it almost all other powers, or at least will in process of time draw all other after it; it is the great mean of protection, security, and defence, in a good government, and the great engine of oppression and tyranny in a bad one. This cannot fail of being the case, if we consider the contracted limits which are set by this constitution, to the late governments, on this article of raising money. No state can emit paper money — lay any duties, or imposts, on imports, or exports, but by consent of the Congress; and then the net produce shall be for the benefit of the United States. The only mean therefore left, for any state to support its government and discharge its debts, is by direct taxation; and the United States have also power to lay and collect taxes, in any way they please. Every one who has thought on the subject, must be convinced that but small sums of money can be collected in any country, by direct taxe[s], when the foederal government begins to exercise the right of taxation in all its parts, the legislatures of the several states will find it impossible to raise monies to support their governments. Without money they cannot be supported, and they must dwindle away, and, as before observed, their powers absorbed in that of the general government.

It might be here shewn, that the power in the federal legislative, to raise and support armies at pleasure, as well in peace as in war, and their controul over the militia, tend, not only to a consolidation of the government, but the destruction of liberty. — I shall not, however, dwell upon these, as a few observations upon the judicial power of this government, in addition to the preceding, will fully evince the truth of the position.

The judicial power of the United States is to be vested in a supreme court, and in such inferior courts as Congress may from time to time ordain and establish. The powers of these courts are very extensive; their jurisdiction comprehends all civil causes, except such as arise between citizens of the same state; and it extends to all cases in law and equity arising under the constitution. One inferior court must be established, I presume, in each state at least, with the necessary executive officers appendant thereto. It is easy to see, that in the common course of things, these courts will eclipse the dignity, and take away from the respectability, of the state courts. These courts will be, in themselves, totally independent of the states, deriving their authority from the United States, and receiving from them fixed salaries; and in the course of human events it is to be expected, that they will swallow up all the powers of the courts in the respective states.

How far the clause in the 8th section of the Ist article may operate to do away all idea of confederated states, and to effect an entire consolidation of the whole into one general government, it is impossible to say. The powers given by this article are very general and comprehensive, and it may receive a construction to justify the passing almost any law. A power to make all laws, which shall be necessary and proper, for carrying into execution, all powers vested by the constitution in the government of the United States, or any department or officer thereof, is a power very comprehensive and definite, and may, for ought I know, be exercised in a such manner as entirely to abolish the state legislatures. Suppose the legislature of a state should pass a law to raise money to support their government and pay the state debt, may the Congress repeal this law, because it may prevent the collection of a tax which they may think proper and necessary to lay, to provide for the general welfare of the United States? For all laws made, in pursuance of this constitution, are the supreme lay of the land, and the judges in every state shall be bound thereby, any thing in the constitution or laws of the different states to the contrary notwithstanding. — By such a law, the government of a particular state might be overturned at one stroke, and thereby be deprived of every means of its support.

It is not meant, by stating this case, to insinuate that the constitution would warrant a law of this kind; or unnecessarily to alarm the fears of the people, by suggesting, that the federal legislature would be more likely to pass the limits assigned them by the constitution, than that of an individual state, further than they are less responsible to the people. But what is meant is, that the legislature of the United States are vested with the great and uncontroulable powers, of laying and collecting taxes, duties, imposts, and excises; of regulating trade, raising and supporting armies, organizing, arming, and disciplining the militia, instituting courts, and other general powers. And are by this clause invested with the power of making all laws, proper and necessary, for carrying all these into execution; and they may so exercise this power as entirely to annihilate all the state governments, and reduce this country to one single government. And if they may do it, it is pretty certain they will; for it will be found that the power retained by individual states, small as it is, will be a clog upon the wheels of the government of the United States; the latter therefore will be naturally inclined to remove it out of the way. Besides, it is a truth confirmed by the unerring experience of ages, that every man, and every body of men, invested with power, are ever disposed to increase it, and to acquire a superiority over every thing that stands in their way. This disposition, which is implanted in human nature, will operate in the federal legislature to lessen and ultimately to subvert the state authority, and having such advantages, will most certainly succeed, if the federal government succeeds at all. It must be very evident then, that what this constitution wants of being a complete consolidation of the several parts of the union into one complete government, possessed of perfect legislative, judicial, and executive powers, to all intents and purposes, it will necessarily acquire in its exercise and operation.

Let us now proceed to enquire, as I at first proposed, whether it be best the thirteen United States should be reduced to one great republic, or not? It is here taken for granted, that all agree in this, that whatever government we adopt, it ought to be a free one; that it should be so framed as to secure the liberty of the citizens of America, and such an one as to admit of a full, fair, and equal representation of the people. The question then will be, whether a government thus constituted, and founded on such principles, is practicable, and can be exercised over the whole United States, reduced into one state?

If respect is to be paid to the opinion of the greatest and wisest men who have ever thought or wrote on the science of government, we shall be constrained to conclude, that a free republic cannot succeed over a country of such immense extent, containing such a number of inhabitants, and these encreasing in such rapid progression as that of the whole United States. Among the many illustrious authorities which might be produced to this point, I shall content myself with quoting only two. The one is the baron de Montesquieu, spirit of laws, chap. xvi. vol. I [book VIII]. "It is natural to a republic to have only a small territory, otherwise it cannot long subsist. In a large republic there are men of large fortunes, and consequently of less moderation; there are trusts too great to be placed in any single subject; he has interest of his own; he soon begins to think that he may be happy, great and glorious, by oppressing his fellow citizens; and that he may raise himself to grandeur on the ruins of his country. In a large republic, the public good is sacrificed to a thousand views; it is subordinate to exceptions, and depends on accidents. In a small one, the interest of the public is easier perceived, better understood, and more within the reach of every citizen; abuses are of less extent, and of course are less protected." Of the same opinion is the marquis Beccarari.

History furnishes no example of a free republic, any thing like the extent of the United States. The Grecian republics were of small extent; so also was that of the Romans. Both of these, it is true, in process of time, extended their conquests over large territories of country; and the consequence was, that their governments were changed from that of free governments to those of the most tyrannical that ever existed in the world.

Not only the opinion of the greatest men, and the experience of mankind, are against the idea of an extensive republic, but a variety of reasons may be drawn from the reason and nature of things, against it. In every government, the will of the sovereign is the law. In despotic governments, the supreme authority being lodged in one, his will is law, and can be as easily expressed to a large extensive territory as to a small one. In a pure democracy the people are the sovereign, and their will is declared by themselves; for this purpose they must all come together to deliberate, and decide. This kind of government cannot be exercised, therefore, over a country of any considerable extent; it must be confined to a single city, or at least limited to such bounds as that the people can conveniently assemble, be able to debate, understand the subject submitted to them, and declare their opinion concerning it.

In a free republic, although all laws are derived from the consent of the people, yet the people do not declare their consent by themselves in person, but by representatives, chosen by them, who are supposed to know the minds of their constituents, and to be possessed of integrity to declare this mind.

In every free government, the people must give their assent to the laws by which they are governed. This is the true criterion between a free government and an arbitrary one. The former are ruled by the will of the whole, expressed in any manner they may agree upon; the latter by the will of one, or a few. If the people are to give their assent to the laws, by persons chosen and appointed by them, the manner of the choice and the number chosen, must be such, as to possess, be disposed, and consequently qualified to declare the sentiments of the people; for if they do not know, or are not disposed to speak the sentiments of the people, the people do not govern, but the sovereignty is in a few. Now, in a large extended country, it is impossible to have a representation, possessing the sentiments, and of integrity, to declare the minds of the people, without having it so numerous and unwieldly, as to be subject in great measure to the inconveniency of a democratic government.

The territory of the United States is of vast extent; it now contains near three millions of souls, and is capable of containing much more than ten times that number. Is it practicable for a country, so large and so numerous as they will soon become, to elect a representation, that will speak their sentiments, without their becoming so numerous as to be incapable of transacting public business? It certainly is not.

In a republic, the manners, sentiments, and interests of the people should be similar. If this be not the case, there will be a constant clashing of opinions; and the representatives of one part will be continually striving against those of the other. This will retard the operations of government, and prevent such conclusions as will promote the public good. If we apply this remark to the condition of the United States, we shall be convinced that it forbids that we should be one government. The United States includes a variety of climates. The productions of the different parts of the union are very variant, and their interests, of consequence, diverse. Their manners and habits differ as much as their climates and productions; and their sentiments are by no means coincident. The laws and customs of the several states are, in many respects, very diverse, and in some opposite; each would be in favor of its own interests and customs, and, of consequence, a legislature, formed of representatives from the respective parts, would not only be too numerous to act with any care or decision, but would be composed of such heterogenous and discordant principles, as would constantly be contending with each other.

The laws cannot be executed in a republic, of an extent equal to that of the United States, with promptitude.

The magistrates in every government must be supported in the execution of the laws, either by an armed force, maintained at the public expence for that purpose; or by the people turning out to aid the magistrate upon his command, in case of resistance.

In despotic governments, as well as in all the monarchies of Europe, standing armies are kept up to execute the commands of the prince or the magistrate, and are employed for this purpose when occasion requires: But they have always proved the destruction of liberty, and [are] abhorrent to the spirit of a free republic. In England, where they depend upon the parliament for their annual support, they have always been complained of as oppressive and unconstitutional, and are seldom employed in executing of the laws; never except on extraordinary occasions, and then under the direction of a civil magistrate.

A free republic will never keep a standing army to execute its laws. It must depend upon the support of its citizens. But when a government is to receive its support from the aid of the citizens, it must be so constructed as to have the confidence, respect, and affection of the people. Men who, upon the call of the magistrate, offer themselves to execute the laws, are influenced to do it either by affection to the government, or from fear; where a standing army is at hand to punish offenders, every man is actuated by the latter principle, and therefore, when the magistrate calls, will obey: but, where this is not the case, the government must rest for its support upon the confidence and respect which the people have for their government and laws. The body of the people being attached, the government will always be sufficient to support and execute its laws, and to operate upon the fears of any faction which may be opposed to it, not only to prevent an opposition to the execution of the laws themselves, but also to compel the most of them to aid the magistrate; but the people will not be likely to have such confidence in their rulers, in a republic so extensive as the United States, as necessary for these purposes. The confidence which the people have in their rulers, in a free republic, arises from their knowing them, from their being responsible to them for their conduct, and from the power they have of displacing them when they misbehave: but in a republic of the extent of this continent, the people in general would be acquainted with very few of their rulers: the people at large would know little of their proceedings, and it would be extremely difficult to change them. The people in Georgia and New-Hampshire would not know one another's mind, and therefore could not act in concert to enable them to effect a general change of representatives. The different parts of so extensive a country could not possibly be made acquainted with the conduct of their representatives, nor be informed of the reasons upon which measures were founded. The consequence will be, they will have no confidence in their legislature, suspect them of ambitious views, be jealous of every measure they adopt, and will not support the laws they pass. Hence the government will be nerveless and inefficient, and no way will be left to render it otherwise, but by establishing an armed force to execute the laws at the point of the bayonet — a government of all others the most to be dreaded.

In a republic of such vast extent as the United-States, the legislature cannot attend to the various concerns and wants of its different parts. It cannot be sufficiently numerous to be acquainted with the local condition and wants of the different districts, and if it could, it is impossible it should have sufficient time to attend to and provide for all the variety of cases of this nature, that would be continually arising.

In so extensive a republic, the great officers of government would soon become above the controul of the people, and abuse their power to the purpose of aggrandizing themselves, and oppressing them. The trust committed to the executive offices, in a country of the extent of the United-States, must be various and of magnitude. The command of all the troops and navy of the republic, the appointment of officers, the power of pardoning offences, the collecting of all the public revenues, and the power of expending them, with a number of other powers, must be lodged and exercised in every state, in the hands of a few. When these are attended with great honor and emolument, as they always will be in large states, so as greatly to interest men to pursue them, and to be proper objects for ambitious and designing men, such men will be ever restless in their pursuit after them. They will use the power, when they have acquired it, to the purposes of gratifying their own interest and ambition, and it is scarcely possible, in a very large republic, to call them to account for their misconduct, or to prevent their abuse of power.

These are some of the reasons by which it appears, that a free republic cannot long subsist over a country of the great extent of these states. If then this new constitution is calculated to consolidate the thirteen states into one, as it evidently is, it ought not to be adopted.

Though I am of opinion, that it is a sufficient objection to this government, to reject it, that it creates the whole union into one government, under the form of a republic, yet if this objection was obviated, there are exceptions to it, which are so material and fundamental, that they ought to determine every man, who is a friend to the liberty and happiness of mankind, not to adopt it. I beg the candid and dispassionate attention of my countrymen while I state these objections — they are

1 such as have obtruded themselves upon my mind upon a careful attention to the
2 matter, and such as I sincerely believe are well founded. There are many
3 objections, of small moment, of which I shall take no notice — perfection is not to
4 be expected in any thing that is the production of man — and if I did not in my
5 conscience believe that this scheme was defective in the fundamental principles —
6 in the foundation upon which a free and equal government must rest — I would
7 hold my peace.

8

Federalist 51

To what expedient then shall we finally resort, for maintaining in practice the necessary partition of power among the several departments, as laid down in the constitution? The only answer that can be given is, that as all these exterior provisions are found to be inadequate, the defect must be supplied, by so contriving the interior structure of the government, as that its several constituent parts may, by their mutual relations, be the means of keeping each other in their proper places. Without presuming to undertake a full developement of this important idea, I will hazard a few general observations, which may perhaps place it in a clearer light, and enable us to form a more correct judgment of the principles and structure of the government planned by the convention.

In order to lay a due foundation for that separate and distinct exercise of the different powers of government, which, to a certain extent, is admitted on all hands to be essential to the preservation of liberty, it is evident that each department should have a will of its own; and consequently should be so constituted, that the members of each should have as little agency as possible in the appointment of the members of the others. Were this principle rigorously adhered to, it would require that all the appointments for the supreme executive, legislative, and judiciary magistracies, should be drawn from the same fountain of authority, the people, through channels having no communication whatever with one another. Perhaps such a plan of constructing the several departments, would be less difficult in practice, than it may in contemplation appear. Some difficulties, however, and some additional expense, would attend the execution of it. Some deviations, therefore, from the principle must be admitted. In the constitution of the judiciary department in particular, it might be inexpedient to insist rigorously on the principle; first, because peculiar qualifications being essential in the members, the primary consideration ought to be to select that mode of choice which best secures these qualifications; secondly, because the permanent tenure by which the appointments are held in that department, must soon destroy all sense of dependence on the authority conferring them.

It is equally evident, that the members of each department should be as little dependent as possible on those of the others, for the emoluments annexed to their offices. Were the executive magistrate, or the judges, not independent of the legislature in this particular, their independence in every other, would be merely nominal.

But the great security against a gradual concentration of the several powers in the same department, consists in giving to those who administer each department, the necessary constitutional means, and personal motives, to resist encroachments of the others. The provision for defence must in this, as in all other cases, be made commensurate to the danger of attack. Ambition must be made to counteract ambition. The interest of the man, must be connected with the constitutional rights of the place. It may be a reflection on human nature, that such devices should be necessary to control the abuses of government. But what is government itself, but the greatest of all reflections on human nature? If men were angels, no government would be necessary. If angels were to govern men, neither external nor internal controls on government would be necessary. In framing a government which is to be administered by men over men, the great difficulty lies in this: you must first enable the government to control the governed; and in the next place oblige it to control itself. A dependence on the people is, no doubt, the primary control on the government; but experience has taught mankind the necessity of auxiliary precautions.

This policy of supplying, by opposite and rival interests, the defect of better motives, might be traced through the whole system of human affairs, private as well as public. We see it particularly displayed in all the subordinate distributions of power; where the constant aim is, to divide and arrange the several offices in such a manner as that each may be a check on the other; that the private interest of every individual may be a centinel over the public rights. These inventions of prudence cannot be less requisite in the distribution of the supreme powers of the state.

But it is not possible to give to each department an equal power of self-defence. In republican government, the legislative authority necessarily predominates. The remedy for this inconveniency is, to divide the legislature into different branches; and to render them, by different modes of election, and different principles of action, as little connected with each other, as the nature of their common functions, and their common dependence on the society, will admit. It may even be necessary to guard against dangerous encroachments by still further precautions. As the weight of the legislative authority requires that it should be thus divided, the weakness of the executive may require, on the other hand, that it should be fortified. An absolute negative on the legislature, appears, at first view, to be the natural defence with which the executive magistrate should be armed. But perhaps it would be neither altogether safe, nor alone sufficient. On ordinary occasions, it might not be exerted with the requisite firmness; and on extraordinary occasions, it might be perfidiously abused. May not this defect of an absolute negative be supplied by some qualified connexion between this weaker department, and the weaker branch of the stronger department, by which the latter may be led to support the constitutional rights of the former, without being too much detached from the rights of its own department?

If the principles on which these observations are founded be just, as I persuade myself they are, and they be applied as a criterion to the several state constitutions, and to the federal constitution, it will be found, that if the latter does not perfectly correspond with them, the former are infinitely less able to bear such a test.

There are moreover two considerations particularly applicable to the federal system of America, which place that system in a very interesting point of view.

First. In a single republic, all the power surrendered by the people, is submitted to the administration of a single government; and the usurpations are guarded against, by a division of the government into distinct and separate departments. In the compound republic of America, the power surrendered by the people, is first divided between two distinct governments, and then the portion allotted to each subdivided among distinct and separate departments. Hence a double security arises to the rights of the people. The different governments will control each other; at the same time that each will be controled by itself.

Second. It is of great importance in a republic, not only to guard the society against the oppression of its rulers; but to guard one part of the society against the injustice of the other part. Different interests necessarily exist in different classes of citizens. If a majority be united by a common interest, the rights of the minority will be insecure. There are but two methods of providing against this evil: the one, by creating a will in the community independent of the majority, that is, of the society itself; the other, by comprehending in the society so many separate descriptions of citizens, as will render an unjust combination of a majority of the whole very improbable, if not impracticable. The first method prevails in all governments possessing an hereditary or self-appointed authority. This, at best, is but a precarious security; because a power independent of the society may as well espouse the unjust views of the major, as the rightful interests of the minor party, and may possibly be turned against both parties. The second method will be exemplified in the federal republic of the United States. Whilst all authority in it will be derived from, and dependent on the society, the society itself will be broken into so many parts, interests, and classes of citizens, that the rights of individuals, or of the minority, will be in little danger from interested combinations of the majority. In a free government, the security for civil rights must be the same as that for religious rights. It consists in the one case in the multiplicity of interests, and in the other, in the multiplicity of sects. The degree of security in both cases will depend on the number of interests and sects; and this may be presumed to depend on the extent of country and number of people comprehended under the same government. This view of the subject must particularly recommend a proper federal system to all the sincere and considerate friends of republican government: since it shows, that in exact proportion as the territory of the union may be formed into more circumscribed confederacies, or states, oppressive combinations of a majority will be facilitated; the best security under the republican form, for the rights of every class of citizens, will be diminished; and consequently, the stability and independence of some member of the government, the only other security, must be proportionally increased. Justice is the end of government. It is the end of civil society. It ever has been, and ever will be, pursued, until it be obtained, or until liberty be lost in the pursuit. In a society, under the forms of which the stronger faction can readily unite and oppress the weaker, anarchy may as truly be said to reign, as in a state of nature, where the weaker individual is not secured against the violence of the stronger: and as, in the latter state, even the stronger individuals are prompted, by the uncertainty of their condition, to submit to a government which may protect the weak, as well as themselves: so, in the former state, will the more powerful factions or parties be gradually induced, by a like motive, to wish for a government which will protect all parties, the weaker as well as the more powerful. It can be little doubted, that if the state of Rhode Island was separated from the confederacy, and left to itself, the insecurity of rights under the popular form of government within such narrow limits, would be displayed by such reiterated oppressions of factious majorities, that some power altogether independent of the people, would soon be called for by the voice of the very factions whose misrule had proved the necessity of it. In the extended republic of the United States, and among the great variety of interests, parties, and sects, which it embraces, a coalition of a majority of the whole society could seldom take place upon any other principles, than those of justice and the general good: whilst there being thus less danger to a minor from the will of the major party, there must be less pretext also, to provide for the security of the former, by introducing into the government a will not dependent on the latter: or, in other words, a will independent of the society itself. It is no less certain than it is important, notwithstanding the contrary opinions which have been entertained, that the larger the society, provided it lie within a practicable sphere, the more duly capable it will be of self-government. And happily for the *republican cause*, the practicable sphere may be carried to a very great extent, by a judicious modification and mixture of the *federal principle*.

PUBLIUS

Federalists No. 70

There is an idea, which is not without its advocates, that a vigorous executive is inconsistent with the genius of republican government. The enlightened well-wishers to this species of government must at least hope that the supposition is destitute of foundation; since they can never admit its truth, without at the same time admitting the condemnation of their own principles. Energy in the executive is a leading character in the definition of good government. It is essential to the protection of the community against foreign attacks; it is not less essential to the steady administration of the laws; to the protection of property against those irregular and high-handed combinations which sometimes interrupt the ordinary course of justice; to the security of liberty against the enterprises and assaults of ambition, of faction, and of anarchy. Every man the least conversant in Roman history knows how often that republic was obliged to take refuge in the absolute power of a single man, under the formidable title of dictator, as well against the intrigues of ambitious individuals who aspired to the tyranny, and the seditions of whole classes of the community whose conduct threatened the existence of all government, as against the invasions of external enemies who menaced the conquest and destruction of Rome.

There can be no need, however, to multiply arguments or examples on this head. A feeble executive implies a feeble execution of the government. A feeble execution is but another phrase for a bad execution; and a government ill executed, whatever it may be in theory, must be, in practice, a bad government.

Taking it for granted, therefore, that all men of sense will agree in the necessity of an energetic executive; it will only remain to inquire, what are the ingredients which constitute this energy? How far can they be combined with those other ingredients which constitute safety in the republican sense? And how far does this combination characterize the plan which has been reported by the convention?

The ingredients which constitute energy in the executive are unity; duration; an adequate provision for its support; and competent powers.

The ingredients which constitute safety in the republican sense are a due dependence on the people, secondly a due responsibility.

Those politicians and statesmen who have been the most celebrated for the soundness of their principles and for the justness of their views have declared in favor of a single executive and a numerous legislature. They have with great propriety, considered energy as the most necessary qualification of the former, and have regarded this as most applicable to power in a single hand; while they have, with equal propriety, considered the latter as best adapted to deliberation and wisdom, and best calculated to conciliate the confidence of the people and to secure their privileges and interests.

That unity is conducive to energy will not be disputed. Decision, activity, secrecy, and dispatch will generally characterize the proceedings of one man in a much more eminent degree than the proceedings of any greater number; and in proportion as the number is increased, these qualities will be diminished.

This unity may be destroyed in two ways: either by vesting the power in two or more magistrates of equal dignity and authority, or by vesting it ostensibly in one man, subject in whole or in part to the control and co-operation of others, in the capacity of counselors to him. Of the first, the two consuls of Rome may serve as an example; of the last, we shall find examples in the constitutions of several of the States. New York and New Jersey, if I recollect right, are the only States which have entrusted the executive authority wholly to single men. Both these methods of destroying the unity of the executive have their partisans; but the votaries of an executive council are the most numerous. They are both liable, if not to equal, to similar objections, and may in most lights be examined in conjunction.

The experience of other nations will afford little instruction on this head. As far, however, as it teaches anything, it teaches us not to be enamored of plurality in the executive. We have seen that the Achaeans on an experiment of two Praetors, were induced to abolish one. The Roman history records many instances of mischiefs to the republic from the dissentions between the consuls, and between the military tribunes, who were at times substituted to the consuls. But it gives us no specimens of any peculiar advantages derived to the state from the circumstance of the plurality of those magistrates. That the dissentions between them were not more frequent or more fatal is matter of astonishment, until we advert to the singular position in which he republic was almost continually placed and to the prudent policy pointed out by the circumstances of the state, and pursued by the consuls, of making a division of the government between them. The patricians engaged in a perpetual struggle with the plebians for the preservation of their ancient authorities and dignities; the consuls, who were generally chosen out of the former body, were commonly united by the personal interest they had in the defense of the privileges of their order. In addition to this motive of union, after the arms of the republic had considerably expanded the bounds of its empire, it became an established custom with the consuls to divide the administration between themselves by lot—one of them remaining at Rome to govern the city and its environs; the other taking the command in the more distant provinces. This expedient must no doubt have had great influence in preventing those collisions and rivalships which might otherwise have embroiled the peace of the republic.

But quitting the dim light of historical research, and attaching ourselves purely to the dictates of reason and good sense, we shall discover much greater cause to reject than to approve the idea of plurality in the executive, under any modification whatever.

Wherever two or more persons are engaged in any common enterprise or pursuit, there is always danger of difference of opinion. If it be a public trust or office in which they are clothed with equal dignity and authority, there is peculiar danger of personal emulation and even animosity. From either, and especially from all these causes, the most bitter dissentions are apt to spring. Whenever these happen, they lessen the respectability, weaken the authority, and distract the plans and operations of those whom they divide. If they should unfortunately assail the supreme executive magistracy of a country, consisting of a plurality of persons, they might impede or frustrate the most important measures of the government in the most critical emergencies of the state. And what is still worse, they might split the community into the most violent and irreconcilable factions, adhering differently to the different individuals who composed the magistracy.

Men often oppose a thing merely because they have had no agency in planning it, or because it may have been planned by those whom they dislike. But if they have been consulted, and have happened to disapprove, opposition then becomes, in their estimation an indispensable duty of self-love. They seem to think themselves bound in honor, and by all the motives of personal infallibility, to defeat the success of what has been resolved upon, contrary to their sentiments. Men of upright, benevolent tempers have too many opportunities of remarking, with horror, to what desperate lengths this disposition is sometimes carried, and how often the great interests of society are sacrificed to the vanity, to the conceit, and to the obstinacy of individuals, who have credit enough to make their passions and their caprices interesting to mankind. Perhaps the question now before the public may, in its consequences, afford melancholy proofs of the effects of this despicable frailty, or rather detestable vice, in the human character.

Upon the principles of a free government, inconveniences from the source just mentioned must necessarily be submitted to in the formation of the legislature; but it is unnecessary, and therefore unwise, to introduce them into the constitution of the executive. It is here too that they may be most pernicious. In the legislature, promptitude of decision is oftener an evil than a benefit. The differences of opinion, and the jarrings of parties in that department of the government, though they may sometimes obstruct salutary plans, yet often promote deliberation and circumspection, and serve to check excesses in the majority. When a resolution too is once taken, the opposition must be at an end. That resolution is a law, and resistance to it punishable. But no favorable circumstances palliate or atone for the disadvantages of dissention in the executive department. Here they are pure and unmixed. There is no point at which they cease to operate. They serve to embarrass and weaken the execution of the plan or measure to which they relate, from the first step to the final conclusion of it. They constantly counteract those qualities in the executive which are the most necessary ingredients in its composition—vigor and expedition, and this without any counterbalancing good. In the conduct of war, in which the energy of the executive is the bulwark of the national security, everything would be to be apprehended from its plurality.

It must be confessed that these observations apply with principal weight to the first case supposed—that is, to a plurality of magistrates of equal dignity and authority, a scheme, the advocates for which are not likely to form a numerous sect; but they apply, though not with equal yet with considerable weight to the project of a council, whose concurrence is made constitutionally necessary to the operations of the ostensible executive. An artful cabal in that council would be able to distract and to enervate the whole system of administration. If no such cabal should exist, the mere diversity of views and opinions would alone be sufficient to tincture the exercise of the executive authority with a spirit of habitual feebleness and dilatoriness.

But one of the weightiest objections to a plurality in the executive, and which lies as much against the last as the first plan is that it tends to conceal faults and destroy responsibility. Responsibility is of two kinds—to censure and to punishment. The first is the most important of the two, especially in an elective office. Men in public trust will much oftener act in such a manner as to render them unworthy of being any longer trusted, than in such a manner as to make him obnoxious to legal punishment. But the multiplication of the executive adds to the difficulty of detection in either case. It often becomes impossible, amidst mutual accusations, to determine on whom the blame or the punishment of a pernicious measure, or series of pernicious measures, ought really to fall. It is shifted from one to another with so much dexterity, and under such plausible appearances, that the public opinion is left in suspense about the real author. The circumstances which may have led to any national miscarriage or misfortune are sometimes so complicated that where there are a number of actors who may have had different degrees and kinds of agency, though we may clearly see upon the whole that there has been mismanagement, yet it may be impracticable to pronounce to whose account the evil which may have been incurred is truly chargeable.

"I was overruled by my council. The council were so divided in their opinions that it was impossible to obtain any better resolution on the point." These and similar pretexts are constantly at hand, whether true or false. And who is there that will either take the trouble or incur the odium of a strict scrutiny into the secret springs of the transaction? Should there be found a citizen zealous enough to undertake the unpromising task, if there happened to be a collusion between the parties concerned, how easy is it to cloth the circumstances with so much ambiguity as to render it uncertain what was the precise conduct of any of those parties?

In the single instance in which the governor of this state is coupled with a council—that is, in the appointment to offices, we have seen the mischiefs of it in the view now under consideration. Scandalous appointments to important offices have been made. Some cases indeed have been so flagrant that ALL PARTIES have agreed in the impropriety of the thing. When inquiry has been made, the blame has been laid by the governor on the members of the council; who on their part have charged it upon his nomination; while the people remain altogether at a loss to determine by whose influence their interests have been committed to hands so unqualified and so manifestly improper. In tenderness to individuals, I forbear to descend to particulars.

It is evident from these considerations that the plurality of the executive tends to deprive the people of the two greatest securities they can have for the faithful exercise of any delegated power, *first*, the restraints of public opinion, which lose their efficacy as well on account of the division of the censure attendant on bad measures among a number as on account of the uncertainty on whom it ought to fall; and, *second*, the opportunity of discovering with facility and clearness the misconduct of the persons they trust, in order either to their removal from office or to their actual punishment in cases which admit of it.

In England, the king is a perpetual magistrate; and it is a maxim which has obtained for the sake of the public peace that he is unaccountable for his administration, and his person sacred. Nothing, therefore, can be wiser in that kingdom than to annex to the king a constitutional council, who may be responsible to the nation for the advice they give. Without this, there would be no responsibility whatever in the executive department—an idea inadmissible in a free government. But even there the king is not bound by the resolutions of his council, though they are answerable for the advice they give. He is the absolute master of his own conduct in the exercise of his office and may observe or disregard the council given to him at his sole discretion.

But in a republic where every magistrate ought to be personally responsible for his behavior in office, the reason which in the British Constitution dictates the propriety of a council not only ceases to apply, but turns against the institution. In the monarchy of Great Britain, it furnishes a substitute for the prohibited responsibility of the Chief Magistrate, which serves in some degree as a hostage to the national justice for his good behavior. In the American republic, it would serve to destroy, or would greatly diminish, the intended and necessary responsibility of the Chief Magistrate himself.

The idea of a council to the executive, which has so generally obtained in the State constitutions, has been derived from that maxim of republican jealousy which considers power as safer in the hands of a number of men than of a single man. If the maxim should be admitted to be applicable to the case, I should contend that the advantage on that side would not counterbalance the numerous disadvantages on the opposite side. But I do not think the rule at all applicable to the executive power. I clearly concur in opinion, in this particular, with a writer whom the celebrated Junius pronounces to be "deep, solid and ingenious," that "the executive power is more easily confined when it is one"; that it is far more safe there should be a single object for the jealousy and watchfulness of the people; and, in a word, that all multiplication of the executive is rather dangerous than friendly to liberty.

A little consideration will satisfy us that the species of security sought for in the multiplication of the executive is unattainable. Numbers must be so great as to render combination difficult, or they are rather a source of danger than of security. The united credit and influence of several individuals must be more formidable to liberty than the credit and influence of either of them separately. When power, therefore, is placed in the hands of so small a number of men as to admit of their interests and views being easily combined in a common enterprise, by an artful leader, it becomes more liable to abuse and more dangerous when abused, than if it be lodged in the hands of one man, who, from the very circumstance of his being alone, will be more narrowly watched and more readily suspected, and who cannot unite so great a mass of influence as when he is associated with others. The decemvirs of Rome, whose name denotes their number, were more to be dreaded in their usurpation than any ONE of them would have been. No person would think of proposing an executive much more numerous than that body; from six to a dozen have been suggested for the number of the council. The extreme of these numbers is not too great for an easy combination; and from such a combination America would have more to fear than from the ambition of any single individual.

A council to a magistrate, who is himself responsible for what he does, are generally nothing better than a clog upon his good intentions, are often the instruments and accomplices of his bad, and are almost always a cloak to his faults.

I will only add that, prior to the appearance of the Constitution, I rarely met with an intelligent man from any of the States who did not admit, as the result of experience, that the UNITY of the executive of this State was one of the best of the distinguishing features of our Constitution.

PUBLIUS

Federalist No. 78

We proceed now to an examination of the judiciary department of the proposed government.

In unfolding the defects of the existing Confederation, the utility and necessity of a federal judicature have been clearly pointed out. It is the less necessary to recapitulate the considerations there urged as the propriety of the institution in the abstract is not disputed; the only questions which have been raised being relative to the manner of constituting it, and to its extent. To these points, therefore, our observations shall be confined.

The manner of constituting it seems to embrace these several objects: 1st. The mode of appointing the judges. 2nd. The tenure by which they are to hold their places. 3d. The partition of the judiciary authority between different courts and their relations to each other.

First. As to the mode of appointing the judges: this is the same with that of appointing the officers of the Union in general and has been so fully discussed in the two last numbers that nothing can be said here which would not be useless repetition.

Second. As to the tenure by which the judges are to hold their places: this chiefly concerns their duration in office; the provisions for their support, and the precautions for their responsibility.

According to the plan of the convention, all the judges who may be appointed by the United States are to hold their offices *during good behavior*; which is conformable to the most approved of the State constitutions, and among the rest, to that of this State. Its propriety having been drawn into question by the adversaries of that plan is no light symptom of the rage for objection which disorders their imaginations and judgments. The standard of good behavior for the continuance in office of the judicial magistracy is certainly one of the most valuable of the modern improvements in the practice of government. In a monarchy it is an excellent barrier to the despotism of the prince; in a republic it is a no less excellent barrier to the encroachments and oppressions of the representative body. And it is the best expedient which can be devised in any government to secure a steady, upright and impartial administration of the laws.

Whoever attentively considers the different departments of power must perceive that, in a government in which they are separated from each other, the judiciary, from the nature of its functions, will always be the least dangerous to the political rights of the Constitution; because it will be least in a capacity to annoy or injure them. The executive not only dispenses the honors but holds the sword of the community. The legislature not only commands the purse but prescribes the rules by which the duties and rights of every citizen are to be regulated. The judiciary, on the contrary, has no influence over either the sword or the purse; no direction either of the strength or of the wealth of the society, and can take no active resolution whatever. It may truly be said to have neither FORCE nor WILL but merely judgment; and must ultimately depend upon the aid of the executive arm even for the efficacy of its judgments.

This simple view of the matter suggests several important consequences. It proves incontestably that the judiciary is beyond comparison the weakest of the three departments of power; that it can never attack with success either of the other two; and that all possible care is requisite to enable it to defend itself against their attacks. It equally proves that though individual oppression may now and then proceed from the courts of justice, the general liberty of the people can never be endangered from that quarter: I mean, so long as the judiciary remains truly distinct from both the legislative and executive. For I agree that "there is no liberty if the power of judging be not separated from the legislative and executive powers." And it proves, in the last place, that as liberty can have nothing to fear from the judiciary alone, but would have everything to fear from its union with either of the other departments; that as all the effects of such a union must ensue from a dependence of the former on the latter, notwithstanding a nominal and apparent separation; that as, from the natural feebleness of the judiciary, it is in continual jeopardy of being overpowered, awed or influenced by its coordinate branches; and that as nothing can contribute so much to its firmness and independence as permanency in office, this quality may therefore be justly regarded as an indispensable ingredient in its constitution, and in a great measure as the citadel of the public justice and the public security.

The complete independence of the courts of justice is peculiarly essential in a limited Constitution. By a limited Constitution, I understand one which contains certain specified exceptions to the legislative authority; such, for instance, as that it shall pass no bills of attainder, no *ex post facto* laws, and the like. Limitations of this kind can be preserved in practice no other way than through the medium of the courts of justice, whose duty it must be to declare all acts contrary to the manifest tenor of the Constitution void. Without this, all the reservations of particular rights or privileges would amount to nothing.

Some perplexity respecting the right of the courts to pronounce legislative acts void, because contrary to the Constitution, has arisen from an imagination that the doctrine would imply a superiority of the judiciary to the legislative power. It is urged that the authority which can declare the acts of another void must necessarily be superior to the one whose acts may be declared void. As this doctrine is of great importance in all the American constitutions, a brief discussion of the grounds on which it rests cannot be unacceptable.

There is no position which depends on clearer principles than that every act of a delegated authority, contrary to the tenor of the commission under which it is exercised, is void. No legislative act therefore contrary to the constitution can be valid. To deny this would be to affirm that the deputy is greater than his principal; that the servant is above his master; that the representatives of the people are superior to the people themselves; that men acting by virtue of powers may do not only what their powers do not authorize, but what they forbid.

If it be said that the legislative body are themselves the constitutional judges of their own powers and that the construction they put upon them is conclusive upon the other departments it may be answered that this cannot be the natural presumption where it is not to be collected from any particular provisions in the Constitution. It is not otherwise to be supposed that the Constitution could intend to enable the representatives of the people to substitute their *will* to that of their constituents. It is far more rational to suppose that the courts were designed to be an intermediate body between the people and the legislature in order, among other things, to keep the latter within the limits assigned to their authority. The interpretation of the laws is the proper and peculiar province of the courts. A constitution is in fact, and must be regarded by the judges as, a fundamental law. It therefore belongs to them to ascertain its meaning as well as the meaning of any particular act proceeding from the legislative body. If there should happen to be an irreconcilable variance between the two, that which has the superior obligation and validity ought, of course; to be preferred; or, in other words, the Constitution ought to be preferred to the statute, the intention of the people to the intention of their agents.

Nor does this conclusion by any means suppose a superiority of the judicial to the legislative power. It only supposes that the power of the people is superior to both, and that where the will of the legislature, declared in its statutes, stands in opposition to that of the people, declared in the Constitution, the judges ought to be governed by the latter rather than the former. They ought to regulate their decisions by the fundamental laws rather than by those which are not fundamental.

This exercise of judicial discretion in determining between two contradictory laws is exemplified in a familiar instance. It not uncommonly happens that there are two statutes existing at one time, clashing in whole or in part with each other, and neither of them containing any repealing clause or expression. In such a case, it is the province of the courts to liquidate and fix their meaning and operation. So far as they can, by any fair construction, be reconciled to each other, reason and law conspire to dictate that this should be done; where this is impracticable, it becomes a matter of necessity to give effect to one in exclusion of the other. The rule which has obtained in the courts for determining their relative validity is that the last in order of time shall be preferred to the first. But this is mere rule of construction, not derived from any positive law but from the nature and reason of the thing. It is a rule not enjoined upon the courts by legislative provision but adopted by themselves, as consonant to truth and propriety, for the direction of their conduct as interpreters of the law. They thought it reasonable that between the interfering acts of an *equal* authority that which was the last indication of its will, should have the preference.

But in regard to the interfering acts of a superior and subordinate authority of an original and derivative power, the nature and reason of the thing indicate the converse of that rule as proper to be followed. They teach us that the prior act of a superior ought to be preferred to the subsequent act of an inferior and subordinate authority; and that, accordingly, whenever a particular statute contravenes the Constitution, it will be the duty of the judicial tribunals to adhere to the latter and disregard the former.

It can be of no weight to say that the courts, on the pretense of a repugnancy, may substitute their own pleasure to the constitutional intentions of the legislature. This might as well happen in the case of two contradictory statutes; or it might as well happen in every adjudication upon any single statute. The courts must declare the sense of the law; and if they should be disposed to exercise WILL instead of JUDGMENT, the consequence would equally be the substitution of their pleasure to that of the legislative body. The observation, if it proved any thing, would prove that there ought to be no judges distinct from that body.

If, then, the courts of justice are to be considered as the bulwarks of a limited Constitution against legislative encroachments, this consideration will afford a strong argument for the permanent tenure of judicial offices, since nothing will contribute so much as this to that independent spirit in the judges which must be essential to the faithful performance of so arduous a duty.

This independence of the judges is equally requisite to guard the Constitution and the rights of individuals from the effects of those ill humors which the arts of designing men, or the influence of particular conjunctures, sometimes disseminate among the people themselves, and which, though they speedily give place to better information, and more deliberate reflection, have a tendency, in the meantime, to occasion dangerous innovations in the government, and serious oppressions of the minor party in the community. Though I trust the friends of the proposed Constitution will never concur with its enemies in questioning that fundamental principle of republican government which admits the right of the people to alter or abolish the established Constitution whenever they find it inconsistent with their happiness; yet it is not to be inferred from this principle that the representatives of the people, whenever a momentary inclination happens to lay hold of a majority of their constituents incompatible with the provisions in the existing Constitution would, on that account, be justifiable in a violation of those provisions; or that the courts would be under a greater obligation to connive at infractions in this shape than when they had proceeded wholly from the cabals of the representative body. Until the people have, by some solemn and authoritative act, annulled or changed the established form, it is binding upon themselves collectively, as well as individually; and no presumption, or even knowledge of their sentiments, can warrant their representatives in a departure from it prior to such an act. But it is easy to see that it would require an uncommon portion of fortitude in the judges to do their duty as faithful guardians of the Constitution, where legislative invasions of it had been instigated by the major voice of the community.

But it is not with a view to infractions of the Constitution only that the independence of the judges may be an essential safeguard against the effects of occasional ill humors in the society. These sometimes extend no farther than to the injury of the private rights of particular classes of citizens, by unjust and partial laws. Here also the firmness of the judicial magistracy is of vast importance in mitigating the severity and confining the operation of such laws. It not only serves to moderate the immediate mischiefs of those which may have been passed but it operates as a check upon the legislative body in passing them; who, perceiving that obstacles to the success of an iniquitous intention are to be expected from the scruples of the courts, are in a manner compelled, by the very motives of the injustice they meditate, to qualify their attempts. This is a circumstance calculated to have more influence upon the character of our governments than but few may be aware of. The benefits of the integrity and moderation of the judiciary have already been felt in more states than one; and though they may have displeased those whose sinister expectations they may have disappointed, they must have commanded the esteem and applause of all the virtuous and disinterested. Considerate men of every description ought to prize whatever will tend to beget or fortify that temper in the courts; as no man can be sure that he may not be tomorrow the victim of a spirit of injustice, by which he may be a gainer today. And every man must now feel that the inevitable tendency of such a spirit is to sap the foundations of public and private confidence and to introduce in its stead universal distrust and distress.

That inflexible and uniform adherence to the rights of the Constitution, and of individuals, which we perceive to be indispensable in the courts of justice, can certainly not be expected from judges who hold their offices by a temporary commission. Periodical appointments, however regulated, or by whomsoever made, would in some way or other, be fatal to their necessary independence. If the power of making them was committed either to the executive or legislature there would be danger of an improper complaisance to the branch which possessed it; if to both, there would be an unwillingness to hazard the displeasure of either; if to the people, or to persons chosen by them for the special purpose, there would be too great a disposition to consult popularity to justify a reliance that nothing would be consulted but the Constitution and the laws.

There is yet a further and a weighty reason for the permanency of the judicial offices which is deducible from the nature of the qualifications they require. It has been frequently remarked with great propriety that a voluminous code of laws is one of the inconveniences necessarily connected with the advantages of a free government. To avoid an arbitrary discretion in the courts, it is indispensable that they should be bound down by strict rules and precedents which serve to define and point out their duty in every particular case that comes before them; and it will readily be conceived from the variety of controversies which grow out of the folly and wickedness of mankind that the records of those precedents must unavoidably swell to a very considerable bulk and must demand long and laborious study to acquire a competent knowledge of them. Hence it is that there can be but few men in the society who will have sufficient skill in the laws to qualify them for the stations of judges. And making the proper deductions for the ordinary depravity of human nature, the number must be still smaller of those who unite the requisite integrity with the requisite knowledge. These considerations apprise us that the government can have no great option between fit characters; and that a temporary duration in office which would naturally discourage such characters from quitting a lucrative line of practice to accept a seat on the bench would have a tendency to throw the administration of justice into hands less able and less well qualified to conduct it with utility and dignity. In the present circumstances of this country and in those in which it is likely to be for a long time to come, the disadvantages on this score would be greater than they may at first sight appear; but it must be confessed that they are far inferior to those which present themselves under the other aspects of the subject.

Upon the whole, there can be no room to doubt that the convention acted wisely in copying from the models of those constitutions which have established *good behavior* as the tenure of their judicial offices, in point of duration; and that so far from being blamable on this account, their plan would have been inexcusably defective if it had wanted this important feature of good government. The experience of Great Britain affords an illustrious comment on the excellence of the institution.

PUBLIUS

Constitution of the United States of America

We the People of the United States, in Order to form a more perfect Union, establish Justice, insure domestic Tranquility, provide for the common defence, promote the general Welfare, and secure the Blessings of Liberty to ourselves and our Posterity, do ordain and establish this Constitution for the United States of America.

Article. I.

Section. 1. All legislative Powers herein granted shall be vested in a Congress of the United States, which shall consist of a Senate and House of Representatives.

Section. 2. The House of Representatives shall be composed of Members chosen every second Year by the People of the several States, and the Electors in each State shall have the Qualifications requisite for Electors of the most numerous Branch of the State Legislature.

No Person shall be a Representative who shall not have attained to the Age of twenty five Years, and been seven Years a Citizen of the United States, and who shall not, when elected, be an Inhabitant of that State in which he shall be chosen.

Representatives and direct Taxes shall be apportioned among the several States which may be included within this Union, according to their respective Numbers, which shall be determined by adding to the whole Number of free Persons, including those bound to Service for a Term of Years, and excluding Indians not taxed, three fifths of all other Persons. The actual Enumeration shall be made within three Years after the first Meeting of the Congress of the United States, and within every subsequent Term of ten Years, in such Manner as they shall by Law direct. The Number of Representatives shall not exceed one for every thirty Thousand, but each State shall have at Least one Representative; and until such enumeration shall be made, the State of New Hampshire shall be entitled to chuse three, Massachusetts eight, Rhode Island and Providence Plantations one, Connecticut five, New York six, New Jersey four, Pennsylvania eight, Delaware one, Maryland six, Virginia ten, North Carolina five, South Carolina five, and Georgia three.

When vacancies happen in the Representation from any State, the Executive Authority thereof shall issue Writs of Election to fill such Vacancies.

The House of Representatives shall chuse their Speaker and other Officers; and shall have the sole Power of Impeachment.

Section. 3. The Senate of the United States shall be composed of two Senators from each State, chosen by the Legislature thereof, for six Years; and each Senator shall have one Vote.

Immediately after they shall be assembled in Consequence of the first Election, they shall be divided as equally as may be into three Classes. The Seats of the Senators of the first Class shall be vacated at the Expiration of the second Year, of the second Class at the Expiration of the fourth Year, and of the third Class at the Expiration of the sixth Year, so that one third may be chosen every second Year; and if Vacancies happen by Resignation, or otherwise, during the Recess of the Legislature of any State, the Executive thereof may make temporary Appointments until the next Meeting of the Legislature, which shall then fill such Vacancies.

No Person shall be a Senator who shall not have attained to the Age of thirty Years, and been nine Years a Citizen of the United States, and who shall not, when elected, be an Inhabitant of that State for which he shall be chosen.

The Vice President of the United States shall be President of the Senate, but shall have no Vote, unless they be equally divided.

The Senate shall chuse their other Officers, and also a President pro tempore, in the Absence of the Vice President, or when he shall exercise the Office of President of the United States.

The Senate shall have the sole Power to try all Impeachments. When sitting for that Purpose, they shall be on Oath or Affirmation. When the President of the United States is tried, the Chief Justice shall preside: And no Person shall be convicted without the Concurrence of two thirds of the Members present.

Judgment in Cases of Impeachment shall not extend further than to removal from Office, and disqualification to hold and enjoy any Office of honor, Trust or Profit under the United States: but the Party convicted shall nevertheless be liable and subject to Indictment, Trial, Judgment and Punishment, according to Law.

Section. 4. The Times, Places and Manner of holding Elections for Senators and Representatives, shall be prescribed in each State by the Legislature thereof; but the Congress may at any time by Law make or alter such Regulations, except as to the Places of chusing Senators.

The Congress shall assemble at least once in every Year, and such Meeting shall be on the first Monday in December [Modified by Amendment XX], unless they shall by Law appoint a different Day.

Section. 5. Each House shall be the Judge of the Elections, Returns and Qualifications of its own Members, and a Majority of each shall constitute a Quorum to do Business; but a smaller Number may adjourn from day to day, and may be authorized to compel the Attendance of absent Members, in such Manner, and under such Penalties as each House may provide.

Each House may determine the Rules of its Proceedings, punish its Members for disorderly Behaviour, and, with the Concurrence of two thirds, expel a Member.

Each House shall keep a Journal of its Proceedings, and from time to time publish the same, excepting such Parts as may in their Judgment require Secrecy; and the Yeas and Nays of the Members of either House on any question shall, at the Desire of one fifth of those Present, be entered on the Journal.

Neither House, during the Session of Congress, shall, without the Consent of the other, adjourn for more than three days, nor to any other Place than that in which the two Houses shall be sitting.

Section. 6. The Senators and Representatives shall receive a Compensation for their Services, to be ascertained by Law, and paid out of the Treasury of the United States. They shall in all Cases, except Treason, Felony and Breach of the Peace, be privileged from Arrest during their Attendance at the Session of their respective

Houses, and in going to and returning from the same; and for any Speech or Debate in either House, they shall not be questioned in any other Place.

No Senator or Representative shall, during the Time for which he was elected, be appointed to any civil Office under the Authority of the United States, which shall have been created, or the Emoluments whereof shall have been encreased during such time; and no Person holding any Office under the United States, shall be a Member of either House during his Continuance in Office.

Section. 7. All Bills for raising Revenue shall originate in the House of Representatives; but the Senate may propose or concur with Amendments as on other Bills.

Every Bill which shall have passed the House of Representatives and the Senate, shall, before it become a Law, be presented to the President of the United States; If he approve he shall sign it, but if not he shall return it, with his Objections to that House in which it shall have originated, who shall enter the Objections at large on their Journal, and proceed to reconsider it. If after such Reconsideration two thirds of that House shall agree to pass the Bill, it shall be sent, together with the Objections, to the other House, by which it shall likewise be reconsidered, and if approved by two thirds of that House, it shall become a Law. But in all such Cases the Votes of both Houses shall be determined by yeas and Nays, and the Names of the Persons voting for and against the Bill shall be entered on the Journal of each House respectively. If any Bill shall not be returned by the President within ten Days (Sundays excepted) after it shall have been presented to him, the Same shall be a Law, in like Manner as if he had signed it, unless the Congress by their Adjournment prevent its Return, in which Case it shall not be a Law.

Every Order, Resolution, or Vote to which the Concurrence of the Senate and House of Representatives may be necessary (except on a question of Adjournment) shall be presented to the President of the United States; and before the Same shall take Effect, shall be approved by him, or being disapproved by him, shall be repassed by two thirds of the Senate and House of Representatives, according to the Rules and Limitations prescribed in the Case of a Bill.

Section. 8. The Congress shall have Power To lay and collect Taxes, Duties, Imposts and Excises, to pay the Debts and provide for the common Defence and general

Welfare of the United States; but all Duties, Imposts and Excises shall be uniform throughout the United States;

To borrow Money on the credit of the United States;

To regulate Commerce with foreign Nations, and among the several States, and with the Indian Tribes;

To establish an uniform Rule of Naturalization, and uniform Laws on the subject of Bankruptcies throughout the United States;

To coin Money, regulate the Value thereof, and of foreign Coin, and fix the Standard of Weights and Measures;

To provide for the Punishment of counterfeiting the Securities and current Coin of the United States;

To establish Post Offices and post Roads;

To promote the Progress of Science and useful Arts, by securing for limited Times to Authors and Inventors the exclusive Right to their respective Writings and Discoveries;

To constitute Tribunals inferior to the supreme Court;

To define and punish Piracies and Felonies committed on the high Seas, and Offences against the Law of Nations;

To declare War, grant Letters of Marque and Reprisal, and make Rules concerning Captures on Land and Water;

To raise and support Armies, but no Appropriation of Money to that Use shall be for a longer Term than two Years;

To provide and maintain a Navy;

To make Rules for the Government and Regulation of the land and naval Forces;

To provide for calling forth the Militia to execute the Laws of the Union, suppress Insurrections and repel Invasions;

To provide for organizing, arming, and disciplining, the Militia, and for governing such Part of them as may be employed in the Service of the United States, reserving to the States respectively, the Appointment of the Officers, and the Authority of training the Militia according to the discipline prescribed by Congress;

To exercise exclusive Legislation in all Cases whatsoever, over such District (not exceeding ten Miles square) as may, by Cession of particular States, and the Acceptance of Congress, become the Seat of the Government of the United States, and to exercise like Authority over all Places purchased by the Consent of the Legislature of the State in which the Same shall be, for the Erection of Forts, Magazines, Arsenals, dock Yards, and other needful Buildings; —And

To make all Laws which shall be necessary and proper for carrying into Execution the foregoing Powers, and all other Powers vested by this Constitution in the Government of the United States, or in any Department or Officer thereof.

Section. 9. The Migration or Importation of such Persons as any of the States now existing shall think proper to admit, shall not be prohibited by the Congress prior to the Year one thousand eight hundred and eight, but a Tax or duty may be imposed on such Importation, not exceeding ten dollars for each Person.

The Privilege of the Writ of Habeas Corpus shall not be suspended, unless when in Cases of Rebellion or Invasion the public Safety may require it.

No **Bill of Attainder** or **ex post facto** Law shall be passed.

No Capitation, or other direct, Tax shall be laid, unless in Proportion to the Census or Enumeration herein before directed to be taken.

No Tax or Duty shall be laid on Articles exported from any State.

No Preference shall be given by any Regulation of Commerce or Revenue to the Ports of one State over those of another; nor shall Vessels bound to, or from, one State, be obliged to enter, clear, or pay Duties in another.

No Money shall be drawn from the Treasury, but in Consequence of Appropriations made by Law; and a regular Statement and Account of the Receipts and Expenditures of all public Money shall be published from time to time.

No Title of Nobility shall be granted by the United States: And no Person holding any Office of Profit or Trust under them, shall, without the Consent of the Congress, accept of any present, Emolument, Office, or Title, of any kind whatever, from any King, Prince, or foreign State.

Section. 10. No State shall enter into any Treaty, Alliance, or Confederation; grant Letters of Marque and Reprisal; coin Money; emit Bills of Credit; make any Thing but gold and silver Coin a Tender in Payment of Debts; pass any Bill of Attainder, ex post facto Law, or Law impairing the Obligation of Contracts, or grant any Title of Nobility.

No State shall, without the Consent of the Congress, lay any Imposts or Duties on Imports or Exports, except what may be absolutely necessary for executing it's inspection Laws; and the net Produce of all Duties and Imposts, laid by any State on Imports or Exports, shall be for the Use of the Treasury of the United States; and all such Laws shall be subject to the Revision and Controul of the Congress.

No State shall, without the Consent of Congress, lay any Duty of Tonnage, keep Troops, or Ships of War in time of Peace, enter into any Agreement or Compact with another State, or with a foreign Power, or engage in War, unless actually invaded, or in such imminent Danger as will not admit of delay.

Article. II.

Section. 1. The executive Power shall be vested in a President of the United States of America. He shall hold his Office during the Term of four Years, and, together with the Vice President, chosen for the same Term, be elected, as follows:

Each State shall appoint, in such Manner as the Legislature thereof may direct, a Number of Electors, equal to the whole Number of Senators and Representatives to which the State may be entitled in the Congress: but no Senator or Representative, or Person holding an Office of Trust or Profit under the United States, shall be appointed an Elector.

The Electors shall meet in their respective States, and vote by Ballot for two Persons, of whom one at least shall not be an Inhabitant of the same State with themselves. And they shall make a List of all the Persons voted for, and of the Number of Votes for each; which List they shall sign and certify, and transmit sealed to the Seat of the Government of the United States, directed to the President of the Senate. The President of the Senate shall, in the Presence of the Senate and House of Representatives, open all the Certificates, and the Votes shall then be counted. The Person having the greatest Number of Votes shall be the President, if such Number be a Majority of the whole Number of Electors appointed; and if there be more than one who have such Majority, and have an equal Number of Votes, then the House of Representatives shall immediately chuse by Ballot one of them for President; and if no Person have a Majority, then from the five highest on the List the said House shall in like Manner chuse the President. But in chusing the President, the Votes shall be taken by States, the Representation from each State having one Vote; a quorum for this Purpose shall consist of a Member or Members from two thirds of the States, and a Majority of all the States shall be necessary to a Choice. In every Case, after the Choice of the President, the Person having the greatest Number of Votes of the Electors shall be the Vice President. But if there should remain two or more who have equal Votes, the Senate shall chuse from them by Ballot the Vice President.

The Congress may determine the Time of chusing the Electors, and the Day on which they shall give their Votes; which Day shall be the same throughout the United States.

No Person except a natural born Citizen, or a Citizen of the United States, at the time of the Adoption of this Constitution, shall be eligible to the Office of President; neither shall any Person be eligible to that Office who shall not have attained to the Age of thirty five Years, and been fourteen Years a Resident within the United States.

In Case of the Removal of the President from Office, or of his Death, Resignation, or Inability to discharge the Powers and Duties of the said Office, the Same shall devolve on the Vice President, and the Congress may by Law provide for the Case of Removal, Death, Resignation or Inability, both of the President and Vice President, declaring what Officer shall then act as President, and such Officer shall act accordingly, until the Disability be removed, or a President shall be elected.

The President shall, at stated Times, receive for his Services, a Compensation, which shall neither be increased nor diminished during the Period for which he shall have been elected, and he shall not receive within that Period any other Emolument from the United States, or any of them.

Before he enter on the Execution of his Office, he shall take the following Oath or Affirmation: — "I do solemnly swear (or affirm) that I will faithfully execute the Office of President of the United States, and will to the best of my Ability, preserve, protect and defend the Constitution of the United States."

Section. 2. The President shall be Commander in Chief of the Army and Navy of the United States, and of the Militia of the several States, when called into the actual Service of the United States; he may require the Opinion, in writing, of the principal Officer in each of the executive Departments, upon any Subject relating to the Duties of their respective Offices, and he shall have Power to grant Reprieves and Pardons for Offences against the United States, except in Cases of Impeachment.

He shall have Power, by and with the Advice and Consent of the Senate, to make Treaties, provided two thirds of the Senators present concur; and he shall nominate, and by and with the Advice and Consent of the Senate, shall appoint Ambassadors, other public Ministers and Consuls, Judges of the supreme Court, and all other Officers of the United States, whose Appointments are not herein otherwise provided for, and which shall be established by Law: but the Congress may by Law vest the Appointment of such inferior Officers, as they think proper, in the President alone, in the Courts of Law, or in the Heads of Departments.

The President shall have Power to fill up all Vacancies that may happen during the Recess of the Senate, by granting Commissions which shall expire at the End of their next Session.

Section. 3. He shall from time to time give to the Congress Information of the State of the Union, and recommend to their Consideration such Measures as he shall judge necessary and expedient; he may, on extraordinary Occasions, convene both Houses, or either of them, and in Case of Disagreement between them, with Respect to the Time of Adjournment, he may adjourn them to such Time as he shall think proper; he shall receive Ambassadors and other public Ministers; he shall take Care that the Laws be faithfully executed, and shall Commission all the Officers of the United States.

Section. 4. The President, Vice President and all civil Officers of the United States, shall be removed from Office on Impeachment for, and Conviction of, Treason, Bribery, or other high Crimes and Misdemeanors.

Article. III.

Section. 1. The judicial Power of the United States shall be vested in one supreme Court, and in such inferior Courts as the Congress may from time to time ordain and establish. The Judges, both of the supreme and inferior Courts, shall hold their Offices during good Behaviour, and shall, at stated Times, receive for their Services a Compensation, which shall not be diminished during their Continuance in Office.

Section. 2. The judicial Power shall extend to all Cases, in Law and Equity, arising under this Constitution, the Laws of the United States, and Treaties made, or which shall be made, under their Authority; — to all Cases affecting Ambassadors, other public Ministers and Consuls; — to all Cases of admiralty and maritime Jurisdiction; — to Controversies to which the United States shall be a Party; — to Controversies between two or more States; — between a State and Citizens of another State; — between Citizens of different States; — between Citizens of the same State claiming Lands under Grants of different States, and between a State, or the Citizens thereof, and foreign States, Citizens or Subjects.

In all Cases affecting Ambassadors, other public Ministers and Consuls, and those in which a State shall be Party, the supreme Court shall have original Jurisdiction. In all the other Cases before mentioned, the supreme Court shall have appellate Jurisdiction, both as to Law and Fact, with such Exceptions, and under such Regulations as the Congress shall make.

The Trial of all Crimes, except in Cases of Impeachment, shall be by Jury; and such Trial shall be held in the State where the said Crimes shall have been committed;

but when not committed within any State, the Trial shall be at such Place or Places as the Congress may by Law have directed.

Section. 3. Treason against the United States shall consist only in levying War against them, or in adhering to their Enemies, giving them Aid and Comfort. No Person shall be convicted of Treason unless on the Testimony of two Witnesses to the same overt Act, or on Confession in open Court.

The Congress shall have Power to declare the Punishment of Treason, but no Attainder of Treason shall work Corruption of Blood, or Forfeiture except during the Life of the Person attainted.

Article. IV.

Section. 1. Full Faith and Credit shall be given in each State to the public Acts, Records, and judicial Proceedings of every other State. And the Congress may by general Laws prescribe the Manner in which such Acts, Records and Proceedings shall be proved, and the Effect thereof.

Section. 2. The Citizens of each State shall be entitled to all Privileges and Immunities of Citizens in the several States.

A Person charged in any State with Treason, Felony, or other Crime, who shall flee from Justice, and be found in another State, shall on Demand of the executive Authority of the State from which he fled, be delivered up, to be removed to the State having Jurisdiction of the Crime.

No Person held to Service or Labour in one State, under the Laws thereof, escaping into another, shall, in Consequence of any Law or Regulation therein, be discharged from such Service or Labour, but shall be delivered up on Claim of the Party to whom such Service or Labour may be due.

Section. 3. New States may be admitted by the Congress into this Union; but no new State shall be formed or erected within the Jurisdiction of any other State; nor any State be formed by the Junction of two or more States, or Parts of States, without the Consent of the Legislatures of the States concerned as well as of the Congress.

The Congress shall have Power to dispose of and make all needful Rules and Regulations respecting the Territory or other Property belonging to the United States; and nothing in this Constitution shall be so construed as to Prejudice any Claims of the United States, or of any particular State.

Section. 4. The United States shall guarantee to every State in this Union a Republican Form of Government, and shall protect each of them against Invasion; and on Application of the Legislature, or of the Executive (when the Legislature cannot be convened), against domestic Violence.

Article. V.

The Congress, whenever two thirds of both Houses shall deem it necessary, shall propose Amendments to this Constitution, or, on the Application of the Legislatures of two thirds of the several States, shall call a Convention for proposing Amendments, which, in either Case, shall be valid to all Intents and Purposes, as Part of this Constitution, when ratified by the Legislatures of three fourths of the several States, or by Conventions in three fourths thereof, as the one or the other Mode of Ratification may be proposed by the Congress; Provided that no Amendment which may be made prior to the Year One thousand eight hundred and eight shall in any Manner affect the first and fourth Clauses in the Ninth Section of the first Article; and that no State, without its Consent, shall be deprived of its equal Suffrage in the Senate.

Article. VI.

All Debts contracted and Engagements entered into, before the Adoption of this Constitution, shall be as valid against the United States under this Constitution, as under the Confederation.

This Constitution, and the Laws of the United States which shall be made in Pursuance thereof; and all Treaties made, or which shall be made, under the Authority of the United States, shall be the supreme Law of the Land; and the Judges in every State shall be bound thereby, any Thing in the Constitution or Laws of any State to the Contrary notwithstanding.

The Senators and Representatives before mentioned, and the Members of the several State Legislatures, and all executive and judicial Officers, both of the United States and of the several States, shall be bound by Oath or Affirmation, to support this Constitution; but no religious Test shall ever be required as a Qualification to any Office or public Trust under the United States.

Article. VII.

The Ratification of the Conventions of nine States, shall be sufficient for the Establishment of this Constitution between the States so ratifying the Same.

[Bill of Rights]

First Amendment

Congress shall make no law respecting an establishment of religion, or prohibiting the free exercise thereof; or abridging the freedom of speech, or of the press; or the right of the people peaceably to assemble, and to petition the Government for a redress of grievances.

Second Amendment

A well regulated Militia, being necessary to the security of a free State, the right of the people to keep and bear Arms, shall not be infringed.

Third Amendment

No Soldier shall, in time of peace be quartered in any house, without the consent of the Owner, nor in time of war, but in a manner to be prescribed by law.

Fourth Amendment

The right of the people to be secure in their persons, houses, papers, and effects, against unreasonable searches and seizures, shall not be violated, and no Warrants shall issue, but upon probable cause, supported by Oath or affirmation, and particularly describing the place to be searched, and the persons or things to be seized.

Fifth Amendment

No person shall be held to answer for a capital, or otherwise infamous crime, unless on a presentment or indictment of a Grand Jury, except in cases arising in the land or naval forces, or in the Militia, when in actual service in time of War or public danger; nor shall any person be subject for the same offence to be twice put in jeopardy of life or limb; nor shall be compelled in any criminal case to be a witness against himself, nor be deprived of life, liberty, or property, without due process of law; nor shall private property be taken for public use, without just compensation.

Sixth Amendment

In all criminal prosecutions, the accused shall enjoy the right to a speedy and public trial, by an impartial jury of the State and district wherein the crime shall have been committed, which district shall have been previously ascertained by law, and to be informed of the nature and cause of the accusation; to be confronted with the witnesses against him; to have compulsory process for obtaining witnesses in his favor, and to have the Assistance of Counsel for his defence.

Seventh Amendment

In Suits at common law, where the value in controversy shall exceed twenty dollars, the right of trial by jury shall be preserved, and no fact tried by a jury, shall be otherwise re examined in any Court of the United States, than according to the rules of the common law.

Eighth Amendment

Excessive bail shall not be required, nor excessive fines imposed, nor cruel and unusual punishments inflicted.

Ninth Amendment

The enumeration in the Constitution, of certain rights, shall not be construed to deny or disparage others retained by the people.

Tenth Amendment

The powers not delegated to the United States by the Constitution, nor prohibited by it to the States, are reserved to the States respectively, or to the people.

[Additional Amendments to the Constitution] 11-27

Eleventh Amendment [Proposed 1794; Ratified 1798]

The Judicial power of the United States shall not be construed to extend to any suit in law or equity, commenced or prosecuted against one of the United States by Citizens of another State, or by Citizens or Subjects of any Foreign State.

Twelfth Amendment [Proposed 1803; Ratified 1804]

The Electors shall meet in their respective states, and vote by ballot for President and Vice President, one of whom, at least, shall not be an inhabitant of the same state with themselves; they shall name in their ballots the person voted for as President, and in distinct ballots the person voted for as Vice President, and they shall make distinct lists of all persons voted for as President, and of all persons voted for as Vice President, and of the number of votes for each, which lists they shall sign and certify, and transmit sealed to the seat of the government of the United States, directed to the President of the Senate; — The President of the Senate shall, in the presence of the Senate and House of Representatives, open all the certificates and the votes shall then be counted; — The person having the greatest number of votes for President, shall be the President, if such number be a majority of the whole number of Electors appointed; and if no person have such majority, then from the persons having the highest numbers not exceeding three on the list of those voted for as President, the House of Representatives shall choose immediately, by ballot, the President. But in choosing the President, the votes shall be taken by states, the representation from each state having one vote; a quorum for this purpose shall consist of a member or members from two thirds of the states, and a majority of all the states shall be necessary to a choice. And if the House of Representatives shall not choose a President whenever the right of choice shall devolve upon them, before the fourth day of March next following, then the Vice President shall act as President, as in the case of the death or other constitutional disability of the President. — The person having the greatest number of votes as Vice President, shall be the Vice President, if such number be a majority of the whole number of Electors appointed, and if no person have a majority, then from the two highest numbers on the list, the Senate shall choose the Vice President; a quorum for the purpose shall consist of two thirds of the whole number of Senators, and a majority of the whole number shall be necessary to a choice. But no person constitutionally ineligible to the office of President shall be eligible to that of Vice President of the United States.

Thirteenth Amendment [Proposed 1865; Ratified 1865]

Section. 1. Neither slavery nor involuntary servitude, except as a punishment for crime whereof the party shall have been duly convicted, shall exist within the United States, or any place subject to their jurisdiction.

Section. 2. Congress shall have power to enforce this article by appropriate legislation.

Fourteenth Amendment [Proposed 1866; Ratified 1868]

Section. 1. All persons born or naturalized in the United States, and subject to the jurisdiction thereof, are citizens of the United States and of the State wherein they reside. No State shall make or enforce any law which shall abridge the privileges or immunities of citizens of the United States; nor shall any State deprive any person of life, liberty, or property, without due process of law; nor deny to any person within its jurisdiction the equal protection of the laws.

Section. 2. Representatives shall be apportioned among the several States according to their respective numbers, counting the whole number of persons in each State, excluding Indians not taxed. But when the right to vote at any election for the choice of electors for President and Vice President of the United States, Representatives in Congress, the Executive and Judicial officers of a State, or the members of the Legislature thereof, is denied to any of the male inhabitants of such State, being twenty one years of age, and citizens of the United States, or in any way abridged, except for participation in rebellion, or other crime, the basis of representation therein shall be reduced in the proportion which the number of such male citizens shall bear to the whole number of male citizens twenty one years of age in such State.

Section. 3. No person shall be a Senator or Representative in Congress, or elector of President and Vice President, or hold any office, civil or military, under the United States, or under any State, who, having previously taken an oath, as a member of Congress, or as an officer of the United States, or as a member of any State legislature, or as an executive or judicial officer of any State, to support the Constitution of the United States, shall have engaged in insurrection or rebellion against the same, or given aid or comfort to the enemies thereof. But Congress may by a vote of two thirds of each House, remove such disability.

Section. 4. The validity of the public debt of the United States, authorized by law, including debts incurred for payment of pensions and bounties for services in suppressing insurrection or rebellion, shall not be questioned. But neither the United States nor any State shall assume or pay any debt or obligation incurred in aid of insurrection or rebellion against the United States, or any claim for the loss or emancipation of any slave; but all such debts, obligations and claims shall be held illegal and void.

Section. 5. The Congress shall have power to enforce, by appropriate legislation, the provisions of this article.

Fifteenth Amendment [Proposed 1869; Ratified 1870]

Section. 1. The right of citizens of the United States to vote shall not be denied or abridged by the United States or by any State on account of race, color, or previous condition of servitude.

Section. 2. The Congress shall have power to enforce this article by appropriate legislation.

Sixteenth Amendment [Proposed 1909; Questionably Ratified 1913]

The Congress shall have power to lay and collect taxes on incomes, from whatever source derived, without apportionment among the several States, and without regard to any census or enumeration.

Seventeenth Amendemnt [Proposed 1912; Ratified 1913]

The Senate of the United States shall be composed of two Senators from each State, elected by the people thereof, for six years; and each Senator shall have one vote. The electors in each State shall have the qualifications requisite for electors of the most numerous branch of the State legislatures.

When vacancies happen in the representation of any State in the Senate, the executive authority of such State shall issue writs of election to fill such vacancies: Provided, That the legislature of any State may empower the executive thereof to make temporary appointments until the people fill the vacancies by election as the legislature may direct.

This amendment shall not be so construed as to affect the election or term of any Senator chosen before it becomes valid as part of the Constitution.

Eighteenth Amendment [Proposed 1917; Ratified 1919; Repealed 1933 (See Amendment 21, Section 1)]

Section. 1. After one year from the ratification of this article the manufacture, sale, or transportation of intoxicating liquors within, the importation thereof into, or the exportation thereof from the United States and all territory subject to the jurisdiction thereof for beverage purposes is hereby prohibited.

Section. 2. The Congress and the several States shall have concurrent power to enforce this article by appropriate legislation.

Section. 3. This article shall be inoperative unless it shall have been ratified as an amendment to the Constitution by the legislatures of the several States, as provided in the Constitution, within seven years from the date of the submission hereof to the States by the Congress.

Nineteenth Amendment [Proposed 1919; Ratified 1920]

The right of citizens of the United States to vote shall not be denied or abridged by the United States or by any State on account of sex.

Congress shall have power to enforce this article by appropriate legislation.

Twentieth Amendment [Proposed 1932; Ratified 1933]

Section. 1. The terms of the President and Vice President shall end at noon on the 20th day of January, and the terms of Senators and Representatives at noon on the 3d day of January, of the years in which such terms would have ended if this article had not been ratified; and the terms of their successors shall then begin.

Section. 2. The Congress shall assemble at least once in every year, and such meeting shall begin at noon on the 3d day of January, unless they shall by law appoint a different day.

Section. 3. If, at the time fixed for the beginning of the term of the President, the President elect shall have died, the Vice President elect shall become President. If a President shall not have been chosen before the time fixed for the beginning of his term, or if the President elect shall have failed to qualify, then the Vice President elect shall act as President until a President shall have qualified; and the Congress may by law provide for the case wherein neither a President elect nor a Vice President elect shall have qualified, declaring who shall then act as President, or the manner in which one who is to act shall be selected, and such person shall act accordingly until a President or Vice President shall have qualified.

Section. 4. The Congress may by law provide for the case of the death of any of the persons from whom the House of Representatives may choose a President whenever the right of choice shall have devolved upon them, and for the case of the death of any of the persons from whom the Senate may choose a Vice President whenever the right of choice shall have devolved upon them.

Section. 5. Sections 1 and 2 shall take effect on the 15th day of October following the ratification of this article.

Section. 6. This article shall be inoperative unless it shall have been ratified as an amendment to the Constitution by the legislatures of three fourths of the several States within seven years from the date of its submission.

Twenty-first Amendment [Proposed 1933; Ratified 1933]

Section. 1. The eighteenth article of amendment to the Constitution of the United States is hereby repealed.

Section. 2. The transportation or importation into any State, Territory, or possession of the United States for delivery or use therein of intoxicating liquors, in violation of the laws thereof, is hereby prohibited.

Section. 3. This article shall be inoperative unless it shall have been ratified as an amendment to the Constitution by conventions in the several States, as provided in the Constitution, within seven years from the date of the submission hereof to the States by the Congress.

Twenty-second Amendment [Proposed 1947; Ratified 1951]

Section. 1. No person shall be elected to the office of the President more than twice, and no person who has held the office of President, or acted as President, for more than two years of a term to which some other person was elected President shall be elected to the office of the President more than once. But this Article shall not apply to any person holding the office of President when this Article was proposed by the Congress, and shall not prevent any person who may be holding the office of President, or acting as President, during the term within which this Article becomes operative from holding the office of President or acting as President during the remainder of such term.

Section. 2. This article shall be inoperative unless it shall have been ratified as an amendment to the Constitution by the legislatures of three fourths of the several States within seven years from the date of its submission to the States by the Congress.

Twenty-third Amendment [Proposed 1960; Ratified 1961]

Section. 1. The District constituting the seat of Government of the United States shall appoint in such manner as the Congress may direct:

A number of electors of President and Vice President equal to the whole number of Senators and Representatives in Congress to which the District would be entitled if it were a State, but in no event more than the least populous State; they shall be in addition to those appointed by the States, but they shall be considered, for the purposes of the election of President and Vice President, to be electors appointed by a State; and they shall meet in the District and perform such duties as provided by the twelfth article of amendment.

Section. 2. The Congress shall have power to enforce this article by appropriate legislation.

Twenty-fourth Amendment [Proposed 1962; Ratified 1964]

Section. 1. The right of citizens of the United States to vote in any primary or other election for President or Vice President, for electors for President or Vice President, or for Senator or Representative in Congress, shall not be denied or abridged by the United States or any State by reason of failure to pay any poll tax or other tax.

Section. 2. The Congress shall have power to enforce this article by appropriate legislation.

Twenty-fifth Amendment [Proposed 1965; Ratified 1967]

Section. 1. In case of the removal of the President from office or of his death or resignation, the Vice President shall become President.

Section. 2. Whenever there is a vacancy in the office of the Vice President, the President shall nominate a Vice President who shall take office upon confirmation by a majority vote of both Houses of Congress.

Section. 3. Whenever the President transmits to the President pro tempore of the Senate and the Speaker of the House of Representatives his written declaration that he is unable to discharge the powers and duties of his office, and until he transmits to them a written declaration to the contrary, such powers and duties shall be discharged by the Vice President as Acting President.

Section. 4. Whenever the Vice President and a majority of either the principal officers of the executive departments or of such other body as Congress may by law provide, transmit to the President pro tempore of the Senate and the Speaker of the House of Representatives their written declaration that the President is unable to discharge the powers and duties of his office, the Vice President shall immediately assume the powers and duties of the office as Acting President.

Thereafter, when the President transmits to the President pro tempore of the Senate and the Speaker of the House of Representatives his written declaration that no inability exists, he shall resume the powers and duties of his office unless the Vice President and a majority of either the principal officers of the executive department or of such other body as Congress may by law provide, transmit within four days to the President pro tempore of the Senate and the Speaker of the House of Representatives their written declaration that the President is unable to discharge the powers and duties of his office. Thereupon Congress shall decide the issue, assembling within forty eight hours for that purpose if not in session. If the Congress, within twenty one days after receipt of the latter written declaration, or, if Congress is not in session, within twenty one days after Congress is required to assemble, determines by two thirds vote of both Houses that the President is unable to discharge the powers and duties of his office, the Vice President shall continue to discharge the same as Acting President; otherwise, the President shall resume the powers and duties of his office.

Twenty-sixth Amendment [Proposed 1971; Ratified 1971]

Section. 1. The right of citizens of the United States, who are eighteen years of age or older, to vote shall not be denied or abridged by the United States or by any State on account of age.

Section. 2. The Congress shall have power to enforce this article by appropriate legislation.

Twenty-seventh Amendment [Proposed 1789; Ratified 1992; Second of twelve Articles comprising the Bill of Rights]

No law, varying the compensation for the services of the Senators and Representatives, shall take effect, until an election of Representatives shall have intervened.

Letter from a Birmingham Jail

Martin Luther King, Jr.
April 16, 1963

My Dear Fellow Clergymen,

While confined here in the Birmingham City Jail, I came across your recent statement calling our present activities "unwise and untimely." Seldom, if ever, do I pause to answer criticism of my work and ideas ... But since I feel that you are men of genuine good will and your criticisms are sincerely set forth, I would like to answer your statement in what I hope will be patient and reasonable terms.

I think I should give the reason for my being in Birmingham, since you have been influenced by the argument of "outsiders coming in." I have the honor of serving as president of the Southern Christian Leadership Conference, an organization operating in every Southern state with headquarters in Atlanta, Georgia. We have some 85 affiliate organizations all across the South ... Several months ago our local affiliate here in Birmingham invited us to be on call to engage in a nonviolent direct action program if such were deemed necessary. We readily consented.

In any nonviolent campaign there are four basic steps: 1) collection of the facts to determine whether injustices are alive; 2) negotiation; 3) self-purification; and 4) direct action. We have gone through all of these steps in Birmingham ... Birmingham is probably the most thoroughly segregated city in the United States. Its ugly record of police brutality is known in every section of the country. Its unjust treatment of Negroes in the courts is a notorious reality. There have been more unsolved bombings of Negro homes and churches in Birmingham than in any city in this nation. These are the hard, brutal, and unbelievable facts. On the basis of these conditions Negro leaders sought to negotiate with the city fathers. But the political leaders consistently refused to engage in good faith negotiation.

Then came the opportunity last September to talk with some of the leaders of the economic community. In these negotiating sessions certain promises were made by the merchants—such as the promise to remove the humiliating racial signs from the stores. On the basis of these promises Reverend Shuttlesworth and the leaders of the Alabama Christian Movement for Human Rights agreed to call a moratorium on any type of demonstrations. As the weeks and months unfolded we realized that we were the victims of a broken promise. The signs remained. As in so many experiences in the past, we were confronted with blasted hopes, and the dark shadow of a deep disappointment settled upon us. So we had no alternative except that of preparing for direct action, whereby we would present our very bodies as a means of laying our case before the conscience of the local and national community. We were not unmindful of the difficulties involved. So we decided to go through the process of self-purification. We started having workshops on nonviolence and repeatedly asked ourselves the questions, "are you able to accept the blows without retaliating?" "Are you able to endure the ordeals of jail?"

You may well ask, "Why direct action? Why sit-ins, marches, etc.? Isn't negotiation a better path?" You are exactly right in your call for negotiation. Indeed, this is the purpose of direct action. Nonviolent direct action seeks to create such a crisis and establish such creative tension that a community that has constantly refused to negotiate is forced to confront the issue.

My friends, I must say to you that we have not made a single gain in civil rights without legal and nonviolent pressure. History is the long and tragic story of the fact that privileged groups seldom give up their privileges voluntarily. Individuals may see the moral light and give up their unjust posture; but as Reinhold Niebuhr has reminded us, groups are more immoral than individuals.

We know through painful experience that freedom is never voluntarily given by the oppressor; it must be demanded by the oppressed. Frankly I have never yet engaged in a direct action movement that was "well timed," according to the timetable of those who have not suffered unduly from the disease of segregation. For years now I have heard the word "Wait!" It rings in the ear of every Negro with a piercing familiarity. This "wait" has almost always meant "never." It has been a tranquilizing Thalidomide, relieving the emotional stress for a moment, only to give birth to an ill-formed infant of frustration. We must come to see with the distinguished jurist of yesterday that "justice too long delayed is justice denied." We have waited for more than 340 years for our constitutional and God-given rights. The nations of Asia and Africa are moving with jetlike speed toward the goal of political independence, and we still creep at horse and buggy pace toward the gaining of a cup of coffee at a lunch counter.

I guess it is easy for those who have never felt the stinging darts of segregation to say wait. But when you have seen vicious mobs lynch your mothers and fathers at will and drown your sisters and brothers at whim; when you have seen hate-filled policemen curse, kick, brutalize, and even kill your black brothers and sisters with impunity; when you see the vast majority of your 20 million Negro brothers smothering in an airtight cage of poverty in the midst of an affluent society; when you suddenly find your tongue twisted and your speech stammering as you seek to explain to your six-year-old daughter why she can't go to the public amusement park that has just been advertised on television, and see the tears welling up in her little eyes when she is told that Funtown is closed to colored children, and see the depressing clouds of inferiority begin to form in her little mental sky, and see her begin to distort her little personality by unconsciously developing a bitterness toward white people; when you have to concoct an answer for a five-year-old son who is asking in agonizing pathos: "Daddy, why do white people treat colored people so mean?" when you take a cross country drive and find it necessary to sleep night after night in the uncomfortable corners of your automobile because no motel will accept you; when you are humiliated day in and day out by nagging signs reading "white" men and "colored" when your first name becomes "nigger" and your middle name becomes "boy" (however old you are) and your last name becomes "John," and when your wife and mother are never given the respected title of "Mrs." when you are harried by day and haunted by night by the fact that you are a Negro, living constantly at tip-toe stance, never quite knowing what to expect next, and plagued with inner fears and outer resentments; when you are forever fighting a degenerating sense of "nobodiness"—then you will understand why we find it difficult to wait. There comes a time when the cup of endurance runs over, and men are no longer willing to be plunged into an abyss of injustice where they experience the bleakness of corroding despair. I hope, sirs, you can understand our legitimate and unavoidable impatience.

I must make two honest confessions to you, my Christian and Jewish brothers. First, I must confess that over the last few years I have been gravely disappointed with the white moderate. I have almost reached the regrettable conclusion that the Negro's great stumbling block in the stride toward freedom is not the White citizens' "Councilor" or the Ku Klux Klanner, but the white moderate who is more devoted to "order" than to justice; who prefers a negative peace which is the absence of tension to a positive peace which is the presence of justice; who constantly says "I agree with you in the goal you seek, but I can't agree with your methods of direst action" who paternistically feels that he can set the timetable for another man's freedom; who lives by the myth of time and who constantly advises the Negro to wait until a "more convenient season." Shallow understanding from people of good will is more frustrating than absolute misunderstanding from people of ill will. Lukewarm acceptance is much more bewildering than outright rejection.

You spoke of our activity in Birmingham as extreme. At first I was rather disappointed that fellow clergymen would see my nonviolent efforts as those of an extremist. I started thinking about the fact that I stand in the middle of two opposing forces in the Negro community. One is a force of complacency made up of Negroes who, as a result of long years of oppression, have been so completely drained of self-respect and a sense of "somebodiness" that they have adjusted to segregation, and a few Negroes in the middle class who, because of a degree of academic and economic security, and at points they profit from segregation, have unconsciously become insensitive to the problems of the masses. The other force is one of bitterness and hatred and comes perilously close to advocating violence. It is expressed in the various black nationalist groups that are springing up over the nation, the largest and best known being Elijah Muhammad's Muslim movement. This movement is nourished by the contemporary frustration over the continued existence of racial discrimination. It is made up of people who have lost faith in America, who have absolutely repudiated Christianity, and who have concluded that the white man in an incurable "devil."

The Negro has many pent-up resentments and latent frustrations. He has to get them out. So let him march sometime; let him have his prayer pilgrimages to the city hall; understand why he must have sit-ins and freedom rides. If his repressed emotions do not come out in these nonviolent ways, they will come out in ominous expressions of violence. This is not a threat; it is a fact of history. So I have not said to my people, "Get rid of your discontent." But I have tried to say that this normal and healthy discontent can be channeled through the creative outlet of nonviolent direct action.

In spite of my shattered dreams of the past, I came to Birmingham with the hope that the white religious leadership in the community would see the justice of our cause and, with deep moral concern, serve as the channel through which our just grievances could get to the power structure. I had hoped that each of you would understand. But again I have been disappointed. I have heard numerous religious leaders of the South call upon their worshippers to comply with a desegregation decision because it is the law, but I have longed to hear white ministers say follow this decree because integration is morally right and the Negro is your brother. In the midst of blatant injustices inflicted upon the Negro, I have watched white churches stand on the sideline and merely mouth pious irrelevancies and sanctimonious trivialities. In the midst of a mighty struggle to rid our nation of racial and economic injustice, I have heard so many ministers say, "Those are social issues with which the Gospel has no real concern," and I have watched so many churches commit themselves to a completely other-worldly religion which made a strange distinction between body and soul, the sacred and the secular.

1 I hope this letter finds you strong in the faith. I also hope that circumstances will
2 soon make it possible for me to meet each of you, not as an integrationist or a civil
3 rights leader, but as a fellow clergyman and a Christian brother. Let us all hope
4 that the dark clouds of racial prejudice will soon pass away and the deep fog of
5 misunderstanding will be lifted from our fear-drenched communities and in some
6 not too distant tomorrow the radiant stars of love and brotherhood will shine over
7 our great nation with all of their scintillating beauty.

8 Yours for the cause of Peace and Brotherhood,

9 **M. L. King, Jr.**

10

Keynes v. Hayek Lyrics

Fear the Boom and Bust

We've been going back and forth for a century

[Keynes] I want to steer markets,

[Hayek] I want them set free

There's a boom and bust cycle and good reason to fear it

[Hayek] Blame low interest rates.

[Keynes] No... it's the animal spirits

[Keynes Sings:]

John Maynard Keynes, wrote the book on modern macro

The man you need when the economy's off track, [whoa]

Depression, recession now your question's in session

Have a seat and I'll school you in one simple lesson

BOOM, 1929 the big crash

We didn't bounce back—economy's in the trash

Persistent unemployment, the result of sticky wages

Waiting for recovery? Seriously? That's outrageous!

I had a real plan any fool can understand

The advice, real simple—boost aggregate demand!

C, I, G, all together gets to Y

Make sure the total's growing, watch the economy fly

We've been going back and forth for a century

[Keynes] I want to steer markets,

[Hayek] I want them set free

There's a boom and bust cycle and good reason to fear it

[Hayek] Blame low interest rates.

[Keynes] No... it's the animal spirits

You see it's all about spending, hear the register cha-ching

1   Circular flow, the dough is everything

2   So if that flow is getting low, doesn't matter the reason

3   We need more government spending, now it's stimulus season

4   So forget about saving, get it straight out of your head

5   Like I said, in the long run—we're all dead

6   Savings is destruction, that's the paradox of thrift

7   Don't keep money in your pocket, or that growth will never lift...

8   because...

9   Business is driven by the animal spirits

10   The bull and the bear, and there's reason to fear its

11   Effects on capital investment, income and growth

12   That's why the state should fill the gap with stimulus both...

13   The monetary and the fiscal, they're equally correct

14   Public works, digging ditches, war has the same effect

15   Even a broken window helps the glass man have some wealth

16   The multiplier driving higher the economy's health

17   And if the Central Bank's interest rate policy tanks

18   A liquidity trap, that new money's stuck in the banks!

19   Deficits could be the cure, you been looking for

20   Let the spending soar, now that you know the score

21   My General Theory's made quite an impression

22   [a revolution] I transformed the econ profession

23   You know me, modesty, still I'm taking a bow

24   Say it loud, say it proud, we're all Keynesians now

25   We've been goin' back n forth for a century

26   [Keynes] I want to steer markets,

27   [Hayek] I want them set free

28   There's a boom and bust cycle and good reason to fear it

29   [Keynes] I made my case, Freddie H

30   Listen up , Can you hear it?

31   Hayek sings:

1   I'll begin in broad strokes, just like my friend Keynes

2   His theory conceals the mechanics of change,

3   That simple equation, too much aggregation

4   Ignores human action and motivation

5   And yet it continues as a justification

6   For bailouts and payoffs by pols with machinations

7   You provide them with cover to sell us a free lunch

8   Then all that we're left with is debt, and a bunch

9   If you're living high on that cheap credit hog

10   Don't look for cure from the hair of the dog

11   Real savings come first if you want to invest

12   The market coordinates time with interest

13   Your focus on spending is pushing on thread

14   In the long run, my friend, it's your theory that's dead

15   So sorry there, buddy, if that sounds like invective

16   Prepared to get schooled in my Austrian perspective

17   We've been going back and forth for a century

18   [Keynes] I want to steer markets,

19   [Hayek] I want them set free

20   There's a boom and bust cycle and good reason to fear it

21   [Hayek] Blame low interest rates.

22   [Keynes] No... it's the animal spirits

23   The place you should study isn't the bust

24   It's the boom that should make you feel leery, that's the thrust

25   Of my theory, the capital structure is key.

26   Malinvestments wreck the economy

27   The boom gets started with an expansion of credit

28   The Fed sets rates low, are you starting to get it?

29   That new money is confused for real loanable funds

30   But it's just inflation that's driving the ones

31   Who invest in new projects like housing construction

1   The boom plants the seeds for its future destruction

2   The savings aren't real, consumption's up too

3   And the grasping for resources reveals there's too few

4   So the boom turns to bust as the interest rates rise

5   With the costs of production, price signals were lies

6   The boom was a binge that's a matter of fact

7   Now its devalued capital that makes up the slack.

8   Whether it's the late twenties or two thousand and five

9   Booming bad investments, seems like they'd thrive

10   You must save to invest, don't use the printing press

11   Or a bust will surely follow, an economy depressed

12   Your so-called "stimulus" will make things even worse

13   It's just more of the same, more incentives perversed

14   And that credit crunch ain't a liquidity trap

15   Just a broke banking system, I'm done, that's a wrap.

16   We've been goin' back n forth for a century

17   [Keynes] I want to steer markets,

18   [Hayek] I want them set free

19   There's a boom and bust cycle and good reason to fear it

20   [Hayek] Blame low interest rates.

21   [Keynes] No it's the animal spirits

22

Fight of the Century

INTRO: John Maynard Keynes. F. A. Hayek Round Two. Round 2.0 Same economists. Same beliefs. New microphones. New Mustaches. Let's go. Let's go. Let's go.

KEYNES:

Here we are. Peace out. Great Recession. Thanks to ME. As you see. We're not in a depression. Recovery. Destiny. If you follow my lesson. More Keynes. Here I come. Line up for the procession.

HAYEK:

We brought out the shovels and we're still in a ditch. And still digging. Don't you think it's time for a switch from that hair of the dog. Friend the party is over, the long run is here, it's time to get sober.

KEYNES:

Are you kidding? My cure works perfectly fine. Have a look. The recession ended in '09. I deserve credit. Things would have been worse. All the estimates prove it. I'll go chapter and verse.

HAYEK:

Econometricians, they're ever too pious. Are they doing real science or confirming their bias? Their Keynesian models are tidy and neat. But that top down approach is a fatal conceit.

KEYNES:

We could have done better if we'd only spent more. Too bad that only happens when there's a world war. You can carp all you want about stats and regression. Do you deny that world war cut short the Depression?

HAYEK:

Wow. One data point and you're jumping for joy. The last time I checked wars only destroy. There was no multiplier. Consumption just shank as we used scarce resources for every new tank. Pretty perverse to call that prosperity. Ration meat. Ration butter. A life of austerity. When that war spending ended, your friends cried disaster. Yet the economy thrived and grew faster.

KEYNES:

You too only see what you want to see. The spending on war clearly goosed GDP. Unemployment was over, almost down to zero. That's why I'M the master. That's why I'M the hero.

HAYEK:

Creating employment is a straight forward craft when the nation's at war and there's a draft. If every worker were staffed in the army and fleet we'd have full employment and nothing to eat.

HAYEK:

Jobs are a means, not the end in themselves. People work to live better, to put food on the shelves. Real growth means production of what people demand. That's entrepreneurship, not your central plan.

KEYNES:

My solution is simple and easy to handle. It's spending that matters. Why's that such a scandal. Money sloshes through the pipes and the sluices. Revitalizing the economy's juices. It's just like an engine that's stalled and gone dark. To bring it to life we need a quick spark. Spending the life blood that gets the flow going. Were it goes doesn't matter. Just Get Spending Flowing.

HAYEK:

You see slack in some sectors as a general glut. But some sectors are health only some in a rut. So spending's not free, that's the heart of the matter. Too much is wasted as cronies get fatter.
The economy's not a car. There's no engine to stall. No experts can fix it. There's no "it" at all. The economy is us. Put away your wrenches, the economy is organic.

KEYNES:

So what would YOU do to help those unemployed? This is the question you seem to avoid. When we're in a mess, would you have us just wait, doing nothing until markets equilibrate?

HAYEK:

I don't wanna do nothing, there's plenty to do. The question I ponder is who plans for whom. Do I plan for myself or I leave it to you. I want plans by the many, not by the

1 few. Let's not repeat what created our troubles. I want real growth not a series of

2 bubbles. Stop bailing out losers, let prices work. If we don't try to steer them they

3 won't go berserk.

4 KEYNES:

5 Come on are you kidding? Don't Wall Street gyrations challenge the world view of self

6 regulation? Even you must admit that lesson we've learned is more oversight is

7 needed or else we'll get burned.

8 HAYEK:

9 Oversight? The government's long been in bed with those Wall Street execs and the

10 firms that they've bled. Capitalism is about profit and loss. You bail out the losers

11 there is no end to the cost. The lesson I've learned is how little we know. The world is

12 complex, not some circular flow. The economy is not a class you master in college, to

13 think otherwise is the pretense of knowledge.

14 KEYNES:

15 You've been on your high horse and you are off to the races. I look at the world on a

16 case-by-case basis. When people are suffering I roll up my sleeves and do what I can

17 to cure our disease. The future's uncertain, our outlooks are frail. That's why markets

18 are so prone to fail. In a volatile world we need more discretion so state intervention

19 can counter depression.

20 HAYEK:

21 People aren't chess men you move on a board at your whim, their dreams and desires

22 ignored. With political incentives, discretion's a joke. Those dials are twisting – just

23 mirrors and smoke. We need stable rules and real market prices so prosperity

24 emerges and cuts short the crisis. Give us a chance so we can discover the most

25 valuable ways to serve one another.

26

Fifteen Required Cases

Marbury v. Madison (1803)

Explanation

SCOTUS was in its infancy and like Federalist Paper 78 said, was the weakest branch. Hamilton assured Anti-Federalists like Brutus that it would have "no influence over either the sword or the purse, ...It may truly be said to have neither FORCE nor WILL, but merely judgment." He quotes the godfather of the three branches theory, Montesquieu: "Of the three powers [...], the judiciary is next to nothing." Congress controlled the flow of money and the President the military, courts did not have nearly the same clout from a constitutional design standpoint. The Judiciary would depend on the political branches to uphold its judgments.

By 1800, the Federalists and Anti-Federalists had settled into political parties, and Marshall, the Chief Justice was a Federalist. So, he had no problem when outgoing president John Adams, a fellow strong central government man, appointed a bunch of Federalist judges at the last minute. It only helped Adam's cause that Marshall hated the new farmer-is-the-backbone-of-America Thomas Jefferson as much as he did. When the man who was supposed to get a job from Adams, Marbury, did not, he appealed his case directly to the Supreme Court. It seemed that Marshall would order Jefferson to deliver the job notice to Adams's hire. Except for one thing: the Supreme Court has no enforcement power.

So, Marshall did something ingenious. He found a way to secure a victory for his branch, the judicial, without starting a fight with Jefferson he could not win. Marshall knew Jefferson would ignore the court order. Much more than a mere personal insult, this would have devasting effects on the Supreme Court's future.

Just a little more background. Congress had passed a law, the Judiciary Act of 1803, that allowed Marbury to take his case directly to the Supreme Court instead of going to a lower federal court first. Marshall ruled that a law cannot change the Constitution, which is apparent in Article III about who can skip the lower federal courts and go straight to SCOTUS. The Constitution's Article III does not give the highest court original jurisdiction in very few instances.

List the areas of SCOTUS original jurisdiction here:

By striking down a law, Marshall established that his branch could review acts of Congress. However, what about the court's power concerning the executive? Note that the importance of justices' written opinions shows that the reasoning of the court is as critical as its "yes" or "no" rulings. Marshall wrote that if Congress' act had been constitutional, then SCOTUS could have told the president what he had to do. That is, the court has the power to review the actions of the executive. It just had not needed to use said power in this case because Congress passed a law it should not have. Marshall got to call the president out while flexing the court's muscle on Congress. Checkmate.

John Marshall found a way to get one of the first precedents in the court's development to state, on the record, that it was a co-equal branch of the other two branches. Because it has no enforcement power, Marshall had no way of making the executive branch follow its order. Rather than coercion, SCOTUS' authority rests on its legitimacy, which depends on the perception that it is impartial and insulated from the politics of the moment. The belief in the court's impartiality is the source of its power.

Issues

Does Marbury have a right to the job Adams gave him, and can he sue the federal government for it? Does the Supreme Court have the authority to order the executive branch to deliver the commission granting Marbury the job?

Constitutional Clauses and Federal Law

Article III, Section 2, Clause 2 of the U.S. Constitution
"In all cases affecting ambassadors, other public ministers and consuls, and those in which a state shall be party, the Supreme Court shall have original jurisdiction. In all the other cases before mentioned, the Supreme Court shall have appellate jurisdiction, both as to law and fact, with such exceptions, and under such regulations as the Congress shall make."

The Judiciary Act of 1789
This Act authorized the Supreme Court to "issue writs of mandamus ... to persons holding office under the authority of the United States."

McCulloch v. Maryland (1823)

Explanation

To regulate the economy and secure loans for itself, the federal government created a banking system to carry out its **enumerated powers** and to carry out the commerce powers granted by the Constitution. Maryland disagreed that the federal government could establish a bank on its territory since such a power is not listed in the Constitution. The Constitution spells out the federal power to fund the military and build post offices, but the list of its powers in Article I, Section 8 does not include a federal bank. The federal government claimed that a bank was "necessary and proper," citing the clause that so alarmed the Antifederalists. This clause, through its elasticity, implies power that the federal government needs to carry out its enumerated powers like coining money and determining how much money to print. In defiance of what it saw as federal overreach, Maryland taxed the federal bank. The federal employee in charge of writing the check to Maryland, McCullough, refused to pay.

Basing its decision on the Necessary and Proper Clause and the Supremacy Clause, SCOTUS ruled 1. a state cannot tax the federal government and 2. The list of enumerated powers implied other, more specific powers, like establishing a bank.

Issues

Did Congress have the authority under the Constitution to commission a national bank? If so, did the state of Maryland have the authority to tax a branch of the national bank operating within its borders?

Constitutional Text and Amendments

U.S. Constitution, Article I, Section 8, Clause 18 (Necessary and Proper Clause)
"The Congress shall have Power... To make all Laws which shall be necessary and proper for carrying into Execution the foregoing Powers and all other Powers vested by this Constitution in the Government of the United States, or in any Department or Officer thereof."

U.S. Constitution, Article VI, Clause 2 (Supremacy Clause)
"This Constitution, and the Laws of the United States which shall be made in Pursuance thereof; and all Treaties made, or which shall be made, under the Authority of the United States, shall be the supreme Law of the Land; and the Judges in every

1 State shall be bound thereby, any Thing in the Constitution or Laws of any state to the
2 Contrary notwithstanding."
3
4 **U.S. Constitution, Amendment X**
5 "The powers not delegated to the United States by the Constitution, nor prohibited by
6 it to the states, are reserved to the states respectively, or to the people."
7

United States v. Lopez (1995)

Explanation

The federal congress wanted to get tough on guns on school campuses. It passed the Gun Free Zones Act to give harsher sentences than state laws for illegal gun possession on or near school properties. A young man, Lopez, broke state and federal laws when he brought a pistol to school. After Texas official arrested him, the feds showed up and pulled rank, arresting him for a federal crime.

His lawyer argued that the federal government had taken the commerce clause's reach too far. How, Lopez asked, did him having a gun on a high school campus impact "commerce between the states?" The federal government pointed to property values going down and thwarted educations. It is hard to get a good education when gun violence is a threat, the argument went. SCOTUS sided with state governments and limited the commerce clauses' application to more commercial activities. Lopez ended up being tried under state laws and got a much lighter sentence than the federal one he would have served.

From June 22, 2001 Time Magazine:

Eighteen-year-old Alfonso Lopez Jr. was just six weeks short of his high school graduation when, in March 1992, he was caught carrying a .38-cal. handgun on school grounds. The San Antonio, Texas senior suddenly found himself in deep trouble. Thanks to a law Congress had passed two years earlier that banned guns within 1,000 ft. of a school, Lopez had little chance of escaping a six-month prison sentence.

Little chance, that is, until Lopez's court-appointed defense attorney decided that his client's case was hopeless enough to warrant a bold gamble. Lopez had a daring lawyer who threw the equivalent of a Hail Mary pass in the final two seconds of the Super Bowl. Lopez's lawyer argued that the federal government acted in violation of the principle of federalism. Pushing back against the federal Gun-Free School Zones Act, Lopez's side wanted to draw the line between state power and federal government overreach. Going back to the arguments in McCulloch v. Maryland, the state of Florida (representing Lopez) saw the federal government's dominion as limited to only those powers explicitly spelled out in the U.S. Constitution in Article 1, Section 8. Remaining areas of authority, such as law enforcement and education, are jealously cloistered behind the 10th Amendment's powers reserved to the states. Up until Lopez's case, however, the Supreme Court had permitted the federal government to breach certain portions of this wall, using the Commerce Clause.

In a shocking majority ruling, SCOTUS agreed with Lopez's lawyer that the Gun-Free School Zones Act of 1990 is unconstitutional. The court rejected arguments based on the Commerce Clause, like guns in schools contribute to violence, which in turn hampers students' learning and hurts the economy by making students less productive. In doing so, the court went against decades of precedent in clipping the wings of the Commerce Clause. The court was deeply divided, however. Justice Stephen Breyer, who called the majority ruling "extraordinary," took the unusual position of reading from the bench a portion of his dissent, which argued that "gun-related violence in and around schools is a commercial, as well as a human problem."

Lopez won his case and faced state, non-felony charges. Avoiding a federal charge allowed him to handle firearms for a living in the U.S. Marine Corps, something he could not have done with a felony conviction. An irony of federalism: extra layers of governments over him gave Lopez more, not fewer, rights.

Issue
Did Congress have the power to pass the Gun-Free School Zones Act under its Commerce Clause power?

Constitutional Clauses and Supreme Court Precedents

Article 1, Section 8, Clause 3 of the U.S. Constitution
"The Congress shall have the power ...to regulate Commerce with foreign Nations, and among the several States, and with the Indian Tribes..."

Article 1, Section 8, Clause 18 of the U.S. Constitution
"The Congress shall have the power ...to make all laws which shall be necessary and proper for carrying into execution the foregoing powers, and all other powers vested by this Constitution in the Government of the United States, or in any Department or Officer thereof."

Wickard v. Filburn (1942)

To increase wheat prices during the Great Depression, Congress passed a law limiting the amount of wheat that some farmers could grow. A lowly wheat farmer, Wickard, argued that Congress could not use the Commerce Clause to stop him from growing wheat for personal consumption. He had not sold his wheat, and, therefore, did not take part in interstate commerce. The Supreme Court
ruled that Congress could regulate a farmer's wheat crop because the production of wheat is a commercial activity that has interstate consequences. The Court reasoned that Congress might regulate intrastate activities that, if taken all together, would substantially affect interstate commerce. If many farmers decided to grow their wheat and not buy it on the market, they would substantially affect interstate commerce.

Heart of Atlanta Motel v. U.S. (1964)

The Civil Rights Act of 1964 made racial discrimination in public places, including hotels, illegal. An Atlanta hotel refused to serve black customers. The hotel argued that Congress did not have the power to pass the law under the Commerce Clause. The Supreme Court ruled against the hotel, concluding that "commerce" includes travel from state to state, and that racial discrimination in hotels can affect travel from state to state. Congress can, therefore, prohibit discrimination in hotels because, in the aggregate, it affects interstate commerce.

Citizens United v. FEC (2010)

Explanation

Madison's minority faction became a problem, just like Brutus said it would in a republic as large as the United States. Brutus argued that legislators would not be able to represent everyone in large legislative districts where today, one congressman represents an average of 750,000 residents. Campaigning for so many votes has become more and more expensive. Commercials and other advertising are not free. Today, Congress spends nearly $6 billion on its elections every two years (do not forget 1/3 of the Senate). 435 in the House + 33 Senators = 468 running every two years. Divided per delegate, that is $12,820,512 for each two-year election cycle. As the wealth divide gets more extensive by the year, those at the top can fund candidates favorable to their particular interests. Laws were passed to prevent this apparent corruption of policymaking. Laws like the FECA and the BCRA aimed to limit the power of a moneyed minority faction (special interest) pushing for narrow, short term gains at the expense of the nation's overall good. The FECA limited money that flowed to directly to candidates. But as water finds a way around obstacles, money found its way to candidates through political parties. After the FECA, donors could still give directly to candidates but with strict spending limits (making money hard rather than soft). The big money from rich individuals and corporations switched channels, from candidates to their political parties. In an early case, Buckley v. Valeo, donors challenged this law under the 1st Amendment's free speech guarantee. SCOTUS ruled that spending money was an expression of their political views. Buckley did uphold provisions in the FECA that required donors and the recipients of their funds to be transparent, requiring the identify of donors and the amounts they had given be made public. So, big money started to flow in another direction: groups formed that were neither candidates' campaigns nor political parties. To accept money, a group must register with the IRS and declare its type of organization. However, charities, churches, education institutions and philanthropic organizations do not have to pay taxes. So the new political groups formed to receive the big bucks registered as though they were one of these groups in the IRS code parts 501(c) and 527. The 501(c) groups called themselves "political action committees" that claimed to be on a mission to inform voters. In reality, they were conduits for unlimited sums of money special interests were dying to inject into the system. Congress responded to this apparent workaround of the rules by passing another money-in-politics law, the BCRA, which would harden the soft money flowing to these groups. One of these groups, Citizens United, claimed that limiting their taking and spending of money was a violation of their 1st Amendment free speech rights. The court granted them a writ of certiorari and followed stare decisis and even expanded the "money is speech" rule set in Buckley. Outside groups, including corporations, cannot be limited in what they say. They are not a part of the political system but are instead private. The speech of private actors cannot be limited in the same way that the speech of political parties, campaigns, and candidates can. Presently, "super PACs" collect and spend record amounts with each election cycle, and Brutus is surely rolling in his grave.

Issue

This case is about how and when companies and other organizations can spend their own money to advocate the election or defeat of a candidate.

It asks, "does a law that limits the ability of corporations and labor unions to spend their own money to advocate the election or defeat of a candidate violate the First Amendment's guarantee of free speech?"

Law and Supreme Court Precedents

The Bipartisan Campaign Reform Act (BRCA) of 2002 (AKA McCain-Feingold Act)

Among other things, this federal law banned any corporation (for-profit or non-profit) or union from paying for "electioneering communications." It defined an "electioneering communication" as a broadcast, cable, or satellite communication that named a federal candidate within 60 days of a general election or 30 days of a primary.

In 2003, in a case called McConnell v. FEC, the Supreme Court said that the portion of the BCRA about electioneering communications was constitutional.

Buckley v. Valeo (1974)

The Court found that governmental restriction of independent expenditures in campaigns, the limitation on expenditures by candidates from their own personal or family resources, and the limitation on total campaign expenditures did violate the First Amendment.

Baker v. Carr (1962)

Explanation

Many states like Tennessee had not changed their legislative districts in decades. Tennessee had not since the census of 1900, which was over 60 years. Over that time, numerous individuals moved from the country to cities, shifting the balance of the population. Thus, a critical number of legislative districts wound up uneven—for instance, a county with 500 individuals and an urban region with 5,000 individuals each would have a single representative in the state legislature. Before the court granted a writ of cert to Baker, disgruntled voters appealed to federal courts, yet federal courts deferred to state laws and would not hear these cases. The federal courts said voters should fix the problem, claiming the issue was "political."

Courts were hesitant to meddle when state legislative branches settled an issue that was a state's issue according to the Constitution. By 1962, the court had become more willing to step into areas it had avoided earlier in its history. The court had to choose between two principles: equality and federalism. The court sided with the 14th Amendment's Equal Protection Clause and stepped over a line previous courts dared not cross, ruling on how state legislatures organize their voters.

Issue

Do federal courts have the power to decide cases regarding reapportionment and redistricting of state legislative districts or does the federal government have a duty to offer equal protection to voters regarding state voting laws?

Constitutional Articles and Amendments and Supreme Court Precedents

Article III, section 2 of the U.S. Constitution

"The judicial Power shall extend to all Cases, in Law and Equity, arising under this Constitution, the Laws of the United States, and Treaties made, or which shall be made, under their Authority...."

14th Amendment to the U.S. Constitution

No State shall...deny to any person within its jurisdiction the equal protection of the laws."

Article I, Section 2

The U.S. Constitution empowers the Congress to carry out the census in "such manner as they shall by Law direct." Since the number of representatives each state gets in the House depends on population, the census data is vitally related to how much say each state has in national affairs. National and state governments redraw congressional districts every ten years as directed by the census.

Shaw v. Reno (1993)

Explanation

First, let us get the irony of this case out of the way. In a historically racist state, white voters successfully pressed a case that they were being discriminated against. This is a "reverse-racism" case, not a case about racism.

States like North Carolina had not integrated their schools by 1964, ten years after Brown. Nor had they lifted laws keeping black residents from registering to vote. About twenty years separated 1993 from a time when North Carolina and the rest of the Deep South remained apartheid states. The main contention of SCOTUS's ruling is that by 1993 America had moved to a post-racial society under a "color-blind" Constitution.

North Carolina's population was 20% black but had never had a black representative in Congress. The 1990 census showed that North Carolina's population had increased, giving it two more seats in Congress (from 11 to 13). The Voting Rights Act (1965) required that state legislatures in the Deep South get their redistricting plans approved by the federal government since they might be racist. North Carolina had politicians in office who boasted of their KKK membership (and leadership positions), so the request seemed reasonable to many observers. In short, black residents who had suffered unimaginable discrimination were being represented by members of the Klan. Seeing this, the Justice Department (federal enforcer) ordered the North Carolina legislature to create two districts that would be majority black. For the first time since Reconstruction, the state's black residents would have representation in the national legislature.

White residents like Shaw balked at a federal order that was motivated by race. The Supreme Court agreed. The majority said that racial classifications of citizens conflict with a free society and with the American political value of equality. Borrowing from the language of the Civil Rights Movement, SCOTUS declared that racial classifications of any sort promote the belief that individuals should be judged by the color of their skin. The justices concluded that racial gerrymandering, even for the best purposes, may "balkanize us into competing racial factions; it threatens to carry us further from the goal of a political system in which race no longer matters."

Issue

Did the North Carolina residents' claim that the 1990 redistricting plan discriminated based on race raise a valid constitutional issue under the 14th Amendment's Equal Protection Clause?

Constitutional Amendments

14th Amendment to the U.S. Constitution
"Nor shall any state...deny to any person within its jurisdiction the equal protection of the laws."

15th Amendment to the U.S. Constitution
"The right of citizens of the United States to vote shall not be denied or abridged by the United States or by any State on account of race, color, or previous condition of servitude."

Brown v. Board of Education of Topeka (1954)

Explanation

The NAACP's Thurgood Marshall successfully argued that segregation violated the 14th Amendment's Equal Protection rights of black students. While SCOTUS's decision was a rejection of the racism inherent in Plessy, Brown's outcome has been far from an integrated society. Remember, the court has no enforcement power, and it had ordered states to act against the white supremacy attitudes state leaders had been elected to uphold. Instead of following the court order, Southern states resisted. Ten years after Brown, Mississippi had not enrolled a single black student in its white public schools. Half the Southern states revoked the teaching license of anyone who supported integration. After the Voting Rights Act gave the vote to Southern black parents, politicians had to pay more attention to the 1954 order to integrate. Upon doing so, the black middle class took a devastating blow, as education was the main field of black professionals, the bulk of whom lost their jobs as schools integrated. The discourse published upon Brown's 50th anniversary is instructive of the problematic legacy of Brown v. Board.

Issue

Does segregation of public schools by race violate the Equal Protection Clause of the 14th Amendment?

Constitutional Amendments and Precedent

14th Amendment to the U.S. Constitution

"No State shall...deny to any person within its jurisdiction the equal protection of the laws."

Plessy v. Ferguson (1896)

The Supreme Court declared that segregation was legal as long as facilities provided to each race were equal. The justices reasoned that the legal separation of the races did not automatically imply that the black race was inferior. They also advised that legislation and court rulings could not overcome social prejudices. Justice Harlan wrote a strong dissent, arguing that segregation violated the Constitution because it permitted and enforced inequality among people of different races.

On the occasion of the 50th anniversary of the Supreme Court's Brown v. Board of Education decision, Sam Tanenhaus, the editor of the Book Review, moderated a discussion of the historic ruling between Cornel West, whose new book, "Democracy Matters," will be published in September, and Henry Louis Gates Jr., whose latest book is "African American Lives."

Unintended Consequences Of the Brown Decision (NYT May 16,2004)

Gates. I was born in 1950. Brown v. Board's in 1954. Schools in Mineral County, W.Va., which is about three hours west of D.C., integrated in 1955. I started school in 1956. So my entire life, because of Brown v. Board, I went to integrated schools. My town had 2,100 people in 1950, 386 of whom were black. So you can see just from the stats why integration occurred so quickly. It was inefficient to have two separate school systems. [So] they fired all the black teachers except one from the elementary school and one, the principal, from the high school and integrated them into the white staff at the white schools.

For me the most problematic aspect of Brown was the fundamental premise that separate inherently spelled unequal. Curiously enough, I find myself agreeing with Clarence Thomas when he argues that there was a perverse aspect to the logic of Brown v. Board.

West. But I think it's really important to keep in mind what the vital options at a particular historical moment are. Given America's vicious legacy of white supremacy, [the Brown legal team] had to argue against separate but equal because that's already inscribed in Plessy v. Ferguson.

Gates. You're absolutely correct. In their time they had no choice. But they also happened to have believed that all-black institutions were inherently inferior and that many of them would disappear very quickly, and all the better for it. In 1937 Richard Wright wrote that once the goals of a nation's civil rights movement are realized, Negro literature as an institution would disappear. We would produce a new kind of integrated society. And we see that legacy in many of the reform movements that abound today trying to address the problem of resegregation.

West. There's a certain complication here. When Charles Hamilton Houston takes over the deanship in 1929 at Howard, he tries to Harvard-ize it. He realized Howard could not even begin to compete with Harvard. But he also knew that after a decade or two Howard would be better than many white law schools, though maybe not Harvard. Now in that sense he doesn't believe that the black folk by themselves are inferior vis-à-vis white institutions, only the elite white institutions. They're going to outcompete a lot of the white law schools. Why? Because he's bringing in some top-notch black professors, and white professors too.

Schenck v. U.S. (1919)

Explanation

Upon entry into WWI, the U.S. Congress passed the Espionage Act (1917) which forbade actions that would "cause insubordination, disloyalty, mutiny, refusal of duty, in the military" or to obstruct military recruiting. Many Americans were arrested and convicted under this law during World War I, including one Mr. Schenck, who campaigned against the draft. Schenck lost the case, but more importantly, it is the language that SCOTUS used in its ruling. The majority claimed that statements that "create a clear and present danger" are not protected. Just as "free speech would not protect a man in falsely shouting fire in a theatre and causing a panic," the Constitution does not protect efforts to discourage enlistment in the armed forces. If effective, the court reasoned, Schenck's action would undoubtedly have been dangerous.

Issue

Did Schenck's conviction under the Espionage Act for criticizing the draft violate his First Amendment right to freedom of speech?

Constitutional Amendment

Amendment I
Congress shall make no law ... abridging the freedom of speech....

Tinker v. Des Moines Independent Community School District (1969)

Explanation

This case may be challenging to understand if one knows nothing of the Vietnam War (1954-1975). Politicians claimed it was a war against communism on the side of democracy and freedom. What the country saw and heard on television and read in newspapers showed a different picture. Nightly news programs showed footage only seen in rated "R" movies today. These images of the cost of war turned many against a conflict so far away and vaguely defined. Many, including the Tinker children, decided to protest the war. Borrowing a method from the Civil Rights Movement where students wore buttons to protest Jim Crow practices, the Tinkers wore black armbands to school in protest of the war. The school board met and issued a rule against such action. The school district expelled them until they came to school armband-less. They fought the school all the way to SCOTUS.

In a decision school personal everywhere hated, SCOTUS ruled that students have constitutional rights and deserve equal protection and due process. In this case, the court not only scored a victory for free speech rights but extended the federal government's reach farther than it had ever gone. By intervening between students and their school board, the court further incorporated the First Amendments' free speech provision. The Supreme Court's language still inspires: "First Amendment rights, applied in light of the special characteristics of the school environment, are available to teachers and students. It can hardly be argued that either students or teachers shed their constitutional rights to freedom of speech or expression at the schoolhouse gate...."

Issue

Does a prohibition against the wearing of armbands in public school, as a form of symbolic speech, violate the students' freedom of speech protections guaranteed by the First Amendment?

Constitutional Amendments

U.S. Constitution, Amendment I

Congress shall make no law ... abridging the freedom of speech....

1   **14th Amendment to the U.S. Constitution**

2   "No State shall...deny to any person within its jurisdiction the equal protection of the

3   laws nor shall any State deprive any person of life, liberty, or property, without due

4   process of law...."

5

New York Times Co. vs. U.S. (1971)

Explanation

The stated reasons for the Vietnam War were usually vague and a little confusing. Vietnam had not attacked American land or interests, nor did it possess vital resources or sit in a strategic place on the globe. "Domino theory" was offered: if we allowed one country to fall to communism, then a scary amount of other nations would fall to the red menace. The pictures and newsreels and mounting deaths soured the public's opinion of the war. By the end of the war, there would be over 50,000 U.S. deaths and over 1 million Vietnamese (this is a low-end estimate; the higher guess is over 3 million). American's willingness to stay in such a war became more and more questionable as images from the war played continuously on the news.

American presidents felt that they had good reasons to fight the war, but these were hard to sell to the public. No president wanted to be the first to lose a war. The country's prestige was on the line--the U.S. had to show the rest of the world it would not back down. But how long would such reasons inspire Americans to send their loved ones in harm's way? Was the conflict worth sums enough to build new schools in every American community? In response to declining approval for U.S. involvement in Vietnam, presidents assured the U.S. public that it was a fight for democracy that the U.S. was winning. Neither of these contentions turned out to be true, and the first light shed on this truth came as the result of stolen documents.

At some level of government, the truth with its hard facts must be accessible so policymakers can make responsible decisions. While the public may be misinformed and even propagandized, military planners must have an accurate analysis of the decisions made before them. That is, they have to know the real history they are acting within. The machine must be visible to those who work it. So, the Pentagon hired a team of researchers to write an accurate account of the U.S. involvement in Vietnam. The papers, which would come to be known as The Pentagon Papers, painted a bleak picture. American politicians had lied about the causes of the war and knew they had been losing the war and lied when they said it could be won. One of the authors of these documents saw the gap between the truth and the government's public accounts and decided to leak the documents, though it meant he would probably go to jail.

The stolen documents went first to the New York Times. The paper contacted the government to verify that the documents were what the leaker (Daniel Ellsberg) said they were. Indeed, they were the official government accounts of the history of the Vietnam War. The government confirmed the latter but then got a federal court to order the NYT not to publish the documents. The governmental prevention of publication is called prior restraint, and this would become the test case for whether the U.S. government had such power. SCOTUS ruled that it did not, taking a comprehensive view of the First Amendment's freedom of the press clause. Their final publication, in addition to the graphic news coverage of the war, pulled public opinion from the government's grasp and fueled anti-war sentiment.

Issue

Did the government's efforts to prevent two newspapers from publishing classified information given to them by a government leaker violate the First Amendment protection of freedom of the press?

Constitutional Amendment

First Amendment to the U.S. Constitution
"Congress shall make no law...abridging the freedom of speech, or of the press"

Engel v. Vitale (1962)

Explanation

Back in the day, folks prayed before school. Students in New York classrooms would salute the U.S. flag and voluntarily recite this school-provided prayer, which had been New York's Department of Education: "Almighty God, we acknowledge our dependence upon Thee, and we beg Thy blessings upon us, our parents, our teachers and our country." A combination of Christians, Jews, and atheists brought suit against NY schools on the ground that the state of New York was imposing religion on students. SCOTUS agreed with those against the prayer, regardless of how vague it left the concept of "God." Still, the court ruled, it is an Establishment Clause violation because it is a religious activity that comes from the government.

Issue

Does the recitation of a prayer in public schools violate the Establishment Clause of the First Amendment?

Constitutional Amendment

First Amendment to the U.S. Constitution

"Congress shall make no law respecting an establishment of religion, or prohibiting the free exercise thereof…"

Wisconsin v. Yoder (1972)

Explanation

The First Amendment has two religious clauses, the Establishment Clause and the **Free Exercise Clause**. The first protects one from the government imposing religion or religious activity on citizens while the second protects those citizen's religious practices. Together, they hold up the principle of the separation between church and state held dear at the founding.

This case regards the freedom of parents to practice their religion despite conflict with state laws. Since children are not full citizens, their parents' rights are considered here. While I don't expect you to accept that middle school aged humans have no rights, we'll move on along...

The Yoders did not think education beyond the eighth grade was necessary. Indeed, they believed it would be harmful. Their children would become exposed to the pornographic lyrics so prevalent in today's music along with scores of other violations against their church's code of conduct. When it came time to register for ninth grade, the Yoders kept their children at home. Shortly thereafter, they were arrested under their states compulsory school laws. The Yoder parents sued Wisconsin for violating their free exercise rights.

In short, the court agreed with the parents, ruling against Wisconsin's argument that it needed to make people get an education so they could become productive and informed. Please note the inclusion of the 14th Amendment in this case. Why was it brought in? The students' parents were claiming "equal protection" from a school board law. They needed the incorporation power of the 14th Amendment's "No state shall" language to apply to their school board. In Yoder, for the first time, SCOTUS got between the relationship of a state and its citizens over the matter of the establishment of religion. Thus, Yoder incorporated the 1st Amendment Establishment Clause against the states per the 14th Amendment's "No state shall...."

Issue

Under what conditions does the state's interest in promoting compulsory education override parents' First Amendment right to free exercise of religion?

Constitutional Amendments and Supreme Court Precedents

First Amendment to the U.S. Constitution
"Congress shall make no law respecting an establishment of religion, or prohibiting the free exercise thereof..."

14th Amendment to the U.S. Constitution
"...nor shall any State deprive any person of life, liberty, or property, without due process of law..."

McDonald v. City of Chicago (2010)

Explanation

In legal terms, the story of McDonald is the same story as Heller (see below) but importantly, in a state jurisdiction. While D.C. is a federal zone, McDonald's gun was taken by Chicago, Illinois. So, McDonald's federal 2nd Amendment challenge was against a state. If McDonald won, the 2nd Amendment, as interpreted in Heller, would be applied to all the states. It would be incorporated. McDonald won.

Issue

Does the Second Amendment right to keep and bear arms apply to state and local governments through the 14th Amendment and thus limit Chicago's ability to regulate guns?

Constitutional Amendments and Supreme Court Precedents

Second Amendment to the U.S. Constitution
"A well regulated Militia, being necessary to the security of a free State, the right of the people to keep and bear Arms, shall not be infringed."

14th Amendment to the U.S. Constitution
"No State shall make or enforce any law which shall abridge the privileges or immunities of citizens of the United States; nor shall any state deprive any person of life, liberty, or property, without due process of law...."

District of Columbia v. Heller (2008)
The District of Columbia, which is a federal city and not a state, had a ban on handguns. The Court decided that the Second Amendment guarantees an individual right to gun ownership, which the federal (or D.C.) government may not infringe. For the first time in U.S. history, the 2nd Amendment was taken to mean that individuals have a right to own guns for self-defense. Not that one can have whatever guns he likes. Heller makes clear that states and the federal government can still pass laws regulating guns. In Heller, the court drew the line at banning a whole class of weapon commonly used for self-defense by millions of its citizens.

1

Gideon v. Wainwright (1963)

Explanation

Clarence Earl Gideon did or did not break into the Bay Harbor Pool room. He claimed that he did not and wanted a lawyer to argue his case. Being poor, he asked his state, Florida, to provide one per the Sixth Amendment's right to counsel clause. Florida responded by reminding the petitioner that it only provided lawyers to defendants accused of capital crimes--crimes for which one may receive the death penalty. So, Gideon did an amateurish job of representing himself and lost. From jail, he wrote a writ of certiorari that SCOTUS granted in 1963. If he won, the Sixth Amendment would be incorporated against all of the states. Imagine the impact: one man wins a case, and suddenly every state has to provide anyone they arrest with a lawyer, even for speeding tickets. He won, so anyone can get a state-paid lawyer if unable to hire one, even for a speeding ticket.

Issue

Does the Sixth Amendment's right to counsel in criminal cases extend to defendants in state courts, even in cases in which the death penalty is not a possible sentence?

Constitutional Amendments

U.S. Constitution, Amendment VI

"In all criminal prosecutions, the accused shall enjoy the right . . . to have the Assistance of Counsel for his defense."

U.S. Constitution, Amendment XIV

"...nor shall any State deprive any person of life, liberty, or property, without due process of law...."

Roe v. Wade (1973)

Explanation

In 1970, Texas resident Jane Roe (a fictional name used in court documents to protect the plaintiff's identity) filed a lawsuit against Henry Wade, the district attorney of Dallas County, Texas, challenging a Texas law making abortion illegal except by a doctor's orders to save a woman's life. In her lawsuit, Roe alleged that the state laws were unconstitutionally vague and abridged her right of personal privacy, protected by the First, Fourth, Fifth, Ninth, and Fourteenth Amendments.

From Ozey.com:

Inherent in the Due Process Clause of the Fourteenth Amendment is a fundamental "right to privacy" that protects a pregnant woman's choice whether to have an abortion. However, this right is balanced against the government's interests in protecting women's health and protecting "the potentiality of human life." The Texas law challenged in this case violated this right.

Justice Harry Blackmun delivered the opinion for the 7-2 majority of the Court.

First, the Court considered whether the case was moot, concluding that it was not. When the subject of litigation is "capable of repetition yet evading review," a case need not be dismissed as moot. Pregnancy is a "classic justification for a conclusion of nonmootness."

The Due Process Clause of the Fourteenth Amendment protects against state action the right to privacy, and a woman's right to choose to have an abortion falls within that right to privacy. A state law that broadly prohibits abortion without respect to the stage of pregnancy or other interests violates that right. Although the state has legitimate interests in protecting the health of pregnant women and the "potentiality of human life," the relative weight of each of these interests varies over the course of pregnancy, and the law must account for this variability.

In the first trimester of pregnancy, the state may not regulate the abortion decision; only the pregnant woman and her attending physician can make that decision. In the second trimester, the state may impose regulations on abortion that are reasonably related to maternal health. In the third trimester, once the fetus reaches the point of "viability," a state may regulate abortions or prohibit them entirely, so long as the laws contain exceptions for cases when abortion is necessary to save the life or health of the mother.

Issue

Does the U.S. Constitution protect the right of a woman to obtain an abortion?

Constitutional Amendments and Supreme Court Precedents

Constitutional Text, Amendments and Case Law

Ninth Amendment to the U.S. Constitution

"The enumeration in the Constitution, of certain rights, shall not be construed to deny or disparage others retained by the people."

14th Amendment to the U.S. Constitution

"No State shall make or enforce any law which shall abridge the privileges or immunities of citizens of the United States; nor shall any state deprive any person of life, liberty, or property, without due process of law; nor deny to any person within its jurisdiction the equal protection of the laws."

U.S. Constitution, Amendment X

"The powers not delegated to the United States by the Constitution, nor prohibited by it to the states, are reserved to the states respectively, or to the people."

Griswold v. Connecticut (1965)

In 1879, Connecticut passed a law that banned the use of any drug, medical device, or other instrument in furthering contraception. Connecticut law criminalized providing counseling to married people regarding birth control. Estelle Griswold provided such services to women and was arrested. Her case begged the Court to consider whether the Constitution protects the right of marital privacy against state restrictions.

The Supreme Court ruled that the Connecticut law violated the Constitution because it invaded the privacy of married couples to make decisions about procreation. The Court identified privacy as a value fundamental to the American way of life and the other basic rights found in the penumbra of the Bill of Rights (including the First, Third, Fourth, and Ninth Amendments).

As of this writing, many states have passed laws in clear violation of the precedent set in Roe v. Wade. The states imagine that lower federal courts will strike the laws down. They hope that the Supreme Court will grant writs of certiorari to their appeals

1   and reverse Roe. Since SCOTUS has five declared conservative justices, opponents of
2   Roe have reason to hope.

3   In Roe, the majority found that aborting a pregnancy was a privacy right and
4   protected by the liberty part of the Due Process Clause of the 14th Amendment. It
5   based its decision on the privacy rights recognized in Griswald's "zone of privacy"
6   idea. Basing its decision on Griswold, SCOTUS ruled that a woman's right to privacy
7   is implied in the First, Fourth, Fifth, Ninth, and 14th Amendments. The government
8   has since stayed out of this area of personal choice.

9   Since Roe's 1973 decision, SCOTUS has heard many cases regarding abortion.
10 In the end, the court has followed the principle of stare decisis, upholding a privacy
11 right to abort an unwanted pregnancy. It has been in these cases, like Casey v. Planned
12 Parenthood, where the debate over the constitutionality of abortion has developed.

13 On one side, "pro-choice" advocates have argued more on equality grounds
14 rather than use the privacy argument as we saw in Griswold. The argument is that
15 women, not men (even Supreme Court justices), should determine what a woman
16 does with her body and anything within it. Such decisions should belong to individual
17 women, one in four of whom will have an abortion in their lives.

18 The other, "pro-life" side sees the issue as advocacy for the fetus, which they
19 see as an unborn person that is entitled to due process life protection. While they
20 differ on the scientific point when life which is entitled to state protection begins, they
21 maintain that the government has a place in protecting the life of unborn human
22 beings. States and the federal government (and the male policymakers in them) must
23 step in to protect the life of the unborn as much as it does in keeping its citizens'
24 property and lives free from criminal violations. Lastly, abortion is not mentioned in
25 the Constitution and should be an issue decided by the states under their 10th
26 Amendment reserved powers.

27

28

29

30

31

32

33

34

35

36

1

2

3

4

5

6

7

8

9

10

11

12

13

14

15

16

17

18

19

20

21

22

23

24

25

26

27

28

29

1
2
3
4
5
6
7
8
9
10
11
12
13
14
15
16
17
18
19
20
21
22
23
24
25

26

27

Made in the USA
Monee, IL
28 March 2021